Praise for *What Happened to Catholicism*

"Over a century ago, Pope Pius X issued an encyclical that dissected a new, subtle, seductive super-heresy. It took subjectivism and scientism as premises and demanded the reinterpretation and reconfiguration of all of Catholicism. That heresy was Modernism. The fruits, or rather ruins, lie all around us today, yet Catholics have been steeped in it for so long that they need help discerning the traditional Faith from the distorted parody. Kennedy Hall offers us a valuable tool in carrying out this much-needed discernment."

— **Dr. Peter A. Kwasniewski,** *Tradition and Sanity* Substack; Author, *The Holy Bread of Eternal Life*

"Kennedy Hall has written an uncomfortable book, for it exposes truths about today's Church that most of us don't want to admit — specifically, that we're all influenced by what Pope St. Pius X called the 'synthesis of all heresies.' How did this happen, and how deeply does Modernism infect the practice of Catholicism in our time? These are important questions, and Hall attempts to answer them directly and honestly. For this, we all should be grateful, even if, at times, we might not like the answers he gives. If we are going to reform and renew the Church in our day, we need to overcome any hurdles in our way, and, as Hall expertly shows, Modernism is the biggest hurdle of them all."

— **Eric Sammons,** Editor in Chief, *Crisis Magazine*

"Kennedy Hall has produced what will be one of the most useful books published for many years. He is able to explain the beliefs of, and problems with, Modernism not only with incredible accuracy but in a style that is understandable and accessible. Too many people give up reading Pius X's *Pascendi Dominici Gregis* because it is somewhat difficult for a reader of today to understand. Further, Modernism purposefully makes itself opaque and difficult to understand as a technique of deception. Kennedy explains history, philosophy, and the crisis in the Church in terms any person of goodwill can understand. I highly recommend this book."

— **Brian M. McCall**, Editor in Chief, *Catholic Family News*

"Kennedy Hall has put together a concise piece of research on one of the most important, yet misunderstood, influences of the modern world — Modernism. With clarity and charity, Kennedy does a forensic deep dive into the philosophical underpinnings of what Pope St. Pius X called the 'synthesis of all heresies,' a subtle secular humanism that has affected every aspect of religious, philosophical, and social life. This book is a must-read for all serious Catholics and a clarion call for a return to tradition and the *depositum fidei*."

— **Dan Schneider, Ph.D.**, Author, *The Liber Christo Method*

What Happened to Catholicism

Kennedy Hall

WHAT HAPPENED TO CATHOLICISM

The Heresy Behind the Current Crisis

Manchester, New Hampshire

Copyright © 2025 by Kennedy Hall

Printed in the United States of America. All rights reserved.

Cover design by LUCAS Art & Design, Jenison, MI.

Cover image: *Portrait of Pius X* (1904), by Alessandro Milesi, Wikimedia Commons, public domain.

Scripture quotations are from the Douay-Rheims edition.

Excerpts from the English translation of the *Catechism of the Catholic Church* for use in the United States of America copyright © 1994, United States Catholic Conference, Inc.—Libreria Editrice Vaticana. English translation of the *Catechism of the Catholic Church: Modifications from the Editio Typica* copyright © 1997, United States Conference of Catholic Bishops—Libreria Editrice Vaticana.

No part of this book may be reproduced, stored in a retrieval system, or transmitted in any form, or by any means, electronic, mechanical, photocopying, or otherwise, without the prior written permission of the publisher, except by a reviewer, who may quote brief passages in a review.

Crisis Publications
Box 5284, Manchester, NH 03108
1-800-888-9344

www.CrisisMagazine.com

paperback ISBN 979-8-88911-286-0
ebook ISBN 979-8-88911-287-7

Library of Congress Control Number: 2024952373

First printing

To Fr. Michel Rion, thank you.
Tu es sacerdos in aeternum

Contents

Foreword by Matt Gaspers ix
Introduction xiii
1. An Enemy Has Done This 1
2. The Philosophical Origins of Modernism 7
3. The Theological Origins of Modernism 27
4. Pope Pius X Addresses the Gravity of the Situation . . . 41
5. An Attack on the Foundations of Philosophy and Religion: Agnosticism and Vital Immanence. 47
6. The Lurking Force behind the Modernist Evolution of Religion. 59
7. The Modernist Misunderstanding of the Origin and Development of Dogma 67
8. The Modernist as Believer 83
9. How Modernism Distorts the Relationship between Faith and Science 101
10. How Modernism Uses Contradiction 113
11. The Modernist as Theologian 123

12. How Modernism Destroys a True Understanding
    of History. 131
13. How Modernism Butchers Sacred Scripture 145
14. Modernist Reform: The Confusion of Vatican II. 161
15. The New Theology behind the New Springtime 185
16. Modernist Reform Activated:
    The Conciliar Revolution in Action 211
17. Modernist Worship: The Liturgy of the Revolution . . . 233
18. The Pride of Modernism Rages More Than Ever. 259
19. The Solution 267
    Conclusion: The Immaculate Virgin,
    the Destroyer of All Heresies 277
    About the Author. 285

Foreword

On his first day in office, in addition to signing a flurry of executive orders, President Joe Biden led a virtual swearing-in ceremony for "Day One Presidential Appointees" — that is, administrative staff for the White House and various governmental agencies.

A few minutes into his remarks, Biden told his new subordinates that "we owe your families, we owe your families, because those of you working in the White House, [and] those who will be working in other agencies, you're gonna work like the devil [an interesting choice of words]. We all do. We put in long hours. And it shouldn't be something that you should do unless you really care about it a great deal."

He returned a few minutes later to this theme of the need for his appointees to be passionate about their work:

> So, you shouldn't be doing this unless you feel it. I always say, a simple proposition: I trust people more who, the idea and the concern starts in their gut, goes to their heart, and is to be [sic] able to articulate it by a good brain, rather than the person who thinks of it intellectually but never feels it. The people you can count on are the ones that starts [sic] in the gut, works their [sic]

way to the heart, and have the intellectual capacity to do what needs to be done."[1]

Aside from noting his significant gaffes, the first thing that occurred to me upon hearing these words was: "Wow, spoken like a true Modernist."
Let me explain.

Modernism, as Pope St. Pius X says in his encyclical *Pascendi Dominici Gregis* (1907), is "the synthesis of all heresies," and it leads to "the destruction not of the Catholic religion alone but of all religion" (39). The reason for its destructive power is that it attacks not this or that truth but rather *the nature of truth itself*.

According to Modernism, truth is not something external to man (an objective reality to which the human intellect must conform); rather, it is *immanent in man*, something that mysteriously bubbles up from the depths of his subconscious, or "gut," to quote Joe Biden. When this philosophical error is applied to religion, the result is that Catholicism — the unique deposit of divinely revealed truths — becomes merely one expression of the "religious sentiment" of believers (as St. Pius X calls it throughout *Pascendi*) who adhere to a particular tradition as a matter of cultural heritage or personal preference. And since cultures and preferences evolve over time, so should religious dogma.[2]

---

[1] "President Biden Swears in Day One Presidential Appointees in a Virtual Ceremony," The White House, January 20, 2021, YouTube video, 11 mins., 7 secs. https://www.youtube.com/watch?v=sRXE5Xl Wnt4&t=391s.

[2] This is precisely why St. Pius X prescribed the following in his Oath Against Modernism (1910): "I sincerely accept that the doctrine of the faith was handed down to us in the same sense and always with the same meaning from the Apostles through the orthodox Fathers; I therefore entirely reject the heretical theory of an evolution of the dogmas, namely, that they change from one meaning to another, different from the one that the Church previously held. I also condemn any error that substitutes for the divine legacy entrusted to the Spouse of Christ, to be faithfully guarded by her, a philosophical system or a

In this way, Modernists "pervert the eternal concept of truth" (*Pascendi* 13) and relativize everything that falls outside the realm of empirical science (yet, even there, they are prone to take certain liberties, such as pretending that biological males can somehow become females while retaining their Y chromosomes). In essence, the Modernist system is rooted in *agnosticism*, that is, skepticism regarding the ability of the human intellect to attain sure knowledge of immaterial things.

What, then, is "faith" for the Modernist? In short, it is a matter of *feelings* rather than objective certitude based on reason and revelation. As Joe Biden would say, it "starts in the gut," whereas St. Thomas Aquinas rightly defines faith as "*an act of the intellect* assenting to the divine truth at the command of the will moved by the grace of God."[3]

Those with eyes to see and ears to hear recognize that the Catholic Church has been in a state of grave crisis for several decades now, following the close of the Second Vatican Council (1962–1965). What many — including the vast majority of the Church's hierarchy — fail to grasp, however, is that *Modernism is at the root of the crisis*, which is why they consistently fail to address it in any meaningful way. In light of this tragic reality, Kennedy Hall is to be commended all the more for writing this book, one that should be read by every Catholic of every rank and station.

---

creation of human reflection that gradually formed through human effort and is to be perfected in the future through unlimited progress" (Denzinger-Hünermann [DH] 3541).

[3] *Summa Theologiae* II-II, q. 2, a. 9, emphasis added. St. Pius X likewise emphasized in his Oath Against Modernism: "I hold with certainty and I sincerely confess that faith is not a blind inclination of religion welling up from the depths of the subconscious under the impulse of the heart and the inclination of a morally conditioned will but is a genuine assent of the intellect to a truth that is received from outside by hearing. In this assent, given on the authority of the all-truthful God, we hold to be true what has been said, attested to, and revealed by the personal God, our Creator and Lord" (DH 3542).

Using St. Pius X's *Pascendi* as his framework, Hall methodically explains the origins of Modernism, including all the major players (both philosophical and theological), and guides readers through the saintly pontiff's systematic refutation of Modernist errors and deceitful methods — the very same we see on display at every level of the Church today, from those who subvert "the old theology" and seek to replace it with "a new theology which shall follow the vagaries of their philosophers" (*Pascendi* 18).

Thankfully, after diagnosing the disease, St. Pius X also prescribed the remedies necessary to expel Modernism from the Mystical Body of Christ, and Hall discusses this toward the end of this book. If I may be so bold, I would add that the ultimate remedy is contained in one simple phrase: *return to Tradition* — to that "which the Lord gave, was preached by the Apostles, and was preserved by the Fathers," in the words of St. Athanasius.[4]

On that note, I am reminded of what St. Pius X wrote to the French bishops of his day: "The true friends of the people are neither revolutionaries nor innovators: they are traditionalists."[5] By exposing Modernism and all its various facets, Kennedy Hall has proven himself a true friend of the people and a faithful son of the Church. May God reward his efforts by granting this book a wide readership, which it richly deserves.

Matt Gaspers
September 3, 2024
Feast of St. Pius X

---

[4] *Four Letters to Serapion of Thmuis* 1, 28.
[5] *Notre Charge Apostolique* (August 25, 1910).

Introduction

What Happened to Catholicism?

If you have picked up this book, it is likely that you have asked yourself, at least in some way, "What happened to Catholicism?" Whether it is the state of your parish, the state of your alma mater, or the sad state of so many Catholic families in which loved ones have fallen away, you have the good sense to try to understand how things have gotten so bad. Granted, there are a few bright spots in the Church, but anyone with good sense recognizes that something is wrong, or many things are wrong.

Perhaps you are one of the many souls who, around ten years ago, started to get the sense that something was "off" as Pope Francis started to say strange things on airplanes. Or perhaps when a pagan idol was paraded into St. Peter's, you realized that things had gone astray. Maybe it was when your religious-exemption letter was rejected by your employer during the Covid tyranny, because Pope Francis had referred to taking the new injection as an "act of love," that you really "woke up" to how bad things are.

Some readers may have seen the present state of the Church developing for decades and, although saddened, are not surprised that we are now in the realm of absurdity wherein the Vatican wastes time and resources on the dreadful Synod on Synodality.

Whatever your situation, you rightfully have questions that you need answered; you *know* that the Church is in a crisis of epic proportions. This book will provide clarity on the disease that undergirds the crisis, and you will find that it is a disease that we were warned about over a century ago by Pope St. Pius X.

The Heresy behind the Current Crisis

It has been my experience, and perhaps yours, that the crisis in the Church is often explained as a result of corruption, scandal, and the workings of malevolent groups. Now, this is true, as much of what befalls us is the result of the efforts or sins of high-ranking churchmen and high-ranking members of secret societies, such as the Freemasons. Far be it from me to suggest that investigating these things is a waste of time. If we want to get to the root of the problem, however, we must go *deeper*.

Consider the Freemasons, for example. What is it that is so evil about them? Pope after pope has condemned them historically, and it is not because of their funny aprons or ridiculous ceremonies. The reason their philosophy is so evil is that it advocates for the *antithesis* of Catholic doctrine. Freemasonry advocates for the equality of all religions, for universal brotherhood based on shared humanity rather than shared Baptism, and for the disestablishment of perennial governmental systems so that revolutionaries may lead nations. In short, Freemasonry is evil because it is Liberalism, and if no lodges were ever established, it would still be just as great an evil for Liberalism to spread by other means.

Now, this is but one example, but the point is that it is the *heretical doctrine* that is the vilest element of Freemasonry and not machinations of Freemasons or the secret rituals or blood oaths, as creepy as they may be.

In 1907, Pope Pius X published an encyclical called *Pascendi Dominici Gregis* — often referred to simply as *Pascendi* — that outlines the doctrines of a new heresy that he spoke of as if it were the greatest heresy possible. He called it the "synthesis of all heresies," which is no small feat considering how many heresies have existed. This means that it contains not only the errors of Liberalism — Freemasonry — but of every heretical and erroneous idea you can imagine.

Arianism, pantheism, dualism, Gnosticism, scientism, materialism, subjectivism, relativism, rationalism, Protestantism, and more are all synthesized in some way in this new heresy. St. Pius X called this heresy Modernism because it arose in modern times — what we call modernity — and not because everything modern is heretical.

Pope Pius X was the first pope to be canonized in almost five hundred years, and *Pascendi* should be considered his magnum opus; but you would be hard-pressed to find anyone who has read the encyclical. Certainly, most laymen have never read it, and it is not likely that most priests formed in seminaries since Vatican II have read it either. Now, it is not an easy document to read, and it is quite lengthy, especially considering that papal bulls did not used to be as long as they are now. It was written by a genius who employed a great depth of vocabulary, and the document was issued to the bishops of the world. Thus, it was not written in a way that is easily understandable to average readers — that is, unless they like to read old encyclicals while constantly referring to dictionaries and philosophy manuals.

Nonetheless, it is a *shocking* document to read when we look back on the last few decades in the Church. St. Pius X warned of and explained the cause of *everything* that has befallen us. After reading *Pascendi* for the first time, I was left wondering whether many of the theologians and prelates of our day *had* read the document — and had read it not as a condemnation but as a "how-to" manual.

In *Pascendi*, Pius X told us that Modernism would destroy biblical scholarship; he told us that Modernism would lead to a complete overhaul of the Mass and all the sacraments; he told us that perennial doctrines would be ignored or rejected by theologians; he told us that Modernists would advocate for limitless ecumenism to the point where all religions were seen as true; and he even told us that Modernism would lead to something like the Synod on Synodality, if you can believe it.

The Scope of This Book

As was mentioned, *Pascendi* can be hard to read, so I present to you a book that breaks down Pius X's work in a way that can be understood, along with examples of how Modernism has infected virtually every corner of the Church, even in places we would least expect it. Of course, a distinction must be made here, as the Church, properly understood, is the Mystical Body of Christ, and in that there is no blemish. Nonetheless, God gave us free will, and He allows sinners to operate within the institutions that represent the Mystical Body on Earth, so we cannot be shocked when we find heresies and heretics in our midst.

Pius X follows in his landmark encyclical a particular order that he deemed necessary to expose fully the heresy of Modernism from root to fruit. He begins with questions of philosophy, moves to doctrine, explains how those doctrines are applied, and then offers a remedy. I have chosen to follow his lead, not only because he was a saintly pope but because Modernism is so multifaceted and pernicious that it must be dealt with in a precise manner and with the requisite philosophical foundation in order to be properly understood. While remaining faithful to Pius X's work, I have endeavored to explain Modernism in relatable terms that the average reader can understand.

I believe that you will come to believe the same thing I have: that the crisis in the Church *is* the heresy of Modernism and that it is therefore of the utmost importance that we understand it fully.

Let us begin.

1

An Enemy Has Done This

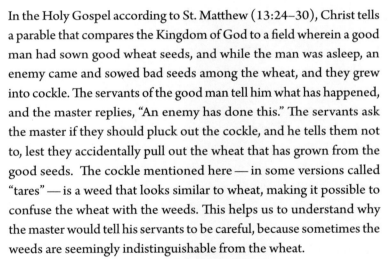

In the Holy Gospel according to St. Matthew (13:24–30), Christ tells a parable that compares the Kingdom of God to a field wherein a good man had sown good wheat seeds, and while the man was asleep, an enemy came and sowed bad seeds among the wheat, and they grew into cockle. The servants of the good man tell him what has happened, and the master replies, "An enemy has done this." The servants ask the master if they should pluck out the cockle, and he tells them not to, lest they accidentally pull out the wheat that has grown from the good seeds. The cockle mentioned here — in some versions called "tares" — is a weed that looks similar to wheat, making it possible to confuse the wheat with the weeds. This helps us to understand why the master would tell his servants to be careful, because sometimes the weeds are seemingly indistinguishable from the wheat.

This parable stands as a warning for us as to the nature of heresies and heretics in the Church because it is often the case that heresies are, at first glance, indistinguishable from orthodox Catholic doctrine. Heresies employ expansive philosophical terms, they appeal to Scripture, and it is almost always the case that heretics themselves are highly intelligent. For all of these reasons, we can all confuse a heresy for a true doctrine of the Church.

Also, the parable tells us that the infiltration of bad seeds into the field is a *crime*, and it is done under the cover of darkness, which warns us that evil can befall us without our seeing it coming.

Modernism, as will be argued in this book, is in full bloom in the Church, and we can confidently say that an *enemy has done this*; therefore, to understand the depth of the problem, we must investigate how this has happened.

What Is Modernism?

As was mentioned in the introduction, Pope Pius X called Modernism the "synthesis of all heresies," which should give us pause. The heresies that the Church has had to deal with are numerous and present ideas that are highly convincing; this is why so many Catholics and theologians have fallen prey to heresies. Because of this, we could say that Modernism contains in it the complexity and sophistication of the mass of heresies that have plagued the Church. This makes it easily adaptable, pernicious, and invasive.

Modernism can be defined as a heresy that, seeking to reconcile the Catholic Faith with key tenets of modern philosophy (notably, agnosticism, subjectivism, and progressivism or evolutionism), reduces the Faith to subjective religious experience and reduces dogmatic truths to mere symbols or metaphors that must continually evolve in order to remain alive.

No defined truth or sacred tradition of the Church is safe as long as Modernism abounds. Modernism necessarily results in sweeping reforms that deform every aspect of ecclesial life. The Modernist commitment to tenets of modern philosophy has created a situation wherein every binding truth is up for reinterpretation, to the point where the authorities in the Church seem to be in a state of perpetual questioning rather than teaching.

The entire thrust of the Church since Vatican II has been animated by a spirit of change, which is labeled "renewal" and "newness"; by the time Catholics attempt to understand the new thing presented to them, there is another novelty they must contend with. The New Mass, for example, was published only in 1969 and has already been revised numerous times, and the norms for what is permitted during Mass have changed as well. When you were growing up, it may have been that girls could not be altar servers, but now they can; it may have been that only priests could read from the pulpit, but now both men and women can do so; it may have been that only priests could distribute Holy Communion, but now you are likely to find multiple queues in parishes on Sundays, with men and women distributing Communion under both species.

The *Catechism of the Catholic Church*, in print for barely thirty years, has been revised numerous times as well, to the point where the long-standing doctrine of the permissibility of the death penalty has now been reversed.

I could go on with examples.

This state of constant change, and ultimately confusion, was not the standard in the Church before Modernism became the theological norm. Yes, missals had been revised, but not at the rate they are revised now or to the same extent. And if we consider the Roman Catechism or the Catechism of Pope Pius X, for example, we simply do not find new editions every few years to reflect new theological insights from new popes. In fact, the Roman Catechism, published in 1566, was *never* revised. This is because the Catholic Faith does not change, and therefore we do not need revisions.

The insistence on subjective experience as a barometer of religious truth has led Catholics into strange spiritual practices and has given rise to a host of movements within the Church, many of them borrowed from outside the Church. Under the guise of "inculturation" (adopting other cultures into Catholic spirituality), we have seen pagan practices take place in Catholic settings, such as when Pope Francis visited Canada and a Native elder performed a "smudging" ceremony to cleanse the room of bad spirits in the presence of the Holy Father.

Dioceses around the world are in a constant state of experimentation with new programs supposedly designed to bring Catholics back to Church. Yet, because progress never stops and things always evolve, these programs can never last, and before you know it, a new program is needed.

Everything is in a state of flux in the Church because of Modernism, and, until the Church is cleansed of it, we can be certain that something new will be around the corner because the thing that was new five minutes ago is now old and no longer works.

The Crime Scene

As was mentioned above, the sowing of bad seeds in the field under cover of darkness was a crime, and it happened when it was least expected. In the same way, Modernism has spread into the veins of the Church. Heresy is a crime against God and the Truth.

Perhaps you have seen a detective show or read a mystery novel in which the author begins the story with the crime. Those in the audience see the crime happen at the outset, and they know something evil has happened, but they may not know *who* committed the crime, or, if they do, they do not know *how*. So, in comes the detective in the next scene with his forensic team and police colleagues to assess the crime scene. There may be blood spattered on the walls or shattered glass on the floor beside the murder weapon. The detective looks around, perhaps he notices clues here and there, and he eventually leaves the crime scene, and the real work begins.

The scene of the crime tells him only so much, so he must branch out and look in other places. If he has a lead, he must follow it; he might track down a person who may be able to tell him something about a hunch. If he finds another clue, it might lead him down another path to make sense of what he has newly discovered. He may discover things that lead him to a library or even a scientist or a professor to help him understand something he happened upon that he has never seen before.

Along the way, the detective finds that he even has to get into the mind of the criminal, to the point where he learns to think like him so that he can understand things the way the criminal does. In fact, a good detective will understand the mind of the criminal better than the criminal understands himself.

The process is painstaking and exhausting, but eventually, after much work, the detective arrives at a theory of what happened. If he has done his work diligently, he will find his man, expose the crime, and explain how the whole thing took place.

This is what Pope Pius X did when he investigated the crime of Modernism. He took on the task of understanding Modernism better than Modernists, and he exposed the whole system. We have all seen the Modernist crime scene — we are living in it! — and in order to understand it, we must follow Pius X's lead and start from the beginning to understand who committed the crime, and how and why they did it. To do that, we will have to begin our quest by traveling back hundreds of years to understand the bad seeds sown in the field that grew into the errors of Modern Philosophy, which make the crime of Modernism possible.

2

The Philosophical Origins of Modernism

Long before Modernism arose in the realm of Catholic theology, the seeds of misleading philosophy were planted in the intellectual milieu. Theology is the study of God and divine things, and we must use philosophical concepts in order to do that well. During the centuries that followed Christ's mission on Earth, Catholic prelates and theologians adopted the philosophical tools of the great thinkers of antiquity, such as Plato, Socrates, and Aristotle. Although these ancient thinkers were pagans and did not have the aid of divine revelation to correct some of their shortcomings, their thought was grounded in reality, and they equipped their intellectual disciples with the necessary tools to conform their minds to the order of nature and the natural law.

For this reason, Catholic priests and theologians were formed with the philosophical teachings stemming from these schools of thought. St. Augustine, for example, was heavily Platonist or Neo-Platonist in his thinking, and St. Thomas Aquinas utilized the precision and wisdom of Aristotle to explain the Catholic Faith with clarity and accuracy. The use of clear philosophical terms and categories is indispensable in Catholic theology, and when we see a degradation in the study of philosophy, we can expect to see a degradation in the study of theology. It is for this reason that we must consider the philosophical ideas that spread throughout the intellectual milieu and how they acted as precursors to the rise of Modernism.

To do this, we must navigate through a historical sketch of the philosophical and theological errors and dangers that have culminated in this great heresy. Among many Catholics today, it is common to opine that Modernism is just a "modern" problem and that it has something to do with modern man or modern times. This is partly true, insofar as Modernism has flowered like a noxious weed in the so-called modern era. But, if we look to the past, we find that the roots of Modernism go back hundreds of years.

As you progress through this book, it will become evident that the errors of Modernism can be found in intellectual tendencies and persuasions as much as or more than in outright heretical statements, which are often absent from works tinged with the Modernist spirit. Modernism is happy to take its time festering in the mind after years and decades. Many great heresies can be compared to mortal sins, such as murder and adultery, in that it is clear that the person who had done such an action has transgressed the moral law. But, in the case of Modernism, we see instead the adoption of a mildly bad habit, such as gambling, which becomes such a part of a person's life that he eventually goes bankrupt after years of losing bits of money here and there. For this reason, it is also extremely difficult, perhaps even impossible in the natural sense, to shake someone out of Modernism. A priest once told me that Modernism is a psychological disease like an intellectual cancer, and it takes many rounds of difficult and almost fatal medical intervention to cure the ailment.

Modernism did not begin yesterday, or even at the time of Pius X. For our purposes, it is useful to consider the rise of nominalism, which was popularized by William of Ockham.

William of Ockham

William of Ockham was a philosopher who lived in the thirteenth and fourteenth centuries and who protested against the method of

Scholastic and Aristotelian philosophy of St. Thomas Aquinas. The *Catholic Encyclopedia* calls his writings "controversial" and states that he advocated a sort of "secular absolutism." This means, in essence, that he believed that the State should not be subject to the pope in a temporal sense. This erroneous persuasion in political philosophy would be condemned five centuries after his death by Pope Bl. Pius IX in his *Syllabus of Errors*, most notably in numbers 54 and 55. Statement 54 of the *Syllabus* condemns the notion that the temporal authorities "are not only exempt from the jurisdiction of the Church, but are superior to the Church in deciding questions of jurisdiction." Similarly, statement 55 condemns the notion that "the Church ought to be separated from the State, and the State from the Church."

These two errors, although perhaps not expressed in such exact terms at the time of Ockham, are at the heart of Liberalism, which is the philosophical framework at the heart of modern Western nation-states. Perhaps the greatest error of Liberalism is the notion of religious liberty, which, in our day, is presented as a sacrosanct virtue of modern civilized states.

Some readers may be surprised to see religious liberty referred to as an error, so I should define what we mean by it and what we do not. First, we must distinguish between a positive liberty and a negative liberty; a positive liberty is a liberty that is posited as a good in and of itself, such as the freedom to live, or what we might call the right to life; a negative liberty is something that is *tolerated* but not desired. Catholic teaching has been clear throughout the centuries that only Catholicism can have a true positive liberty in the State, while other religions can be tolerated for social reasons. This may seem antithetical to modern political thinking because even conservative political thought in modern times trumpets religious liberty as one of the highest ideals. As Catholics, however, we must understand that *error has no rights*, and therefore, heresy and false religion can have no positive right to be promoted or practiced publicly, even if they are tolerated in the private lives of citizens.

Now, we must also consider what is at stake when we herald religious liberty, as such, as a good or something that should be considered a positive right in a society; by doing so, we are giving equal rights to Christ and the Devil in the public square. This may seem hyperbolic, but all false religions must necessarily be inspired by Satan, even if many good and moral people who follow them do not believe so and do not want to follow the Devil. For this reason, Catholic states during the reign of Christendom always professed Catholicism as the State religion, and whether other religions were allowed to be practiced was a prudential decision made by politicians. Islam and Judaism, for example, were always heavily restricted in Catholic states. If we fall for the notion that religious liberty is a *good* thing in a society, then we must believe that it would be *good* for a false religion to be free to influence citizens as much as Catholicism. While it is understandable that we should never force anyone to convert — of course we shouldn't — we should also understand that false religions should be restricted like any other harmful thing.

For example, we would not think it was okay for a society to profess legally that citizens are free to poison themselves and teach others how to poison themselves. Religious poison is much worse than physical poison; physical poison kills the body, but spiritual poison kills the soul and can lead to damnation.

Pope Pius VIII, Pope Gregory XVI, Pope Pius IX, and Pope Leo XIII all wrote triumphantly against Liberalism, but like all weeds, it still grows where it is unwelcome.

Although Liberalism — and its most damnable error of the "separation of Church and State" — applies primarily to the political and social sphere, it is this Liberalism that lays the foundation for Modernism. Although there is a distinction between Church and State, the traditional Catholic understanding is that there is no pure *separation* between them. Of course, there are exterior differences, and we would not say that the parliament is the same as the synod, even if the modern synod is nothing more than a parliament of religion. The heart of Christian civilization is the *Mass*, as John Senior so wonderfully explained in *The Restoration of Christian Culture*, and therefore Christian society cannot exist with Church and State in opposition to one another. Instead, the State must be at the service of the Church, as the body is at the service or under the dominion of the soul.

Society, in many ways, is a collection of families, and Christian society is a collection of Christian families. What we call Christendom is really the Christian religion lived by Christians in their homes and communities. If the Faith is the heart of civilization, then the State is the infrastructure built to house and protect the heart. In the same way that it would be impossible for a man to say he is a Christian and has a Christian family that is separate from the Church, it is impossible for a Christian nation to say it is separate from the Church.

Granted, there are very few nations left that are Christian in the official sense, as most Western nations have declared themselves secular in the aftermath of so many revolutions. Nonetheless, it is important to remember that Ockham's errors pertaining to the relation between Church and State arose when states were officially and legally Catholic. While we do not have Catholic states like we once did, the effect of his errors has filtered into the philosophical underpinnings of the post-Christian West, and Catholic discourse has not been immune to this. The Catholic principles remain because they are true and are based on the Church's perennial teaching, which does not change when opinions change. A non-Christian nation will undoubtedly reject the authority of the Church, as a non-Christian rejects Christ, and the consequences will be what they will be in the long run.

Furthermore, politics is related to human activity and human society, which the Church has an obligation to speak on. Also, many elements of political activity are distinctly concerned with moral and religious matters, and the Church has rightful authority in this sphere.

Even local political decisions, which may seem trivial, may possess a distinctly moral element: Is it moral — meaning, is it just — to say this road should be fixed and that road should not? Will these decisions hinder a father's ability to provide for his family? Is it ethical to disallow a family to have chickens on their property? And so on.

Even though seemingly mundane, these questions of local governance carry an ethical weight as they affect the professional and familial lives of residents. If a town says that residents cannot have chickens, this will affect what chores are available to children in a given home, a factor that pertains to their moral formation. If a town decides to fix a meeting hall and not a road, those who rely on that road will experience greater wear and tear on their vehicles, and that will affect the family budget. Suffice it to say, there can be no separation in the truest sense between morality and what the State — however small — decides.

Because there can be no meaningful or full separation between politics and ethics, there can be no separation between politics and religion, as morals are heavily governed by religious truth. It may be retorted that not all moral questions are matters of Catholic doctrine because morality can be found in the natural law, and this is, of course, true. But Catholicism is the *only* true religion, and therefore the full truth of morality can be enlightened only by Catholic Truth. And, because Catholicism is the only true religion, this means that out of justice to the Creator, who established His Church, His creatures must give Him what is His due; and He is due the assent to the fullness of Truth enacted in His Creation. So, for a Catholic, there can be no "secular" society in the sense of a nonreligious or multireligious state but only a toleration of non-Catholic beliefs and practices. A Catholic cannot *promote*, which is to say, actively will, any aspect of a false religion, even if he can *allow* or *permit* a non-Catholic practice prudentially and for the sake of public cohesion in a pluralist society.

The result of the State absolutism that was professed by William of Ockham, and became Liberalism, was the false notion that the exterior positive actions of the State could be independent of the Truth of the Faith. This mentality, although starting in the social realm, seeped into the philosophical and psychological realm of Christian thought.

When a society permits or seemingly approves of public sin while still professing to be Catholic, the effect on the believer is that he will eventually come to believe that exterior action can exist in contradiction to interior reality. If the Catholic State can approve willingly of heterodox activity but still be Catholic, then why can't the believer act or believe in a heterodox way while still being Catholic? What results from this error is that religion becomes a private matter, and any talk of the social reign of Christ the King is null and void.

This demonstrates how Liberalism, although mainly political, set the stage for moral and religious subjectivism, which ultimately became Protestantism, which, far from being a result of doctrinal differences or of one man's desire to beget an heir, was really a revolution against the Church and the State.

Nominalism

The most difficult error of Ockham, however, was *nominalism*, which is an error in philosophy. In essence, nominalism is the denial that the intellect can understand abstract or universal concepts or that such concepts even exist. This means that nominalism does not recognize true knowledge of the *essence* or *nature* of a thing and recognizes only the externals, which are really nothing more than categories for the nominalist. In other words, nominalism asserts that everything outside the mind is completely individual and that reality cannot be understood by universal and abstract concepts.

Aristotelian and Thomistic metaphysics — the backbone of Catholic philosophy — tell us that something has a *form* and an *essence*. A dog has the form of a dog and the essence of a dog. A dog looks like, or has the form of, a dog because it is really a dog. It does not look like a dog yet is really something else. Ockham's error is in saying that we cannot know the essence of a dog but can only categorize what dogs look like by characteristics that seem "doggish."

The consequences of nominalism may not be obvious at first glance because it seems almost like something philosophers concern themselves with in ivory towers, but the consequences are severe. One author wrote:

> By denying that there is any basis in reality for universals that every human mind can grasp, nominalism moved knowledge away from objectivity and toward subjectivity and prepared the way for further radical propositions in the realms of theology and morality.... If God's acts do not possess a logical, objective nature — as Ockham and his disciples taught — then they are merely the result of a groundless divine will unconcerned with what humans call "reason" or "logic." If that is the case, obviously man cannot use his reason or logic to determine what is just or unjust. Natural law, then, is simply nonsense.[6]

Ockham went so far as to suggest that the Incarnation was important only insofar as God applied value to it and that God could have saved the human race by becoming anything He wanted, even an inanimate object.[7]

The error of nominalism betrays a primordial and scriptural truth, however, as Adam was given the task of "naming" the creatures (Gen. 2:19). Adam did not simply give a descriptor and say, "Well, this looks cowy, so we will call it a cow." On the contrary, Adam had infused knowledge and was therefore in a position to name each thing based on what it *was*, not merely on what it looked like. It would have been impossible for Adam to do otherwise, as he would have had no knowledge of what a cow should look like if he did not know what a cow was. He named the creatures because he *knew* the essence of what the creatures were, not because he thought the creatures looked like something that looked like the creatures.

---

[6] Carl Olson, "The Error of Nominalism," *Catholic Answers Magazine*, October 1, 2005.
[7] Olson, "The Error of Nominalism."

When you or I look at a human being, we understand that a human being looks like a human being because we intrinsically know what a human being is, even if we do not have the language — in infancy, for example — to verbalize what it is. We know that a human being *is* a human being in both its form and its essence, and we understand that nonhuman creatures are not human beings because they have not only different forms but also different essences.

If we adopt nominalism, we ultimately find ourselves in an intellectual trap of living with a disconnect between what we know to be true by our senses and how we describe things. The nominalist lives with an internal contradiction of mind, in which he is forced to say, "Look at those beautiful flowers," when he really means, "Look at those things that appear to have the characteristic of what is called beauty and seem to correspond to the image of what I perceive as flowers because they look like other things I perceive to be flowers."

The result of this thinking is a type of agnosticism and skepticism about the nature of reality because nominalism creates a conundrum wherein we call things by certain names even though they aren't *really* what we call them.

Nominalist thought has given rise to modern trends that are commonplace today. Of course, readers are aware of the modern tendency to describe created things as continually "evolving" in the sense that one thing can give rise to a different type of thing. If we were to break down the notion of the evolution of the species in basic terms, it would be defined either as created things creating themselves or created things creating from themselves things that are different from themselves. This sort of thinking is made possible due to nominalism's denial of the philosophical category of essences. Evolution, both in the metaphysical and the physical realm, requires that there be no essences in the pure sense. This is because a thing with its own essence cannot give rise to a thing with a different essence. For example, a true statement cannot be the same as, or the progenitor of, a false statement, as this would be a contradiction: two plus two equals four; we cannot say that five also comes from two plus two. In Catholic doctrine, when something is defined in a particular way, we cannot say that something that cannot be found in that definition is also part of that doctrine, as it would be an essentially different doctrine. In the physical realm, a fish cannot give birth to a lizard, or a bird to a cat, as the essences of those animals are not shared.

Evolutionists both in the realm of ideas and biological reality must ultimately deny essences as being a real thing in order for their philosophy to work. Our society has adopted nominalism fully, and this is why we are told that as long as a man has surgery and wears female clothing, he is really a female — but that is impossible. While it is true that the man dressed as a woman may appear in some ways to be like a woman, he cannot change his essence from male to female because both his body and his soul — form and essence — are male and not female.

Modernists, as we will see in the work of Pius X, believed that doctrine can evolve and change in its essential meaning; this is a type of nominalist error. But the First Vatican Council made it clear that this is impossible when it stated:

> For the doctrine of the faith which God has revealed is put forward not as some philosophical discovery capable of being perfected by human intelligence, but as a divine deposit committed to the spouse of Christ to be faithfully protected and infallibly promulgated. Hence, too, that meaning of the sacred dogmas is ever to be maintained which has once been declared by holy mother church, and there must never be any abandonment of this sense under the pretext or in the name of a more profound understanding.[8]

---

[8] First Vatican Council, session 3 (April 24, 1870), chap. 4, nos. 13–14, Papal Encyclicals, https://www.papalencyclicals.net/councils/ecum20.htm.

As an example, the doctrine of Transubstantiation — the process of bread and wine changing into the Body and Blood of Our Lord — cannot be understood to mean that the bread and wine do not undergo a substantial change at the Consecration. Thus, if a theologian were to say that he believes in Transubstantiation but were to define it differently from what the dogma truly is, he would be in error.

The nominalism championed by Ockham did not disappear, and his philosophical ideas were never condemned by name. He also espoused the error of fideism, which is the notion that belief in God is strictly a matter of faith alone and not of reason. This error is manifestly in opposition to the solemnly defined teaching of the Church from the First Vatican Council that by reason God can be known to exist: "If anyone says that the one, true God, our creator and lord, cannot be known with certainty from the things that have been made, by the natural light of human reason: let him be *anathema*."[9]

Ockham was eventually excommunicated after coming into conflict with the pope, and he lived his final years with a group of dissident Franciscans.

Fortunately, Ockham's errors did not become common in the realm of Catholic thought, but after the Protestant Revolution, a series of philosophers arose who not only revived nominalism but gave us what can be called modern philosophy and all the metaphysical chaos that came with it.

The Four Horsemen of the Philosophical Apocalypse

Although it would require multiple volumes to investigate in full the profound complexity and confusion of the philosophical systems of Immanuel Kant, Georg Hegel, David Hume, and René Descartes, it would be insufficient if we did not at least present the fundamental ideas of these men because they provide the intellectual framework for Modernism.

---

[9] First Vatican Council, Canons, chap. 2, no. 1.

Kant, Hegel, and Hume were all roughly contemporaneous with one another and are considered paragons of the philosophical systems that emanated from the so-called Enlightenment era (roughly 1685–1815). The Enlightenment is named as such because it is alleged that this era brought forth the "Age of Reason," in which the shackles of the old systems were unchained and man was free to be what traditional religion had stopped him from being. Of course, this era was an intellectual and moral disaster and was filled with some of the most gruesome and bloody conflicts ever seen in human history, typified by the insanity of the French Revolution. If most historians had more sense, they would call this era the Darkening. During this era, Liberalism, Freemasonry, revolution, and regicide all flourished, capitalizing on the Industrial Revolution, which saw a great change in everyday life for the everyday man. If there was any light during the Enlightenment, it was the camouflaged light of Satan, who disguised himself as an angel of light as he preyed on an upturned society in order to upturn the order of Christian civilization.

The world was filled with a love of novelty, and the novel ideas of the four horsemen of the Philosophical Apocalypse — Descartes, Hume, Kant, and Hegel — satisfied the desire for new ideas in an old world.

Descartes

René Descartes (1596–1650) is remembered as a French philosopher and scientist and is heralded in academia as an influential genius of the period between the Renaissance and the Enlightenment. He is most famous for his utterance "Cogito, ergo sum," "I think, therefore I am." It is said that he anguished over the nature of reality for some time, and after locking himself in a confined space, he had a revelatory thought that since he was, in fact, thinking, it was proof that he must exist. At first glance, this notion may seem relatively harmless — after all, thinking is proof that one exists in order to think. It was not that Descartes used this as *a* proof for his existence, however, but that he looked at this idea as *the* proof par excellence that he existed. Putting aside the fact that it is quite strange that a man must agonize over his own existence to the point where he needs to lock himself up in order to prove the idea, the notion itself presents a revolution in philosophy and a break with Scholastic and Hellenistic thought, which had been the backbone of Christian philosophy.

In the philosophy of Aristotle and St. Thomas Aquinas, one first comes into contact with exterior, objective reality and then, secondarily, reflects on his own act of knowledge and comes to self-awareness. In other words, knowledge begins with the sense of the exterior world, and it is a given that the knowledge received by the senses is true knowledge and really known. There can be exceptions, as in the case of intoxication, illusion, and so forth, but this is not because the senses themselves don't work but because what is being sensed is a trick of some sort or because one is impaired in perceiving what his senses are experiencing.

In addition, because Descartes' philosophy starts with self-awareness, it is ultimately prone to subjectivism and even a type of insane confusion. How is one to know that he should trust his judgment of self, given that he cannot — in a sense — trust his own judgment? How is a man to know that the outside world is real, given that his perception could just be his own, and everyone else could perceive things in a completely different manner? Ultimately, this manner of thinking precludes any objective reality, and one is free to believe he is living in simulated reality and may not even exist at all. It is madness, but Descartes' ideas were embraced and expanded upon, and today, there are people — many of them — mad enough to take ideas of living in a simulated reality seriously.

It is said that Descartes maintained that he was a faithful Catholic, despite his disastrous philosophy. This may be true, and I hope he saved his soul, but his veritable insanity became the foundation for the modern philosophers who followed.

Hume

David Hume (1711–1776) was a Scottish philosopher and intellectual known for his influence on the Scottish Enlightenment. He is remembered for his naturalist and skeptical empiricism, which, in reality, presented itself as something like Ockham's nominalism. Hume was not trained as a Scholastic, so his terminology is different from that of the medieval William of Ockham, but his ideas are similar. Hume did not start with self-awareness like Descartes, and he did believe that knowledge received from the exterior senses is real and points to something real. Like Ockham, though, he believed that what is perceived by the senses is merely an image of what is presented by an object, but the "supersensible" (comparable to the Scholastic term "essence") is unknowable. His manner of thinking was different from Descartes', but it contributed to the disorder in philosophical discourse, especially in the English-speaking world.

Kant

Immanuel Kant (1724–1804), along with Georg Hegel, may have been the proto-Modernist philosopher par excellence. Following Hume, he accepted the existence of the physical world and held to Hume's style of subjectivism about the nature of what things are. He also believed that we impose notions such as space and time as well as causality and substance on the natural world. According to Kant, we know only our subjective experience of reality (phenomena) — a logical conclusion from Descartes' ideas — and this results from our imposing of subjective "forms of intuition" and "categories" on raw sensory data. Keeping with Ockham and Hume, the real nature of external things (noumena) is unknowable, and this renders the entire discipline of metaphysics — the pursuit of knowledge of the nature of reality — impossible and futile.

In his *Critique of Pure Reason* (1781), Kant attempts to dismantle the notion of any objective certainty regarding the existence of God, free will, and the immortality of the soul. He proposes what are called "antinomies," which are nearly synonymous with philosophical paradoxes, in an attempt to prove that reason cannot be trusted ultimately, as it could be used to prove and disprove opposite theses. This means that he asserted that contradictory things could be true at the same time, or, better yet, a thing could be true and not true at the same time. It is easy to see how this is false, as it contradicts the basic principle of noncontradiction; X cannot be X and not X at the same time. For example, Kant allegedly proved that the universe had a beginning and is therefore finite (thesis) and also the opposite — namely, that the universe was eternal (antithesis).

As you can imagine, Kant's ideas do not leave the reader with any intellectual satisfaction; instead, they facilitate a state of certain agnosticism, which ironically seems like one of Kant's antinomies — the idea that one could be certain about his uncertainty. In a sense, Kant is like an anti-Thomist in the way that a villain is an ape or mockery of the hero. His method is rigorous, and he seems to consider "both sides," as Thomas Aquinas considers the strongest argument for and against a given topic. But, due to his inherent skepticism about the knowledge of things and his insistence on the subjective nature of reality, Kant's method merely serves to prove that the notion of proof itself is limited, if not futile.

It is a bit ironic that Kant spent a considerable amount of time and effort in the pursuit of knowledge as a way of proving that knowledge itself is ultimately unattainable. Kant's work is, in itself, a contradiction and antinomy of the highest order.

In his later work *Critique of Practical Reason* (1788), Kant attempts to reestablish belief in God in an abstract sense based on the usefulness of belief in a Divine Being for our moral life. Again, it is ironic that a man who significantly rejected the metaphysics necessary to prove that something could be truly good or evil spent much of his time arguing for the necessity of God as an idea because it is good for men to be good. Despite the attempts of Kantians to dress up his religious ideas as sophisticated or groundbreaking, we can say with certainty that Immanuel Kant's idea of God is akin to the popular notion of Santa Claus or the tooth fairy. I would be more inclined, however, to promote belief in Santa Claus than in Kant's notion of God because belief in Jolly Old St. Nick is meant to be whimsical and playful, whereas belief in God in a subjective or relativist sense will lead to a relativist morality that undermines Kant's very insistence that the idea of God is necessary for morality.

Finally, in a third work, called *Religion within the Bounds of Bare Reason* (1793), Kant argued that historical religions are like different ways of dressing up what human reason naturally knows about God. For Kant, it is ultimately the interior life of man that matters, and the external trappings of this or that religion are merely symbols. The real purpose of religion is to foster morally upright behavior. As we will see, Kant's notion of some sort of subconscious religious sense that is in touch with the divine, or is divine itself, is essentially what Pius X will condemn as *vital immanence*, one of the hallmarks of Modernism. And, as we will also see, Kant's inherent agnosticism goes hand in hand with vital immanence and is another pillar of the Modernist system.

Kant's system was clearly condemned by Pope Leo XIII in his encyclical on the state of the education of the clergy, *Depuis le Jour* (1899):

> We are profoundly grieved to learn that ... some Catholics have felt at liberty to follow in the wake of a philosophy which under the specious pretext of freeing human reason from all ideas and from all illusions, denies it the right of affirming anything beyond its own operations, thus sacrificing to a radical subjectivism all the certainties which traditional metaphysics, consecrated by the authority of the strongest thinkers, laid down as the necessary and unshakable foundations for the demonstration of the existence of God, the spirituality and immortality of the soul, and the objective reality of the exterior world. (15)

The German philosopher's system is also castigated by Pope St. Pius X in *Pascendi*.

For a true Catholic to understand and accept Kant is virtually impossible, unless he rejects the basis for all logical thinking, as Pope Leo XIII explains. When reading Kant, one gets the impression that he viewed himself as the "first thinker" tasked with figuring out the nature of reality on his own. It is painfully monotonous to comb through his musings, and most people certainly do not investigate his works with any attention to detail.

Nonetheless, Kant is so popular and adored by so many, perhaps because his conclusions — even if baseless and veritably insane — offer fallen man the subjective morality his lower appetites so desperately desire, dressed up with a veneer of pseudo-sophistication. In other words, Kant's agnostic relativism allows a man to think and act as if the world begins and ends in his own mind and to think he is really smart and moral for believing that.

Hegel

Georg Hegel (1770–1831) followed Kant in many respects but added his own flavor to his predecessor's ideas, most notably by way of positing an evolutionary mentality. Kant taught that noumena were essentially unknowable, but Hegel posited that "noumenal reality is not an unknowable substrate of appearances, but an ever-active process, which in thought and in reality constantly passes into its opposite in order to return to a higher and richer form of itself."[10]

In essence, Hegel posited that the noumenal reality is not really unknown but, instead, is a living process in which reality itself goes back and forth between itself and its opposite (unreality?) in order to produce a higher reality of sorts. We see here the basis for an evolutionary mindset, in which conflicting forces go back and forth with one another so that a "higher" or more evolved reality emerges from the struggle. The substrate for reality itself, according to Hegel, is a struggle for a higher reality that emerges from reality's struggle for its own evolution.

---

[10] William Turner, "Hegelianism," *The Catholic Encyclopedia*, vol. 7 (New York: Robert Appleton Company, 1910), https://www.newadvent.org/cathen/07192a.htm.

The consequences of this mindset in the metaphysical is such that the notion of real evil and real good is ultimately destroyed. Even if one were to posit that there is something like a temporary good and a temporary bad, in the mind of a Hegelian, it is necessary to conclude that eventually a higher reality would emerge from contact with evil, and evil itself is therefore something like an agent of progress.

Now, there is a partial truth in this philosophy, in that a battle with evil can sharpen good actions, thoughts, and so on. As Christians, we would, of course, say that God brings good out of evil, but there is a fundamental difference between the Hegelian view and the Christian view. As Christians, we believe that all that God has created is, in its pure state, good. We do not believe that God creates evil things but that the good things God has made can be used for evil, or that God's intelligent creatures — humans and angels — can do evil things with their free will. Even if a human being does something evil, however, he is still good in the sense that he is a creature God has made.

Furthermore, if the Hegelian concept of synthesis is applied to the physical realm, we find problems there as well because the insinuation is that the created world goes from a lower state to a higher state through a process of conflict. We read, however, that "In the beginning God created heaven, and earth.... And God saw that it was good" (Gen. 1:1, 10). What God has created is *good* in its initial state, and by "good" Scripture means not merely "cool" or "neat" in the colloquial sense but that the creation was done the way God desired it to be done. On the contrary, when we speak of something being "evil" or "bad" in the sense of created things, we speak of something *lacking* something that makes it good. For example, we would say that severe cold is a physical evil because the presence of enough heat to survive is missing. In the moral realm, we would say that fornication is evil, not because there is anything intrinsically wrong with the human action that takes place during fornication but because the bonds of marriage are missing, and they are what would make the action good, which is to say, done as it was intended. In this way, we can say that evil is a privation of the good, and this means that the presence of evil is the absence of good.

Since Hegelian thought leaves us with a creation that is consistently striving within or against itself with opposing forces, we cannot say that there is any real good to be found in that manner of thinking; there are only "opposites" that are neither good nor bad but only incomplete or in transition to something higher. If you have ever studied Eastern religions such as Hinduism, perhaps you have noticed how Hegelian thought is strikingly pantheist, in the sense that existence or reality is something like a transitionary phase wherein the lower things are in a type of conflict as they evolve or move through cycles toward higher phases. In Hindu thought, as in Hegelian thought, the notion of real good and evil is essentially absent because there is no room for it.

We should not be surprised that Hegel was ultimately considered a pantheist or a semi-pantheist. He did not believe that finite things would vanish into the "Absolute," as a Hindu believes that the human soul, or "Atman," is resorbed into "Brahman," but he did believe the Absolute came into existence through finite things. In any event, as complex as his metaphysics is, Hegel's views are strikingly non-Christian, and the consequences of adopting them are severe.

* * *

As will be seen throughout our investigation of Pius X's work on Modernism, the *synthesis of all heresies* is like a religious presentation of the core values of Descartes, Hume, Kant, and Hegel. We will see how the philosophical ideas discussed in this chapter will occur again and again, even if they are called something different. Modernism presents a revolution in religion, a complete break with the traditional Christian view, both theological and philosophical. Like these modern schools, Modernism presents an intellectual prison wherein the believer is trapped by artificial confines that require him to reject tradition, ancient wisdom, and common sense.

3

The Theological Origins of Modernism

Following the philosophical revolution at the turn of the nineteenth century, a revolution occurred in Christian scholarship. I do not say Catholic scholarship, as the movement began within Protestantism. You may have noticed that three of the four philosophers mentioned in the last chapter came from countries deeply affected by Protestantism: Germany (Kant, Hegel) and Scotland (Hume). Consequently, the philosophical developments of these men notably affected Protestant theology. Leaving all polemics about the Protestant heresy aside, Protestant groups, generally speaking, have taken the historical character of the Bible seriously — even if they are missing books of the Bible.

In the aftermath of the Enlightenment, however, given the relativistic and revolutionary character of philosophy departments in the academy, Protestant scholars were essentially given free rein to apply the notions of Kant and the others to biblical scholarship. The radical subjectivism of modern philosophy, combined with a burgeoning scientific enterprise that had gained steam in the wake of the Industrial Revolution, ensured that the Bible was looked at with new and highly skeptical eyes, as if for the first time.

What followed was the phenomenon of the historical-critical method of biblical scholarship. In a nutshell, this method entails a total reconsideration of long-held beliefs, accomplished by the use of modern methods of scholarship.[11] In addition, truth claims from ancient times are interpreted by exegetes with the modern perspective that history necessarily progresses over time, thereby tainting their view of the ancient world with that bias. For example, the first chapters of the book of Genesis are viewed with the understanding that Genesis is a type of creation myth common to Middle Eastern cultures at the time, and therefore the claims of Genesis are interpreted as being written down by authors — who remain unknown — who were writing "all they knew how to write" given the time and culture.

On the one hand, this method is patronizing, as it assumes that ancient men could write only things that reflected their immediate surroundings or experience while modern man is free to be objective and rational; on the other hand, there is a grain of truth — as there is in all heresy — in the method. It is a fact that historical *context* is helpful

---

[11] The historical-critical method essentially starts with a radical skepticism about historical claims. We might say that the scientific method adopted by the natural sciences was imported into scriptural and historical research. For example, an adopter of this method would look at a text saying this or that about an ancient period, and he would not accept the claims of the text unless archaeological or documentary evidence from another source could confirm what was said. While it is true that some modern scholars use this method to the benefit of sound Catholic study, the worst abuses of the method occurred in the nineteenth and twentieth centuries based on historical misconceptions. For example, there was a time when it was believed that the domestication of camels had not been accomplished during the time of Abraham, so when scholars saw that domesticated camels were mentioned in Genesis, they rejected some of the historical character of the book. Archaeological evidence later confirmed, however, that the domestication of camels was as ancient as the biblical timeline, so this assumption was in error. This sort of thinking colored the approach of the adopters of the new method and wrought havoc in the realm of biblical theology. Scholars such as Dr. Scott Hahn and Dr. John Bergsma have used the method in an effort to support the Catholic tradition of biblical theology, but much damage has already occurred.

and at times necessary for understanding literature from another time, but the historical-critical method goes a step further and essentially explains away any claims that contrast with modern perceptions as merely the result of historical forces. It is easy to see how this method could lead to major problems, given the changing opinions of historians about former times, as all types of evidence — archaeological, literary, forensic — often change with new discoveries and methods of inference.

The effect of this on Catholic biblical scholarship will be discussed later, but the result in Protestant biblical scholarship was an almost complete rejection of the historical character of the Bible as a whole. Genesis was merely a myth, Moses may have crossed a portion of a river in Egypt with a few hundred people during low tide, and people labeled as demon-possessed were really just dealing with forms of mania that are better understood by modern Freudians. Many such conclusions were reached by the new biblical scholars, and given modern man's love of all things modern, this method of scholarship became the norm in academia. It should be noted that this was also the age of Marx and Darwin, which meant that the world was seen by more and more academics as a matter of struggle and survival, not to mention as evolutionary, which left no room for the "fairy tale" of biblical history that was supplanted by the myth of apes giving birth to Adam.

The Church's Response to the New Biblical Theology

During this tumultuous time, the Church — mainly through admonitions from popes — condemned the various liberal and Modernist propositions as they emerged. Focusing mainly on the sociopolitical effects of the intellectual and political revolutions, numerous popes released powerful encyclicals castigating the errors of Liberalism, starting with *Mirari Vos* by Pope Gregory XVI, who condemned the Liberalism that had gained a foothold in the secular and academic culture.

In 1864, Pope Pius IX released his famous *Syllabus of Errors*, wherein many of the errors circulating at that time were condemned. The rationalist spirit that exalted individual reason to the place of arbiter over religion was denounced, and important aspects of the new rationalist approach were dealt with. In particular, the notion that revelation was merely a "myth" was addressed. Furthermore, Pius IX condemned the notion that philosophical inquiry could be free from regulation by legitimate authority and any philosophical approach that disregarded divine revelation.

Adding to the weight of Pius IX's condemnations, the First Vatican Council, in 1870, anathematized and exposed various heresies and errors that emanated from modern philosophy and would become the Modernist scheme.[12]

During the second session, Pope Pius IX expressed on behalf of the Church a profession of faith that stated: "Likewise I *accept* sacred scripture according to that sense which holy mother church held and holds, since it is her right to judge of the true sense and interpretation of the holy scriptures; nor will I ever receive and interpret them except according to the unanimous consent of the fathers" (no. 3).

From the third session, the faithful are warned of: "Impiety spreading in every direction.... Many even among the children of the Catholic Church have strayed from the path of genuine piety.... Led away by diverse and strange teachings and confusing nature and grace, human knowledge and divine faith, they are found to distort the genuine sense of the dogmas which Holy Mother Church holds and teaches, and to endanger the integrity and genuineness of the faith" (no. 8). It was also taught that it was "not permissible" to interpret Scripture in a way contrary to the perennial teaching of the Church.

Furthermore, the third session states: "Hence, too, that meaning of the sacred dogmas is ever to be maintained which has once been declared by holy mother church, and there must never be any abandonment of this sense under the pretext or in the name of a more profound understanding" (chap. 4, no. 14).

---

[12] For the full text of the council, visit https://www.papalencyclicals.net/councils/ecum20.htm.

The canons published by the Council were even more powerful.[13] Taking aim at the heart of the new method, as well as the revolution in metaphysics that makes religion unintelligible, under the heading of "On Faith and Reason," the following statement was declared infallibly: "If anyone says that it is possible that at some time, given the advancement of knowledge, a sense may be assigned to the dogmas propounded by the church which is different from that which the church has understood and understands: let him be anathema" (session 3, chap. 4, no. 3).

Hegelian pantheism was condemned by this statement: "If anyone says that the substance or essence of God and that of all things are one and the same: let him be anathema" (canon 1, no. 3). In addition, the underpinnings of evolutionary theory — which came into fashion in the years leading up to Vatican I — were clearly condemned: "If anyone does not confess that the world and all things which are contained in it, both spiritual and material, were produced, according to their whole substance, out of nothing by God; or holds that God did not create by his will free from all necessity, but as necessarily as he necessarily loves himself; or denies that the world was created for the glory of God: let him be anathema" (canon 1, no. 5).

Given all the strong teachings of the popes from that time, it would seem as if the Catholic Church had sufficiently been protected from the dangers of modern philosophy. Sadly, this was not the case.

The late nineteenth century was a time of great upheaval and difficulty for the Church, both in Rome and abroad. France continued with its undulating revolutions, the spirit of which migrated abroad. In the latter half of the nineteenth century, Italy experienced a terrible revolution, which, although not as outwardly bloody as the French,

---

[13] It is traditionally understood that what is infallible from a council is that which is defined explicitly, or when there are statements with an "anathema." Thus, when we find such statements in councils, we can under no circumstances deviate from them.

still caused great harm to Catholic life in Rome. Ireland experienced its famine, which caused massive emigration, largely to the United States, where Catholicism was persecuted in various ways. Spain lost Latin America, piece by piece, as liberal independence movements sprang up in the various nations. Other events could be mentioned as well.

Whatever grip the Holy See and the episcopacy had on the official organs of Catholic doctrine, the societal situation was such that the Catholic faithful could be influenced heavily by states that had gone wrong. It must be remembered that, in many of these situations, Catholic children could not attend Catholic schools, either because there were no such schools available or because the state had suppressed Catholic education. This was the dawn of the public school system in its various iterations, as well as an age when both parents were often forced to work outside the home as rural life was destroyed by the mechanization of farms and traditional artisanal life. This meant that a generation of Catholics would imbibe revolutionary ideas, even if their families were pious and the priests were orthodox from the pulpit. Even Archbishop Marcel Lefebvre — the archetype of a non-liberal — remarked that in his early years, he held liberal ideas, which were rooted out only by the eminent Fr. LeFloch at the French Seminary in Rome.[14]

Suffice it to say, the situation was such that, even in the good orders and seminaries, the influence of the modern age of intellectualism had seeped in. The historical-critical method made its way into Catholic biblical theology, even if not explicitly in contradiction to the will of the popes of that era and the teachings of Vatican I. This included the dialectic struggle of Marxist ideology, which permeated the political and historical philosophy of some Catholic institutions, as did Darwin's pantheistic worldview, which left no room for God the Creator.

---

[14] See his biography by Bernard Tissier de Mallerais for more information on Lefebvre's early years.

The situation became so alarming that Pope Leo XIII added to the already stern condemnations of modern philosophy a condemnation regarding Kantian, Hegelian, and Cartesian errors. In his 1899 encyclical *Depuis le Jour*, Leo XIII wrote: "

> We renew our condemnation of those teachings of philosophy which have merely the name, and which by striking at the very foundation of human knowledge lead logically to universal skepticism and to irreligion. We are profoundly grieved to learn that for some years past some Catholics have felt at liberty to follow in the wake of a philosophy which under the specious pretext of freeing human reason from all preconceived ideas and from all illusions, denies it the right of affirming anything beyond its own operations, thus sacrificing to a radical subjectivism all the certainties which traditional metaphysics, consecrated by the authority of the strongest thinkers, laid down as the necessary and unshakable foundations for the demonstration of the existence of God, the spirituality and immortality of the soul, and the objective reality of the exterior world. It is to be deeply regretted that this doctrinal skepticism, of foreign importation and Protestant origin, should have been received with so much favor in a country so justly celebrated for its love of clearness of thought and expression. (15)

This encyclical, written *on the education of the clergy* and addressed to the French bishops, shows that the virus of modern philosophy, theology, and biblical scholarship had infected even such a great Catholic nation as France. We can hardly expect this to have been the case in only one country, which history proves was surely not the case.

Leo XIII had also addressed to the universal Church his reaffirmation of sound biblical scholarship and interpretation in his encyclical *Providentissimus Deus* (1893), in which the total inerrancy of the Holy Bible was declared to be the necessary consequence of its divine inspiration. He declared that Catholics who approached the Scriptures with methods of criticism that were imbued with the worst abuses of the historical-critical method were transgressing lines of orthodoxy and the boundaries of sound biblical criticism. Leo XIII also established the Pontifical Biblical Commission (PBC) as a mechanism to regulate biblical scholarship within the Church, especially among educational institutions. Among other things, the PBC answered questions regarding the historical nature of the first three chapters of Genesis, the traditionally held view that Moses was the principal author of the Pentateuch, and the authorship of the Gospels. As you can imagine, the PBC came down on the side of traditional scholarship and belief.

Now, the PBC was not established as a congregation or endowed with the charism of infallibility, and this has led some modern outlets and commentators to dismiss its conclusions as not relevant, even if such opinions are permissible. For example, a post on Catholic Answers states: "At one time the Pontifical Biblical Commission was essentially a low-ranking Congregation. Its decisions, though, were not considered to be dogmatic or doctrinal. Its directives were neither infallible nor unchangeable."[15] But this is a mistake and represents a misunderstanding of the purpose of the PBC.[16] The PBC was established to clarify what the Church has always *held to be true* in these matters and not to define or infallibly declare some new doctrinal formula. The answers of the PBC were published with the direct oversight of the popes — including Pope St. Pius X — and did not represent mere theological opinion. In addition, the PBC was established to provide *clarity* in the midst of a sea of error. How can a faithful Catholic simply

---

[15] Fr. Charles Grondin, "Authority of the Pontifical Biblical Commission," Catholic Answers Q&A, accessed January 18, 2025, https://www.catholic.com/qa/authority-of-the-pontifical-biblical-commission.

[16] For a more in-depth history of the PBC, see John Corbett, "The Biblical Commission," *The Catholic Encyclopedia*, vol. 2 (New York: Robert Appleton Company, 1907), http://www.newadvent.org/cathen/02557a.htm.

cast aside clear teaching, given the circumstances? Although the PBC did not possess the charism of infallibility, it did publish teachings held as infallible and did so by leveraging twenty centuries of scholarship and theological study. It is rare that answers from Rome on theological matters are presented with objective infallibility, but what is important is the *content* of what is expressed and not the *mechanism*. For example, if someone were to ask the current Dicastery for the Doctrine of the Faith a question about some previously defined or universally held theological opinion, it would be irresponsible to disregard a response reiterating Catholic teaching because the response in question did not contain the charism of infallibility in how it was written. This approach seems to be legalistic and rely on technicalities rather than on the spirit of what the teaching contains.

This approach is common among Modernists who regard Vatican II as a veritable super council, more important than the Council of Nicaea[17] — even though the popes who oversaw it were clear that the council did not define dogma or invoke the charism of infallibility — and easily disregard whatever came before the 1960s.

Two Fathers of Modernism in the Catholic Church: Alfred Loisy and George Tyrrell

If we could point to two archetypes of the quintessential Modernist, we would do well to discuss Alfred Loisy and George Tyrrell. Pope Pius X's encyclical was written essentially to condemn the errors that these two men most famously (infamously) espoused, and both men were excommunicated after *Pascendi* was released, as they remained obstinate in their heresy.

---

[17] "On June 29, 1975, writing to Archbishop Lefebvre, Paul VI spoke these extraordinary and significant words: 'The Second Vatican Council has no less authority, it is even in certain aspects more important than that of Nicea.'" Quoted in "The Interpretation of Vatican II," FSSPX News, January 1, 1970, https://fsspx.news/en/news/interpretation-vatican-council-ii-9514.

Loisy (1857–1940) was born and raised in France and entered a diocesan seminary at the age of seventeen. As a seminarian, he demonstrated a strong dislike for Scholastic philosophy and formation[18] and preferred liberal and modern thinkers from the Enlightenment, such as Jean-Jacques Rousseau as well as the founders of French liberal Catholicism (Félicité Lamennais, Henri Lacordaire).[19]

It is said that just before his ordination, Loisy was struck with insufferable doubt, asking himself whether the Christian religion as such was nothing but a hoax. After serving as a parish priest in the countryside for a short time, he was sent to teach at the Institut Catholique. Although he was heterodox in his beliefs, which was made manifest later, he was highly intelligent. He lectured on biblical Hebrew and was seen as an expert in the study of the Bible. He adopted the critical methods already spoken of and swiftly came to reject the traditional teachings of the Church on several topics, including the Mosaic authorship of the Pentateuch, the historicity of Genesis, and the authorship and dating of the Gospels. Essentially, Loisy came to see the Bible as a collection of myths. Initially, he published his works with a pseudonym, but eventually he came out of the Modernist closet. Needless to say, his work became famous — or rather infamous — and he was promoted by Modernists. Pope Leo XIII had Loisy and his ilk in mind when he set to correct the record on the Church's interpretation of Scripture as he published his aforementioned encyclicals on the topic and by setting up the PBC.

---

[18] As will be shown during our look into *Pascendi*, a dislike for Thomas Aquinas and other Scholastic sources is a sure sign of Modernism, according to Pius X.

[19] For a detailed discussion on Loisy and Tyrrell, you may watch or listen to a discussion I had with Fr. William MacGillivray, SSPX, an expert instructor and highly praised intellectual. See "The Pope Who Predicted Vatican II: Saint Pius X's teaching on MODERNISM / Father MacGillivray," Mere Tradition with Kennedy Hall, August 26, 2023, https://www.youtube.com/watch?v=8766kw_77JY&t=459s.

Loisy's positions became so extreme that he completely rejected the divinity of Christ and saw Christ as nothing more than a sort of apocalyptic zealot who was killed and thrown into a mass grave. His work was condemned by Rome, and Pope Pius X excommunicated him in 1908 after he had doubled down with the publication of volume 2 of his heretical commentary on the Gospels, *Les Évangiles Synoptiques*. It is said that of the sixty-five propositions condemned by Pope Pius X in his syllabus that accompanied *Pascendi — Lamentabili Sane* — fifty were Loisy's notions and heresies.

Loisy lived and died as an apostate, and at the end of his life, he professed an ambiguous belief in a pantheistic humanitarian positivism — a Hegelian-inspired belief that the Absolute (God) moves through the human race on a progressive march toward the fulfillment of time, not unlike the belief of Hinduism — if he believed in anything at all.

George Tyrrell (1861–1909) was perhaps a more tragic figure than Loisy, and we might say that his approach to Modernism was a little "softer" than Loisy's hard-hearted approach. Of course, the term "soft" is here applied in a relative sense, as his views were still in concrete opposition to the teachings of the Church as his career progressed. If Loisy was the prototypical Modernist, it may be said that Tyrrell planted the seeds of what became Neo-Modernism, even if today's Neo-Modernists are not so bold.

Tyrrell was born to an Anglo-Irish family and was raised in a Calvinist environment, only to convert first to the Anglican Church of Ireland and then to Catholicism. He seems never to have been firm in his faith, uttering the following prayer while he was an Anglican: "O God, if there be a God, save my soul, if I have a soul."

Doubts notwithstanding, he entered the Jesuit novitiate and was eventually ordained. His doubts were not unknown while he was a seminarian; nonetheless, he was put forth for ordination. We can only speculate here, but it seems as if there must have been some sympathy for Tyrrell's Modernist disposition, given that he was ordained even though his predilection was known. At any rate, he was a top-notch academic, as all Modernist academics tend to be. After he was ordained, he wrote for the Jesuit journal *The Month* and began to promote his heterodox ideas.

Among his most erroneous notions, he seemingly denied the existence of Hell on the basis that it was not in keeping with the character of a loving God, and like Loisy, he took a rationalist approach by essentially negating the supernatural or miraculous claims of the Church as a whole. After he caused quite a stir with the release of controversial books in 1898 and 1899, the general superior of the Jesuits demanded that Tyrrell write only for *The Month* and only if heavy editing was first done to his work by more orthodox theologians. One wonders why he was allowed to write at all, even with editors. Eventually, he began to publish anonymously, like Loisy, to avoid the chance that his work would be censored.

He was not a fan — to put it mildly — of Pope St. Pius X, whom he saw as too severe, and was eventually expelled from the Jesuit Order in 1906, after some of his heresies were published in an Italian newspaper. Tyrrell's views were more concerned with the spiritual side of things than those of Loisy, who had functionally become an atheist. Tyrrell believed in the spiritual, but his approach was to immanentize spirituality — that is, to claim that religious faith emerges from within the human consciousness — and to view external religious signs as merely symbolic. According to this concept, faith is not something revealed by God from outside (divine revelation) but rather is an evolution of human religious sentiment that develops naturally within the individual and the community. The condemnation of the heresy of vital immanence outlined by Pius X in *Pascendi* is doubtless directed at the heresies of Tyrrell.

Tyrrell's approach to Modernism was, overall, an attempt to reconcile the Catholic Faith with Modernity and modern scientism. In short, the Church had to "get with the times," according to Tyrrell. He still has supporters today who claim that he was merely a misunderstood genius who, like Cardinal Newman, professed the "development of dogma," but it is clear that he rejected perennial Catholic doctrine. Development of doctrine or dogma does not mean a *change* in dogma, but a *development*, as the word suggests. Thus, we have the perennial belief that at Mass there is a true Sacrifice on the altar, and we have over time developed more precise terminology to express this same reality, but without any substantial change. A true understanding of the development of dogma is not altogether that complicated, even if some make it so. Chesterton, with his classic wit and common sense, explained the concept swimmingly when he wrote: "When we talk of a child being well-developed, we mean that he has grown bigger and stronger with his own strength; not that he is padded with borrowed pillows or walks on stilts to make him look taller. When we say that a puppy develops into a dog, we do not mean that his growth is a gradual compromise with a cat; we mean that he becomes more doggy and not less."[20]

Tyrrell was excommunicated after the release of *Pascendi*, and he died in 1909. He did not renounce his Catholic identity entirely and still believed himself to be part of the Church, even if it was the Church he had reimagined.

There is more that could be said about both Tyrrell and Loisy, but for our purposes, we would do well to move on to the wisdom of St. Pius X, who exposed superbly the true evil of their teachings, and the heresy of Modernism as a whole.

---

[20] Quoted in Edward Feser, "Boundaries of Belief," review of *The Development of Dogma: A Systematic Account*, by Guy Mansini, O.S.B., *First Things*, May 2024, https://www.firstthings.com/article/2024/05/boundaries-of-belief.

4

Pope Pius X Addresses the Gravity of the Situation

Though Popes Pius IX and Leo XIII had addressed the encroaching errors of Modernism head-on, the heresy continued to develop and seemingly gain ground in Catholic scholarship. Responding to the need of the Catholic faithful for a concise condemnation of Modernism as such — not just the various errors of Liberalism and modern scholarship addressed by his predecessors — Pope St. Pius X published his landmark encyclical on September 8, 1907, a feast day traditionally called "Marymas" and known as the Nativity of Mary. Thus, the holy Vicar of Christ entrusted his work to the care of the Blessed Virgin Mary, invoking her title as "Immaculate Virgin, destroyer of heresies" in the final paragraph of the document.

Pope St. Pius X begins his work with an introduction wherein he expresses the purpose of his efforts:

> The office divinely committed to Us of feeding the Lord's flock has especially this duty assigned to it by Christ, namely, to guard with the greatest vigilance the deposit of the faith

delivered to the saints, rejecting the profane novelties of words and oppositions of knowledge falsely so called.[21]

The pope expresses the grave situation facing the Church. Furthermore, he is unambiguous in stating that Modernism is a threat to the very life of the Church and that he fully intends to speak with the weight of his office in an unmistakably doctrinal way. After explaining that the watchfulness of the pope has always been necessary to safeguard the Catholic Faith, he insists that the crisis of Modernism represents a unique threat to the Church by "enemies of the cross of Christ... who are striving, by arts, entirely new and full of subtlety, to destroy the vital energy of the Church, and, if they can, to overthrow utterly Christ's kingdom itself" (1).

After the introduction, Pius X titles the first section of the document "The Gravity of the Situation." Referring to the presence of Modernists, he writes: "They lie hid, a thing to be deeply deplored and feared, in her very bosom and heart, and are the more mischievous, the less conspicuously they appear" (2).

At that time in Church history, the Modernists, although growing in number, did not enjoy the favor of the intellectual institutions of the Church; this is why men such as Tyrrell and Loisy had, at points, published their heresies with pen names. What is striking about the pope's description is that he shows how the Modernists are immoral and duplicitous men. They play with terms and cheat with words, as they are by nature subjectivists or relativists in their doctrines. One does not have to be an expert in theology or psychology to analyze the mindset necessary for one to adopt Modernism. By using our reason and common sense, we can understand that if a man believes the Church has erred or been deficient in her solemn magisterial pronouncements and actions over centuries and centuries, then he has

---

[21] Quotations from this encyclical are taken from the official Vatican translation, and, where appropriate, paragraph numbers are given in parenthetical citations.

necessarily set himself up as the judge of Sacred Tradition and therefore above the wisdom of the Holy Ghost, who has guided the Church throughout tumults and tempests, and through the worst of heresies and revolutions.

The Modernist theologian must necessarily have imbibed some sort of messianic mentality in that he believes that he has somehow been selected and set apart to save the Church from herself. We understand this from a psychological perspective, as those who seek to overhaul an organization of any sort must necessarily believe that they "know better" than the status quo and thus believe themselves to be like arbiters of hidden truth that they have unlocked with their interpretive key and that only they understand. "Thoroughly imbued with the poisonous doctrines taught by the enemies of the Church, and lost to all sense of modesty, [the Modernists] vaunt themselves as reformers of the Church; and, forming more boldly into line of attack, assail all that is most sacred in the work of Christ, not sparing even the person of the Divine Redeemer, whom, with sacrilegious daring, they reduce to a simple, mere man" (2).

Throughout the encyclical, Pius X expands on these themes in great detail, but it is a sign of his genius that, with so few words, he is able to encapsulate the prideful delusion that plagues men afflicted with this spiritual disease.

Not mincing words, Pius X intensifies his castigation of Modernists, saying that God accounts them as "the most pernicious of all the adversaries of the Church" (3). He compares these most pernicious enemies of Christ to men with axes who strike at the very root of the Church, who "proceed to disseminate poison through the whole tree, so that there is no part of Catholic truth from which they hold their hand, none that they do not strive to corrupt" (3).

Modernists are not dummies, according to the pope. On the contrary, they are highly intelligent — devilishly so — and employ "a thousand noxious arts" in their attempts to destroy the Church. He ends the opening section with a stark assessment of the minds of

Modernists, saying that their own "doctrines have given such a *bent to their minds*, that they disdain all authority and brook no restraint; and relying upon a false conscience, they attempt to ascribe to a love of truth that which is in reality the result of pride and obstinacy" (3, emphasis added).

Perhaps in the opening chapters of this book, when we discussed the proto-Modernists in philosophy, you found yourself scratching your head in trying to understand the ideas of Kant, Hegel, and the others. If that is the case, then good! The ideas of so much of modern philosophy are utterly unintelligible when compared with the perennial philosophical tradition of the Church, and even the best of antiquity. In *Out of the Silent Planet*, the first book of C. S. Lewis's space trilogy, his main character learns of the deep truths of the Christian faith through the mediation of some interesting extraterrestrials that the author uses as literary devices to present his allegorical tale of Christian wisdom. In the language of those otherworldly beings, what we would call the Devil is referred to as the "Bent One."

That Pius X described Modernists as having "bent" minds and not merely as men with wrong opinions is quite telling. Men of goodwill who have minds that are not stretched and contorted into ugly shapes are capable of coming to different conclusions about various topics without venturing into the realm of absurd madness. There have always been aspects of doctrine and philosophy that are not yet distilled and crystallized into precise and exact definitions, and reasonable men can disagree on these things in good faith. If we take, however, the dogma of Transubstantiation — the dogma that expresses the real substantial change of bread and wine into the real Body, Blood, Soul, and Divinity of Our Lord — we see that although there was a constant belief in the Real Presence since the dawn of the Church, it wasn't until the Council of Trent that the dogma was defined with an anathema attached as a warning to those who deny it. Men with minds bent against the Truth and the rightful authority of the Church to define dogmas — such as Martin Luther and John Calvin, who mutilated and contorted Christian belief with their incomplete Bibles and heresies that have wrought so much destruction — persist in rejection of Catholic teaching.

A Modernist can be very menacing, like a serial killer of reason and truth; he has created for himself a world of fantasy where, like Pharaoh during the time of Moses, he believes he can call the evening "morning" and the morning "evening," as if he possesses a divine power to bend reality to his will.

5

An Attack on the Foundations of Philosophy and Religion: Agnosticism and Vital Immanence

At the outset of his encyclical, Pope Pius X asserts clearly that the threat of Modernism to the Catholic Church is so grave that a concise and intentional dissection of the heresy is needed to guard the Catholic faithful from the onslaught. After introducing his work and the purpose thereof, he begins with the two principles at the heart of Modernist thought: agnosticism and vital immanence.

You have likely heard the term "agnosticism," but the term "vital immanence" will be new to many. Thankfully, Pius X, being an excellent teacher, provides us with detailed information so that we can understand what these terms mean in full and the part they play in the Modernist heresy.

Agnosticism

"Agnosticism" refers to a philosophical disposition about the nature of truth, which Pius X tells us is at the heart of the religious philosophy of Modernism. Although he does not mention Kant and the others by name, we will see that elements of the reimagination of the nature of truth inherent in modern philosophy are present in the nature of agnosticism as Pius X explains it.

In our day, it is commonly held that a man who identifies as an agnostic is searching for truth and has the humility not to be so rigid and black and white in his beliefs. For example, if you ask any bright-eyed, bushy-tailed college freshman what he thinks about God, it is likely he will tell you that he is an "agnostic" and doesn't believe in "organized religion."

As annoying as answers like this are, and as intellectually lazy as they are at root, one does not, out of nowhere, find himself in adulthood without enough conviction to say yes or no to the vital question of whether God exists. Before a man is an agnostic in the colloquial sense, he must be an agnostic in his philosophical foundation. The question of whether God exists is simultaneously a question of philosophy and theology. It is the starting point for *all* questions because God is the starting point — and ending point — for *all that exists*. "I am Alpha and Omega, the first and the last, the beginning and the end" (Rev. 22:13).

Without belief in God, there can be no belief in belief, as all actions that take place in space and time — whether in the physical or metaphysical realm — hinge upon an inherent purpose or *end*. In the animal realm, for example, even irrational creatures act as if they have a purpose and with what appears as intention. Although the insect that spends its short life building this or that habitat, or the beaver that spends its time constructing a dam in a stream, may be doing so out of instinct and not out of free will, in the way that humans do, it is still clear that they do so because they *must* do so. And why must they do so?

Does an ant colony pop up here and there under this or that mound of sand for no reason at all? Of course not. Whether we understand the complexity of a given ecosystem or not, we understand that the system is a system and is therefore dependent on the various moving parts doing their jobs and that a failure in the chain of nature creates a deficiency that spoils the whole thing.

Human beings are both animal and rational, in that we have not only the body of a mammal but also the intellect of something more angelic. I say "angelic" because the human mind is in some way free from the bounds of physical nature, at least the bounds of physical space, as Augustine mused when he spoke of the faculty of memory in his *Confessions*:

> Behold, in the innumerable fields and dens and caverns of my memory, innumerably filled with kinds of things past numbering, either by their images, as is the case with all bodily things, or by their very presence, as with all of the arts, or by certain notions or marks, as with the affections of the mind — for even when the mind does not feel them, the memory retains what it was like, for whatever is in the memory is also in the mind — I run through all these things, I fly here and there, I pry into them as deeply as I can, but never to the bottom. Such is the power of memory, such is the power of life in man whose very life is a way of dying![22]

Augustine illuminates for us here the power of the mind with his consideration of memory, which illustrates a major difference between man and nonrational animals. Because we are rational, it is impossible, at least with fundamental questions of a metaphysical nature, for us to be truly "agnostic" in the sense that we "don't know." In reality, when it comes to metaphysical considerations, such as the existence of God or a belief in truth claims, we surely make a concrete decision, based on what we *do know* or how we *choose to understand*, that is anything but "agnostic."

If the physical world is governed by laws and physical creatures necessarily act with either intended or instinctual purpose, then how much more so must man, who possesses such a complex faculty as memory,

---

[22] Saint Augustine of Hippo, *Confessions*, trans. Anthony Esolen (Gastonia, NC: TAN Books, 2023), 238.

act with intention and purpose. Why would the agnostic answer that he "does not know" if he did not know that he does not know? How could a man with any sense utter such foolishness as "I am not sure if I believe in God" without an underlying assumption that he knows who God is enough to know that he is not sure if he believes in Him? Agnosticism is really an intellectual trick or sleight of hand wherein a man may profess that he does not — or that we cannot — really *know* things while he relies on a certain knowledge of his uncertainty.

Since it is impossible to be truly agnostic about reality, the agnostic must retreat from his angelic and metaphysical nature and live solely in the realm of the material because, try as he might, he cannot escape the elements of physical nature as he has escaped the bounds of common sense. About this, Pius X states:

> According to this teaching [agnosticism] human reason is confined entirely within the field of phenomena, that is to say, to things that are perceptible to the senses, and in the manner in which they are perceptible; it has no right and no power to transgress these limits. Hence it is incapable of lifting itself up to God, and of recognising His existence, even by means of visible things. From this it is inferred that God can never be the direct object of science, and that, as regards history, He must not be considered as an historical subject. (6)

With this statement, Pius X illustrates how adherence to agnosticism paves the way for a rejection of a reasoned understanding of belief in God and for the notion that truth claims about God, either in revelation or received theology or philosophy, must be doubted with severe skepticism. It is worth noting that agnosticism, as a principle, is similar to relativism or subjectivism — the belief that truth is relative or subjective to persons, places, and time periods — but it is ultimately more fundamental than relativism. Relativism asserts that there is no absolute truth, but in doing so, it asserts an absolute truth — namely, that it is absolutely certain that there is no absolute truth. Agnosticism, however, is at root a skepticism about the nature of truth itself and a principled doubt about the ability to know anything at all with any certainty. It is a slight distinction, but an important one. If we were to think of relativism as a "school" of thought, we might think of agnosticism as a lens through which agnostics see thought itself, or we might conceive of it as an instinct that undergirds an approach to observing reality.

Because of this doubt, Socrates, Aristotle, and Plato must be thrown into the rubbish bin because, in the mind of the Modernist, their philosophical endeavors were plagued with the fatal disease of assuming that it was possible to *know* with certainty about things that could not be explained by brute material processes. For this reason, the Modernist rejects the miraculous and essentially all metaphysical certainty.

Of course, this renders the question of religion utterly absurd, especially the question of the Catholic religion, which is objective and severe in its doctrines and anathemas. No one, however, not even an agnostic, can escape the fact of existing and the experience of reality, no matter how hard he tries. We might call to mind Descartes and his time spent in confinement wherein he tried to prove that he existed, which demonstrates a fundamental doubt about his own existence — so strange.

This paradox creates a need for agnostics — and by extension, Modernists — to deal somehow with fundamental elements of human nature, such as religion, but they must do so without sound metaphysics. In essence, they cannot accept claims or the establishment of binding truth about religion, but they must account for the fact that religion is a universal phenomenon. In order to do this, they employ the principle of vital immanence.

Vital Immanence

Pius X calls agnosticism the "negative part of the system of the Modernist" and calls the "positive side" "vital immanence" (7). What he means is that agnosticism is the destructive side of the Modernist system in that it is a denial of certainty about fact beyond the physical realm; vital immanence is the mechanism used to explain religious belief in the Modernist system.

> Religion, whether natural or supernatural, must, like every other fact, admit of some explanation. But when Natural theology has been destroyed, the road to revelation closed through the rejection of the arguments of credibility, and all external revelation absolutely denied, it is clear that this explanation will be sought in vain outside man himself. It must, therefore, be looked for in man; and since religion is a form of life, the explanation must certainly be found in the life of man. Hence the principle of *religious immanence* is formulated. (7)

For the Modernist, religion cannot be explained from anything *outside* man, and therefore the religious impulse must be something natural to the *interior* of man. This is a dangerous assertion as it is not completely false. As Augustine so famously said at the outset of his *Confessions*, "You have made us for yourself, O Lord, and our hearts are restless until they rest in You." Man, indeed, has a natural inclination toward questions of the divine; it is natural that the soul moves toward its source in some way, as an infant without reason naturally moves toward his mother's breast when he becomes restless due to hunger.

The Modernist, however, makes it impossible for man to find his rest in God because, in the world of agnosticism, God is not a certain external fact but only the personification of a sentiment that begins in the human heart. The infant who roots around on his mother's chest when only minutes old acts on a created impulse that pushes him to search for his mother, who acts as a creator and gives life to her son. He goes to his source for his sustenance, and therefore he is satisfied, even if he must feed again moments later. The agnostic rejects the concrete notion that there is a Creator who can satisfy the longing of his heart, and therefore he must look *inside* himself for his nourishment.

Religious sentiment, according to the Modernist, is a sort of animal instinct in a rational animal; therefore, Pius X, distilling Modernist thinking, states: "This need of the divine, which is experienced only in special and favourable circumstances, cannot, of itself, appertain to the domain of consciousness; it is at first latent within the consciousness, or, to borrow a term from modern philosophy, in the subconsciousness, where also its roots lies hidden and undetected" (7).

What Pius X explains here is that because Modernism disallows us to view religious belief as an assent to an objective, external truth, it asserts that any religious movement in the person is akin to acting on a hidden impulse that propels him to grope about in obscurity as he looks for a way to express an instinct that lies deep within.

Religion is purely personal and is experienced only in the *subconsciousness*, according to this system; therefore, an impassable obstacle is met when there is an attempt to synthesize the created physical world with the subjective, interior, experiential life of man. Simply put, when the Modernist studies man as a physical creature, he finds that man has a nonmaterial impulse that cannot be explained by material phenomena and that cannot fully be *explained away*; he is utterly incapable of encapsulating the truth of religion in an objective sense.

From here, Pius X tells us that there arises a type of *fideism*, which, in essence, refers to *faith in faith itself*. You may recall that William of Ockham adhered to a type of fideism and that Martin Luther's famous — or infamous — doctrine of salvation by "faith alone" is consistent with this thinking. It is easy to see how agnosticism and vital immanence lead to this sort of "blind faith" or "leap of faith" because the ground for objective and verifiable religious faith based on concrete realities has been completely eroded.

Thus, modern man, who has been plagued with this intellectual disease, can refer to "people of faith" when what he means is merely people who profess some sort of belief in a divine reality or even just belief in belief. But this is a complete misunderstanding of what faith is.

When a godparent stands for an infant at Baptism, he is asked by the priest, "What are you asking of God's Church," to which he replies, "Faith."[23] Think of the problem here if a Catholic were to adopt the Modernist notion of faith.

If faith — as it is defined by the heretics — refers to nothing but a mere sentiment of interior voyaging toward an ethereal divinity, then what is the point of Baptism? Leaving aside the dogma of Original Sin, which Modernists must necessarily reject, given their rejection of dogma itself, there could be nothing more futile than to suggest that an infant could receive from the workings of a physical sacrament a change in the nonphysical soul. In addition, there could be nothing to receive! The Modernist notion of faith is inapplicable to an infant to begin with, as only a person with the use of reason can even begin to search his "subconscious" to try to make sense of his immanent religious impulses that pertain to what Modernists refer to as "faith." Naturally, if one were to adopt the Modernist concept of faith, Baptism would be rendered merely symbolic and viewed as an initiation ritual that benefits the community as it welcomes a new member. In reality, this is how many Catholics view Baptism today.

Is it any wonder that Catholics today — if they do baptize their children — wait until they are much older than has been the custom for centuries? At least implicitly, Catholics the world over — and the priests who shepherd them — have ignored or rejected the infallible teaching on the necessity of Baptism.

In addition, Pius X explains how, with the confusion of instinct or sentiment with faith, Modernism asserts that *revelation* itself takes place inside the person (8). As we have established, the Modernist views faith as a type of sentiment, and given that this faith is not an external thing that we assent to or receive at Baptism but something that we come to know only as we progress in age and reason, we must necessarily conclude that this happens by a type of revelation. This

---

[23] Old Latin Rite of Baptism according to the 1962 ritual.

is because, if we consider the fact that all external revealed truth is at least implicitly doubted due to agnosticism, and that vital immanence suggests that religious belief is an expression of what bubbles up inside, Modernism requires a rethinking of revelation itself. Therefore, it is possible, according to Modernism, that God "reveals" religious concepts to each person on an individual basis.

What follows from the logic of the Modernist understanding of these realities is striking: God reveals Himself gradually to each man in a progressive way, and God dwells in some way in the soul of every man so that He can be discovered in a way that is unique to each person and not beholden to how Christians have understood God to have revealed Himself in orthodox Catholic teaching. Pius X summarizes this notion by saying: "And they add: Since God is both the object and the cause of faith, this revelation is at the same time *of* God and *from* God; that is, God is both the revealer and the revealed" (8).

Of course, God does, in a sense, reveal Himself to each person, and I imagine we can all recall moments of grace when we were brought closer to God in ways that are unique to us. It must be remembered, however, that when Pius X speaks here of how Modernists understand revelation, he is explaining that, in Modernism, this supposed revelation is completely relative to the person and each sentiment of revelation is equally valid in all others. Thus, according to Modernist thinking, we have no leg to stand on if we compare the divine revelation given to the sacred authors of the Bible with the musings of Joseph Smith, the founder of Mormonism.

It is easy to see how this mentality puts religious claims from all traditions on an equal footing, at least as regards their particular claims about God and His interaction with human beings. Pius X concludes this section by summarizing the matter: "Hence it is that they make consciousness and revelation synonymous. Hence the law, according to which *religious consciousness* is given as the universal rule, to be put on an equal footing with revelation, and to which all must submit, even the supreme authority of the Church, whether in its teaching capacity, or in that of legislator in the province of sacred liturgy or discipline" (8).

In layman's terms, our perception of being, according to Modernists, is also our understanding of revelation, as God reveals Himself to us individually in a manner that is independent of objective religious truth. Therefore, it is impossible for the Church to require of the faithful the submission of intellect and will. This is because submission of intellect and will to the teachings of the Church is predicated on the notion that the teachings are objective and constitute an obligation if one desires to believe the Catholic Faith to be saved. If Modernism is adopted, even in part, however, there is no ground for authority over another soul if that soul is the subject of uniquely tailored inspiration directly from God, who is both revealed and reveals Himself to them. This manner of thinking renders religion completely subjective and relative to the individual.

Interestingly, Pius X mentions the effect this mentality would have on sacred liturgy. He connects changes in liturgy with the principle of vital immanence, specifically under the aspect of religious consciousness, because of the Modernist reversal of faith and belief. The long-held belief in the Church of *lex orandi, lex credendi* — the law of praying is the law of believing — is based on the fact that sacred liturgy expresses what is believed by Catholics, and therefore, it is doctrinal in nature. This means that a liturgical ceremony of the Church represents what is believed by Catholics as a general rule. If, as the principle of vital immanence would have it, belief is in a state of flux governed by continual revelation to the religious subconscious, then what is prayed at Mass or in any other liturgy must change substantially over time to match the ever evolving and progressing religious sentiments of believers.

The New Mass will be discussed at length in a later chapter, but a short consideration in light of Pius X's teaching is appropriate here.

What do you think a Modernist liturgy would look like? Well, of course, the notion that the liturgy would be unchangeable would be anathema, as God is continually revealed to human beings individually and uniquely, and therefore we could not expect a liturgy to be universal in scope or application. Furthermore, it would be impossible to say that a particular liturgy is a more or less perfect expression of the Holy Sacrifice offered to the Divine Majesty. In addition, since Modernist religion is man-centered, it would be untenable for a liturgy acceptable to these heretics to be God-centered.

Also, given the fact that it is very hard to argue in Modernist terms that man could truly sin against God, since God reveals Himself specially to each man, we could not expect the propitiatory reality of the sacred liturgy to be emphasized. In short, a Modernist liturgy would be tailored for each man or the diverse groups of men; it would change as often as the religious consciousness of men progresses and changes; and it would be seemingly offered to men and for men as an aid for them to participate more fully in the interior state of religious consciousness that bubbles up inside each man, who is also a mystic and a prophet.

As Paul VI stated during a General Audience on November 26, 1969, while speaking about the promulgation of the Novus Ordo Missae: "Understanding of prayer is worth more than the silken garments in which it is royally dressed. Participation by the people is worth more — particularly participation by modern people, so fond of plain language which is easily understood and converted into everyday speech."[24] Paul VI made these remarks in the context of expressing the fundamental reason for the massive changes to the liturgy, after admitting that many of the treasures of sacred liturgical tradition would be lost.

So, according to the pope who published the new missal, the central principle that undergirds the publication of the New Mass rests on the changing needs of "modern people" who require that each of their languages be used so they can understand the Mass. Perhaps I am a bit naive, but I was under the impression that there is no such thing as "modern man" any more than there is such a thing as "happy

---

[24] Cited in Kwasniewski, *Once and Future Roman Rite*, 132 and 389.

man" or "1950s man." Man is man, and his nature is the same in each age, and his need for true religion does not change because days on the calendar are subsequently checked off. Similarly, what is true does not change on Thursday because what was true on Tuesday is no longer valid. The liturgy is the central meeting place of all Catholics where they are formed and initiated into the sacred mystery of Calvary, and Calvary has not changed, nor could it ever change.

It seems that it is at least probable that the Novus Ordo was created with a conception of religion acceptable to Modernism — namely, that man is changing, his needs are changing, his beliefs are changing, so how he prays should change to reflect that.

6

The Lurking Force behind the Modernist Evolution of Religion

After Pope Pius X deals with vital immanence and agnosticism, he swiftly moves on to a sad but inevitable consequence of Modernism: the deformation of religious history. Admittedly, the great pope's words at the outset of this section are a bit hard to decipher at first glance, but this is not because *he* is not clear; rather, the muddled system of the Modernists is so complex and multifaceted — like a spinning hydra — that complexity in explanation is required.

Pius X refers to the "Unknowable" to describe the vague and amorphous "force" that permeates the religious sentiment of man and bubbles up in the religious conscience of all "believers" who experience that continual revelation of ineffable religious truth I spoke of in the last chapter. The so-called Unknowable is something that "belongs to the realm of science and history yet to some extent oversteps their bounds." This is to say that what religious people call divine is nothing more than the supranational sentiment of what is called divinity and which results from "an act of nature containing within itself something mysterious" (9).

Of course, to any believing Catholic — traditional or conservative — this notion is anathema, but it gained ground under the heresiarch Jesuit priest Pierre Teilhard de Chardin. An entire book could be written on Chardin — and has been done; it is not our intention to go on at any greater length than is necessary here, but a short exposé of one of his most damnable ideas is required.

If it were at all possible for a man to be the incarnation of Modernism, it would be Fr. Chardin. Sadly, he is the archetype of the modernist Jesuit who is all too common today, which is such a shame for the good Jesuits, of whom a few remain. He was a self-styled scientist with an obsession with evolutionary theory. For Chardin, the Darwinian theory of evolution was an indisputable fact by which he fashioned his entire worldview — both philosophical and religious.

He believed and professed that matter evolved into spirit and even said that "Christ, too, is saved by Evolution."[25] Of course, such an utterance is nothing but blasphemy, but it is an idea completely consistent with Modernism. Chardin was not referenced in *Pascendi*, as it was not until decades later that he became infamous, but the Modernist principles explained in Pius X's work can be easily recognized in Chardin's work.[26]

Chardin took the notion of a rising and spiritualized "religious consciousness" and developed it into a concept called the "Noosphere."[27] According to Chardinian thinking, the Noosphere is a realm of intellectual frequency — not unlike radio waves or 5G — where the common consciousness of man is in a state of evolutionary flux, and over time, this amorphous meta-consciousness progresses toward a new state as human beings continue to exist. Chardin described it thus: "We must

---

[25] Chardin in *Le Christique*, 1955, quoted in "Unmasking Chardin's Modernist Manifesto," https://www.salvemariaregina.info/Reference/Chardin.html.

[26] It is worth noting that Pius XII's *Humani Generis* deals with the ideas of Chardin and the New Theology.

[27] The term "Noosphere" is derived from the Greek word for mind, *noos*, and the word "sphere" is included to give the impression that there is a "sphere of mind" that is as real as, say, the atmosphere or the biosphere.

enlarge our approach to encompass the formation, taking place before our eyes and arising out of this factor of hominization, of a particular biological entity such as has never before existed on earth — the growth, outside and above the biosphere, of an added planetary layer, an envelope of thinking substance, to which, for the sake of convenience and symmetry, I have given the name of the Noosphere."[28]

In layman's terms, the process of "hominization" — becoming more human through an evolutionary process — results in a layer of "thinking substance," which is to say, a measurable and pseudo-material realm of consciousness that evolves with the species.

What Chardin has done here is take the logic of biological evolution and apply its principles to metaphysical reality. As Catholics, we believe that man is a rational animal, meaning that he has a material nature, which is animal, and a spiritual nature, which is his soul. Man is a body-soul composite; therefore, his material body interacts with its sense perception in this corporeal realm, and his metaphysical or spiritual intellect is housed in his soul. Put it this way: the human brain is not the same thing as the human mind, as the brain itself does not separate from the body at death, as the soul does. But the brain functions in such a manner that we may "access" and interact with the immaterial information we house in our minds that is gathered through sensory experience.

A true evolutionist cannot allow a substantial difference between the body and the soul because the soul cannot be measured or quantified with the instruments of natural science. Of course, we can use the pure science of sound realist philosophy to reason about the presence and nature of the soul — as all great and sane thinkers have done throughout history — and with the help of revelation, we can understand better the nature and mechanisms of the human soul with the aid of theology, which is the "queen of the sciences."

---

[28] Pierre Teilhard de Chardin, *The Formation of the Noösphere*, January 1947, Library of Consciousness, https://www.organism.earth/library/document/formation-of-the-noosphere.

Chardin was not able to let go of his religious sentimentality completely, given his priestly vocation; therefore, he created the cockamamie and completely pseudoscientific idea of the Noosphere to account for the rational but nonphysical reality of mind and consciousness. In a true Hegelian monstrosity, he synthesized the thesis of religion with the antithesis of materialism and gave us spiritualized materialism.

This is the tenet of Modernism that Pius X refers to when he says: "Therefore the *religious sentiment*, which through the agency of *vital immanence* emerges from the lurking places of the subconsciousness, is the germ of all religion, and the explanation of everything that has been or ever will be in any religion" (10). In other words, the proximate life force of humanity known through "vital immanence" evolves in the collective consciousness of man, and from there springs the divinized matter that becomes spiritual consciousness. This Modernist concept, consistent with Chardin's notion of the Noosphere, represents a complete reversal of how Catholicism and the Realist philosophical tradition — Aristotle, Augustine, Aquinas, and so on — view reality. A Catholic believes that God creates man, whereas a Modernist seems to suggest that from man there is a begetting of a superspiritual entity that is a collection of the religious energy or sentiment of the collective of human beings. In a sense, it is as if Modernists are saying that man as a species evolves into God. Again, we see shades of pantheism.

Pius X goes on to describe how the heretical foundations of Modernism lead to further error with regard to religious indifference:

> The sentiment, which was at first only rudimentary and almost formless, gradually matured, under the influence of that mysterious principle from which it originated, with the progress of human life.... [It] is the origin of all religion, even supernatural religion.... The Catholic religion [is not] an exception; it is quite on a level with the rest; for it was engendered, by the process of *vital immanence*, in the consciousness of Christ, who

was a man of the choicest nature, whose like has never been, nor will be. (10)

It may seem counterintuitive that Modernism puts Catholicism on an equal footing with other religions while exalting Christ as the perfect man, but this is understandable when the context is understood. Modernism allows for the belief that some people may be more in line with the ineffable religious sentiment than others. Modernism, however, requires us to believe that what is truly perfect or Christlike in Christ is in what He represents as a matter of *faith* — in the Modernist sense — and not by who He was objectively as a historical figure.

According to Modernism, the Catholic religion emanates from the "consciousness of Christ," and Chardin tells us, "Christ, too, is saved by Evolution." Naturally, the evolutionist *and* the Modernist would have to believe this about Christ because if the heretic wishes to hold on to Christ as a matter of religious sentiment, he must not relegate Christ to an objective historical place that is less evolved than ours.

First, the evolutionist and the Modernist must both hold that humanity is in a state of constant progression and therefore it is impossible to believe that perfection could have been manifested in a former age. Second, if Christ is divine in the way they understand divinity, then Christ's divinity necessarily evolves with the evolving nature of the divine consciousness, which is an amalgamation of the collective experiences of religious people. Third, history itself must be reassessed through the lens of evolution and vital immanence; therefore, Christ must not be subjected to the out-of-date mores and taboos of men of a more "superstitious" age.

Jesus of History, Christ of Faith

The desire to hold on to Christ for religious reasons and the Modernist view of the evolution of history creates a problem for Modernists because the notion that Christ could be so excellent while coming from a period in history that was so primitive is paradoxical. Thus,

Modernism tells us that the true person of Christ has been "disfigured" by accretions of organized religion. Therefore, a reinterpretation of Christ through the lens of Modernist historical viewpoints is required. This means that "everything should be excluded, deeds and words and all else that is not in keeping with His character, circumstances and education, and with the place and time in which He lived," according to how Modernism views history (9).

An example of this would be how Christ institutes an all-male priesthood in the New Testament by including only men as Apostles. A Modernist interpretation of this fact would be something like this: "The sacred authors wrote about the life of Christ given the cultural norms of their time in history, which was male-dominated, but we know that Christ's insistence on an all-male clerical class was either a concession to cultural norms in a less tolerant society or an invention of the authors to aid in the spreading of the new faith in the person of Jesus of Nazareth as the Messiah." In essence, Catholics must have added aspects to the history of Christ that were inventions of the authors, or any "primitive" characteristics present in Christ's ministry were merely concessions by a wise man for the needs of the people at the time. Is it surprising that as the clerics of the Church have become more and more progressive — Modernist — there has been a continual push for female deacons?

For the Modernist, there must be a "Christ of history and Christ of faith," with the former being inferior to the latter, given the nature of the evolution of religious sentiment. This means that there is the "real" person called Jesus of Nazareth who is a historical figure, and there is the divinized Person called Jesus Christ who is the Messiah. And, over time, according to Modernist thought, believers transformed Jesus the historical person into Christ the Person of faith. So, from the religious perspective, there is the "spiritual Christ," who is different from the historical person. As a result, the inerrancy of the Bible is questioned in Modernist thought — following in the footsteps of the tendencies of adopters of the historical-critical method — because what was written by the authors was, in a sense, sentimentalized to reflect how the first believers viewed Christ from a religious perspective. For example, believers who knew Jesus were so moved by His love and charity for others, typified by His willingness to cure the ailments of sick persons, that they "supernaturalized" his interactions with sick persons to the point that Christ is recorded as performing "miraculous healings." Or, when Christ is recorded as adamantly hammering home the Real Presence of His Body in the Eucharist in the Bread of Life Discourse (John 6), this is either the writing style of the author, who thought it important to overemphasize the symbolic nature of the Eucharist, or it is a recording — albeit exaggerated — of Christ's sayings, which He uttered to inspire believers. In any event, the historical reality of Christ and the spiritual beliefs about Christ are, in the Modernist system, juxtaposed.

So, if we were Modernists and wanted to understand the "real" Jesus Christ without all the accretions of history and official theology, we would want to go back to the "sources" and the "early Church" to see who Christ truly was. Of course, there is nothing wrong with going to the sources and appealing to early Church writings, especially the Church Fathers, but the intention behind the investigation makes all the difference. If you were trying to prove to a Protestant friend that the first Christians believed in the Real Presence of Christ in the Eucharist or the perpetual virginity of the Blessed Mother, you would do well to appeal to the strong writings and consensus of the Church Fathers on the subject; on the other hand, if you wanted to demonstrate that the practice of receiving Communion on the tongue was merely a "medieval" practice, you could find a citation from an early writer speaking about receiving in the hand. And even though that practice was not widespread and was later abandoned as liturgical discipline developed along with the deepening understanding that Christ is truly present in every particle of the Eucharist, the Modernist could reply that this development was merely the result of an adaptation to the needs of the time — which are not the needs of "modern man"" — and not the practices of the earliest believers, who were closest to the "historical Jesus."

Ultimately, the Modernist perception of history and the evolution of religion is a bit maddening and can be used to justify virtually any position. Fortunately, the very notion that Christ can be bifurcated into a historical figure and a religious figure is condemned explicitly in Pius X's syllabus of Modernist errors, *Lamentabili Sane*. Condemned proposition 29 of *Lamentabili* states: "It is permissible to grant that the Christ of history is far inferior to the Christ Who is the object of faith." (Note that the propositions in a syllabus of errors such as this one are written in the positive to demonstrate the belief that is condemned.)

At any rate, the Modernist mentality that facilitates the evolution of religion and the rethinking of Christ leads to consequences that touch on Catholic doctrine as a whole. Ultimately, doctrine itself is up for debate when the evolutionary mentality is applied to Truth. This will be discussed in the next chapter.

7

The Modernist Misunderstanding of the Origin and Development of Dogma

Modernist phraseology can be quite confusing, and this makes the detection of Modernist tendencies difficult for even faithful and well-meaning Catholics. This is because Modernism, although it is heresy, seems to differ from other heresies in how it works. When we think of a heresy, we are likely thinking of a set of assertions that stand in stark contradiction to the defined teachings of the Church, such as with Arianism and the various Protestant heresies. With Modernism, however, the most pernicious danger is in the *method* or mechanism, which is to say, *how* Modernism works.

While it is true that the early days of Modernism gave us heretics such as Loisy and Tyrrell, who taught objective errors, the encroachment of Modernism into the veins of the institutions of the Church has been more subtle. What we have seen is an embrace of a Modernist mentality that infects minds and nudges them toward heresy or at least the toleration thereof over a long period. One of the most effective means of forming Catholics to tolerate or embrace Modernism has been the Modernist conception of the origin and development of dogma.

The Origin of Dogma

We may then ask the question, "If Modernists believe in the changing nature of dogma, where do they believe dogma comes from?"

Building on what Pius X explained earlier concerning the modernist notion of continual revelation to "believers," he tells us that Modernism asserts that "God indeed presents Himself to man, but in a manner so confused and indistinct that He can hardly be perceived by the believer" (11). Now, Modernists do not believe that *all* men are unable to understand "confused and indistinct" divine truth because, of course, *they* understand these hidden truths and will tell us all about them!

Given the evolutionary nature of their belief, Modernists trace all religious sentiment back to a "primordial" experience that grows in complexity and evolves with the human race, much as an evolutionist hearkens back to a primordial ooze whence all life came. Therefore, even though they believe in the progression of religion with the progress of man, they must necessarily hold that the purest religious sentiment is one from a bygone age when the accoutrement of human creativity did not sully the original revelation. If you have heard of Jean-Jacques Rousseau (1712–1778), you may have seen a similarity in the Modernist conception of primordial revelation and religion to Rousseau's concept of the "state of nature."

Rousseau believed that human beings lived in their purest way when they lived in a "state of nature" and that this original state was ideal for human society. It was his contention that the advent of states and private-property rights were to blame for a degradation in the human community. In essence, if there were no rules and regulations, Rousseau thought, people would thrive. Now, there is a grain of truth in what he believed, if we consider the negative effect of oppressive overregulation and tampering with the lives of citizens, but he was utterly wrong about history. The most primitive societies, such as those encountered by the explorers of the Americas in the fifteenth and sixteenth centuries, lived in societies that were ghastly compared with European civilization. Of course, this is politically incorrect to say, but it is true. The accounts of the French martyrs, such as St. Jean de Brébeuf, about what they witnessed in New France (Canada) during the age of exploration might make your skin crawl. Even the most sophisticated civilizations, such as that of the Aztecs in Mexico, were as barbaric and merciless as can be envisioned. The point is, the further we go back in history and the more primitive or untouched by Christian civilization a society is, the more we find the opposite of a pure "state of nature."

Modernism looks to the age of primordial religion and offers a Rousseauian perspective that is equally absurd. In addition, Modernism believes in the progress of religion through the collective subconscious of believers, so it is paradoxical, if not self-defeating, that Modernists believe we should look to an imagined past of pure religion while asserting that religion must progress with the times. Which is it? Were the earliest believers the purest in their belief? Or did the collective beliefs of believers evolve over time to better represent the progress of religion?

Modernists are — in their own minds — like carpenters who restore old furniture to their original glory, yet they believe that the furniture should evolve with time and progress to a state or type of furniture. This is the world of contradictions that encapsulates the Modernist intellect. Modernists are both progressives and traditionalists, both the products of evolution and evolved people who hearken to a less evolved time, both materialists and spiritualists. All of this makes any talk of dogma — binding teachings — completely foreign to Catholic thinking.

In fairness to this brand of heretic, they seem to admit their folly because no one can *truly* define any dogma under their system. So they place the origin of dogma in a distant, amorphous time of pure or primitive religion, which they call the "primary formula," while asserting that the dogmas to be taught to believers are expressed in "secondary formulae" (12).

This is to say that the *primary* formula of religious sentiment — the pure revelation or religion from the past — is ineffable and mysterious, and therefore, the best we can do is approximate pure religious truth with formulations that express the psychological experience of believers. These secondary formulations are "mere instruments" (12), according to Pius X, that theologians create to furnish believers with symbolic or imagistic statements that help believers make sense of or express their religious sentiment. In other words, the *real* truth of religion is mysterious and unknown, so the best we can do is try to talk about religion in a way that describes our experience of what is ultimately ineffable.

Now, there is an aspect of truth in this, but only to a degree. Yes, there is much that we do not know about God or spiritual realities, and much of what is unknown to us now will be made clearer in eternity. There is also a lot that we *do know*, however, especially what has been revealed by God through the Sacred Scriptures and what Jesus Christ — true God and true man — revealed to us in the New Testament. Furthermore, the Apostles preserved and distilled for us the Deposit of Faith, of which the Church and her pastors have been the stewards and which has been taught to us throughout the centuries through dogmatic Church teaching. Modernism, however, would have us believe that all the dogmas and teachings, while helpful in a given context, are mere approximations of the unknowable truth that ultimately eludes us.

Taking this into account, the reader should be on guard against Modernist usage of traditional theological terms. Take, for example, the term "sacrament." In the broad sense, a sacrament is a "sign of something secret and hidden (the Greek word is mysterious)."[29] So, in a sense, it is not improper to say that a sacrament is symbolic of something. In the Church, however, we understand that the seven sacraments, although they transmit symbolic meaning, which is not to be undervalued, are not *merely* signs of symbols but are *real* things that

---

[29] Daniel Kennedy, "Sacraments," in *The Catholic Encyclopedia*, vol. 13 (New York: Robert Appleton Company, 1912), https://www.newadvent.org/cathen/13295a.htm.

leave indelible marks on our souls, such as with Baptism, or provide sanctifying grace, such as with Holy Communion.

In other words, according to the orthodox Catholic understanding, sacraments "do not merely signify Divine grace, but in virtue of their Divine institution, they cause that grace in the souls of men."[30]

A Modernist, because he is an agnostic and suffers from a philosophical disease, can use a term such as "sacrament" and apply its meaning as if he believes in it from an orthodox perspective. He can herald the beauty and grandeur of the Holy Eucharist and, in some cases — with very cunning rhetoric — convince even the traditionalist that he believes in the Real Presence of Christ in the Eucharist and believes that a man's soul is significantly helped by the worthy reception thereof.

Do not be fooled, though, because Modernism cheats with words. We must take into consideration that this heresy begins with a complete misunderstanding of *faith itself*, and therefore any talk of "grace" from a "sacrament" according to a Modernist must be understood as a subjectivist religious sentiment. So a Modernist could say in all sincerity that souls receive grace by participating in the Catholic sacramental life; what he means, however, is that the believer is helped in his spiritual quest because he participates in something — the sacraments — from which he derives great meaning. It is a confusion of psychological help with the spiritual perfection received from sanctifying grace. Again, it is partially truthful, because a good mental state can result from a good spiritual state, and there are psychological consolations that we receive from reverent experiences. Nonetheless, Modernism reduces the spiritual to the psychological, which degrades the objectivity of dogmatic truth, given that psychological experience is often relative to context and circumstances.

A major consequence of the Modernist understanding of the origin of dogma occurs when we consider other religions and their teachings

---

[30] Kennedy, "Sacraments."

in light of the Modernist system. This is because, by the Modernist system, there is really no way to suggest that a Buddhist or a Muslim or a Jew is not given "divine help" from his false religion,[31] because dogmas are ultimately symbols of ineffable realities. As you can imagine, any notion that there could be no salvation outside the Church — a dogma that is more serious than a heart attack and is *infallible* — holds no merit. If anything, the Modernists of our day, who are really Neomodernists,[32]

---

[31] As Catholics, we believe that the Jews of the Old Testament practiced the true religion, but the Old Covenant was meant to prepare for the coming of Christ, who gave us the New Covenant. The Judaism that has been practiced since the coming of Christ is not the same as in the Old Testament. For one, there is no more Temple, so there is no more sacrifice, and God willed that the prefiguring sacrifice of the Old Covenant would cease and give place to the Holy Sacrifice of the Mass. Judaism since the time of Christ is necessarily anti-Christ, meaning against the true Messiah; therefore, we say that it is false as it stands today.

[32] Neomodernists are not much different from Modernists but are simply more careful with words and how they express their doctrines. Pope Pius XII condemned the trend of Neomodernism in his encyclical *Humani Generis* (1950), where he wrote in paragraph 15: "Moreover, they assert that when Catholic doctrine has been reduced to this condition, a way will be found to satisfy modern needs, that will permit of dogma being expressed also by the concepts of modern philosophy, whether of immanentism or idealism or existentialism or any other system. Some more audacious assert that this can and must be done, because they hold that the mysteries of faith are never expressed by truly adequate concepts but only by approximate and ever changeable notions, in which the truth is to some extent expressed, but is necessarily distorted. Wherefore they do not consider it absurd, but altogether necessary, that theology should substitute new concepts in place of the old ones in keeping with the various philosophies which in the course of time it uses as its instruments, so that it should give human expression to divine truths in various ways which are even somewhat opposed, but still equivalent, as they say. They add that the history of dogmas consists in the reporting of the various forms in which revealed truth has been clothed, forms that have succeeded one another in accordance with

can also cheat with the word "church" and extend its meaning to the amorphous communities of believers spread throughout the world who have merely different religious traditions dictated by cultural norms. By Modernist logic, there is certainly no ground to stand on in saying that a heretic or an infidel or a man living in perfidy will be excluded from the Beatific Vision, because the sacraments, which are merely symbols — even if more perfect and powerful symbols — express only what is ultimately inexpressible anyway.

The Evolution of Dogma

So, if dogmas are ethereal things that are mere approximations to the truth, then we should expect them to *evolve* according to the Modernist understanding.

Before we consider the words of Pius X, let us define our terms. "Evolution" must be juxtaposed with "adaptation" or "development." For something to evolve, it must change from one thing to another in a substantial way so as to become a different thing that no longer exists in the same way as the former thing. For example, in terms of biological evolution — which I reject wholeheartedly in the sense of *macroevolution* — we would say that if a particular species of ape birthed a type of hominid that was no longer of the same species, the new species would constitute an evolved species — a new type of animal that may have an origin in the former but can no longer procreate with the progenitor, as it is a substantially different kind. We would call this *macroevolution*, meaning a "big" evolution.[33]

---

the different teachings and opinions that have arisen over the course of the centuries."

[33] It must be noted that there is no real consistency of thought with the theory of evolution. Some theorists opine that different species can breed with one another, while others say that the inability to breed constitutes a differentiation in species. Evolutionary theory suffers from a diseased metaphysical underpinning; thus, it is impossible to pin down what evolutionists believe in all cases.

On the other hand, if we look at the animal kingdom, we find various groupings such as canine and feline. Dogs are a perfect example of a *microevolution*, which means a "small" evolution or, better yet, a *development* or *adaptation*. A Chihuahua can be bred with a Great Dane, for example, although this rarely happens and must be done through artificial insemination, given the size differences. Also, a wolf can breed with a dog, as they are both canines and therefore are part of the same species grouping in the animal kingdom. A wolf cannot, however, breed with a mountain lion.

In Catholic dogma, we *cannot* say that there has ever been a true *evolution* of dogma in the sense that one dogma has changed so completely that it means something completely different, but we can say there has been a *development* in dogma. In other words — to use a crude analogy — doctrines may develop as species of dogs may develop over time to the point where we have a more refined and beautiful canine, but dogmas may never evolve until they become a different animal. Modernists necessarily reject this.

Speaking of the Modernist notion about dogmas, Pius X writes: "Hence it is quite impossible to maintain that they express absolute truth: for, in so far as they are *symbols*, they are the images of truth, and so must be adapted to the religious sentiment in its relation to man; and as *instruments*, they are the vehicles of truth, and must therefore in their turn be adapted to man in his relation to the religious sentiment" (13).

Dogma, according to the Modernist, must adapt to man as he changes. Pius X adds that Modernism asserts that "he who believes may pass through different phases.... Thus the way is open to the intrinsic *evolution* of dogma" (13).

Now, it may be retorted that the Church *does* change dogma in some way as man grows in understanding of religious truth. In a certain sense, there is truth to this, but only partially. The dogmas — what is taught and required to be believed — never change, but the formulations of dogmas may develop to be clearer. For example, it is beyond doubt that Catholics have always believed, and the Church has always taught, that when the priest consecrates the bread and wine during Mass, the Holy Eucharist is confected and what is present after the Consecration is the true Body and true Blood of Our Lord. Of course, the accidents — the material appearance — remain, but Christ is truly present in the Eucharist, and we can no longer call what has been consecrated "bread and wine." In this way, we receive Our Lord in Holy Communion truly and substantially. Now, it was not the case in the early centuries that this process of consecration was given a name or described in a way that was binding on Catholics or universally applied in theological discourse. As Catholic theology organically developed, however, the Church eventually did define, at the Council of Trent, the process of the transformation of the bread and wine into the Body and Blood of Our Lord during Mass as *transubstantiation*. What was defined and described with a definitive formulation was something that was always believed — the substantial change that takes place during the Consecration. So, while we may say that the dogma of transubstantiation provided the Church with a new dogmatic formulation, we *cannot* say that any Catholic dogma had changed, much less "evolved." What we see with this example is a *development* of dogma by way of refined formulation of what is already believed and not an *evolution* of one belief into another.

Furthermore, once a dogma is defined *infallibly*, it is no longer permissible for Catholics to debate the topic, although the definition of a particular dogma may spark further developments in theological discourse that help refine adjacent principles and concepts further.

Recall the philosophical origins of Modernism discussed at the outset of this book, and you will see the *fundamental* shift in basic understanding of reality itself that took place largely with Descartes. If it is true that dogma must evolve as man passes "through different phases," then it is *impossible* that dogma remain constant throughout the ages, because a dogma with the philosophical foundation of a thirteenth-century Scholastic will be incomprehensible to a twentieth-century idiot, which is to say, a Hegelian; therefore, the nature of the dogma itself must completely change to express a belief about religion that is wholly different.

A saner theologian from the time of Aquinas would believe that the Real Presence of Christ in the Eucharist means just that: that Christ is really present in an objective way. The Modernist of our day, on the other hand, would say that if Christ is present, it cannot be the way that Thomas Aquinas would have understood it because the nature of "being present" itself can no longer mean what it did for Aquinas!

As Archbishop Lefebvre said: "For the Faith, evolution is death. They speak of a Church that evolves, they want an evolving faith. 'You must submit to the living Church, to the Church of today,' they were writing to me from Rome in the mid seventies, as if the Church of today should not be identical to the Church of yesterday. I answered them, 'Under those conditions, tomorrow it will no longer be what you are saying today!' Those people have no concept of truth, of being. They are Modernists."[34]

Contrariwise, Modernists assert:

> Dogma is not only able, but ought to evolve and to be changed.... In other words, it is necessary that the primitive formula be accepted and sanctioned by the heart; and similarly the subsequent work from which spring the secondary formulas must proceed under the guidance of the heart. Hence it comes that these formulas, to be living, should be, and should remain, adapted to the faith and to him who believes. Wherefore if for any reason this adaptation should cease to exist, they lose their first meaning and accordingly must be changed. (13)

You will notice that Modernists place a noticeable emphasis on the "living" nature of dogma; this is deduced from the principle of *vital*

---

[34] Marcel Lefebvre, *They Have Uncrowned Him* (Saint Marys, KS: Angelus Press, 1988), 16.

immanence, which tells us that religious formulas — dogmas — ought to be "alive" and keep up with the life of the religious sentiment.

This mentality is part and parcel of the general zeitgeist of our social narratives and philosophy in the post-Christian world. Marriage, for example, was once between a man and a woman, and it was for life; now it is between a man and a man, or a woman and a woman, or a man who was a woman and a woman who is neither a man nor a woman, and marriage is no longer viewed as permanent.

Of course, the reader is well aware of the ridiculousness of contemporary beliefs about marriage, but we should consider that these beliefs did not spring up out of nowhere, as if there were no philosophical foundation that facilitated this shift. In reality, the redefinition of marriage, even though it has taken place in the civil sphere and in Protestantism, is an evolution of dogma. While the Catholic Church cannot change the dogma of sacramental marriage, we can surely see that in the practical sense there are legions of priests and baptized Catholics who act as if it has changed.

This is doubtless a consequence of the Modernism that has degraded the formation of so many priests in recent decades. If a priest knows that a couple is living in an objective state of adultery by being civilly "remarried," yet he includes that couple in the sacramental life of his congregation, we must assume that he is confused or malformed about the nature of sanctifying grace and mortal sin. Perhaps he does not believe in transubstantiation and views the Eucharist as symbolic; perhaps he believes that the dogmatic truth of the permanence of sacramental marriage is too old-school and not representative of the modern milieu; perhaps he believes that a couple are not sinning if their consciences do not accuse them of sin. Whatever he believes or doesn't believe, he demonstrates a Modernist outlook by allowing the sacraments to be abused.

We are in absurdity, as we are in a Modernist or even Postmodernist hellscape where the nature of what is true relies on the nature of man who evolves and who feels the truth in his own way, and therefore the truth — which is dependent on the life within man — must change again and again.

In the Church, it is in vogue to talk of "living tradition" as opposed to the historical notion of hard-and-fast "Sacred Tradition." In fact, in the letter that Pope John Paul II wrote wherein he alleged that Archbishop Marcel Lefebvre had excommunicated himself and committed a schismatic act, the Polish pope employed the same term. He wrote: "The root of this schismatic act can be discerned in an incomplete and contradictory notion of Tradition. Incomplete, because it does not take sufficiently into account the living character of Tradition."[35]

Now, whatever one may think about Archbishop Lefebvre, are we really willing to say that he did not understand Sacred Tradition?

To make matters worse, John Paul II continued with a definition taken from the Vatican II document *Dei Verbum*:

> The Second Vatican Council clearly taught, "[tradition] comes from the apostles and *progresses* in the Church with the help of the Holy Spirit. There is a growth in insight into the realities and words that are being passed on. This comes about in various ways. It comes through the *contemplation and study of believers who ponder these things in their hearts*. It comes from the *intimate sense of spiritual realities which they experience*. And it comes from the preaching of those who have received, along with their right of succession in the episcopate, the sure charism of truth."[36] (emphasis added)

Now, given the understanding of Modernism we have from our study of *Pascendi*, let us compare and contrast the words of John Paul II and Pius X. John Paul II claimed that Lefebvre misunderstood Tradition because it develops from the "contemplation and study of believers who ponder these things in their hearts," which comes from the

---

[35] Pope John Paul II, apostolic letter *Ecclesia Dei* (July 2, 1988), no. 4.
[36] *Ecclesia Dei* 4.

"intimate sense of spiritual realities which they experience." Contrast this notion with what Pius X castigated about Modernist doctrine: "In other words, it is necessary that the primitive formula be accepted and *sanctioned by the heart*; and similarly the subsequent work from which spring the secondary *formulas must proceed under the guidance of the heart*. Hence it comes that these formulas, to be *living*, should be, and should remain, *adapted to the faith and to him who believes*" (emphasis added).

Now, if John Paul II, and, by extension, *Dei Verbum*, is alluding to the development of dogma in the Catholic sense, it is hard to see how the aforementioned statement fits the bill. If the statement were merely "Tradition comes from the apostles and progressed in the Church with the help of the Holy Spirit; there is a growth in insight into the realities and words that are being passed on," then we could perhaps see this understanding as in line with the perennial understanding of Sacred Tradition. If it was just this, then we could chalk it up to a Catholic understanding of the development of dogma, given that the Apostles did provide us with the Deposit of Faith given to them, and the Church has been entrusted to the guidance of the Holy Ghost. That being said, the use of the word "progresses" in this context is problematic, given that, for something to progress, it must move forward to a destination, and we cannot say that dogma "moves forward" even if we move forward in our spiritual life or in our understanding of dogma.

But the definition does not stop there, and both Vatican II and Pope John Paul II tell us that Tradition comes from the "contemplation and study of believers who ponder these things in their hearts" and from their "intimate sense of spiritual realities which they experience." This definition of Tradition is highly problematic, and I cannot see how it is not Modernist in spirit and tone. A synonym for the word "sense" is "feeling," which is the same as "sentiment." In reality, the modern definition of Tradition, according to John Paul II and Vatican II, is that Tradition, although it may begin with the Apostles, goes through stages of progress in the intimate religious sentiments of believers, who express these feelings based on their experiences; and, considering pastors are also believers, their preaching expresses these realities as well. While there is mention of the "sure charism of truth" in the Vatican II definition, what truth is protected by this charism? If Tradition comes from religious sentiment and experience, what is true about it? And if it "progresses," does that not mean it is moving *away* from the Apostles toward some unseen final end?

It is not my intention to accuse John Paul II of being a Modernist here, as that is something I have no right to do, and it should be noted that his letter from 1988 "no longer has juridical effect."[37] If the allegation, however, is that one is liable to enter into *schism* if one does not understand Tradition the way John Paul II presented it in his letter, then what are we to make of this?

We must all admit that the words of John Paul II — and, by extension, Vatican II — seem to be in line with the condemned proposition held by the Modernists. If we admit this, are we falling prey to a "schismatic" mentality? It seems to me that, rather than falling prey to a spirit of schism, if we reject or call into question the conciliar definition of Tradition, we are merely heeding the warnings of Pope Pius X about the Modernist definition of Tradition! Does this mean that being anti-Modernist is schismatic?

In the Oath Against Modernism, an oath that Pope John Paul II would have been required to recite when he was a priest, Pope Pius X defined Sacred Tradition as "the absolute and immutable truth preached by the apostles from the beginning, [that] may never be believed to be different, may never be understood in any other way." This understanding of Tradition is a far cry from the notion that it is something that progresses through feelings and experience. So who is correct: Pope Pius X or Vatican II and John Paul II?

---

[37] Cardinal Giovanni Battista Re, *Decree Remitting the Excommunication "Latae Sententiae" of the Bishops of the Society of Saint Pius X*, January 21, 2009, Vatican website.

Now, let us entertain the idea of accepting the teaching of Pius X while also accepting the teaching of Vatican II and John Paul II. How can we do this without accepting a substantial change in dogmatic teaching? If we were to try to reconcile the former with the latter, would we not have to resort to something like a Modernist understanding of the evolution of dogma?

If one is at risk of falling into schism for not understanding Tradition the way it was expressed in the postconciliar era, then we might say that one is at risk of being in schism from Modernism, and therefore in communion with the anti-Modernism of Pius X — Tradition.

To conclude his section on the evolution of dogma, Pius X ends with a scathing rebuke of the Modernists:

> *Blind* that they are, and *leaders of the blind*, inflated with a boastful science, they have reached that pitch of folly where they pervert the eternal concept of truth and the true nature of the religious sentiment; with that new system of theirs *they are seen to be under the sway of a blind and unchecked passion for novelty, thinking not at all of finding some solid foundation of truth, but despising the holy and apostolic traditions, they embrace other vain, futile, uncertain doctrines, condemned by the Church, on which, in the height of their vanity, they think they can rest and maintain truth itself.* (13, emphasis in the original)

Our age in Church history is one in which novelty is always upon us. We live in the Church of the "new Advent," the "new springtime," the "new Pentecost," and we have a "New Mass." Our hierarchs, even popes — especially Pope Francis — have demonstrated that they despise "the holy and apostolic traditions" while "they embrace other vain, futile, uncertain doctrines."

8

The Modernist as Believer

At this point, dear reader, we have become familiar with the philosophical and theological underpinnings of Modernism as explained by Pope Pius X in *Pascendi*. Thus far, we have discussed the origins of the heresy and how Modernist theologians have employed it to pervert theology. Since most readers of this book are not priests or theologians, however, it behooves us to consider what Modernism does to the Catholic believer. After all, even if we are not trained in theology in an official way, we are all catechized, in some cases poorly, by our pastors. So we must assume that Modernism does not remain solely in the realm of academics and clerics and that it could affect each one of us.

The well-known exorcist priest Fr. Chad Ripperger said the following in a conference about Modernism: "Modernism, which is now the heresy in the Church, is so toxic. It's so much in the air that, unless you have a *special grace or unless you really know your faith extraordinarily well*, you are simply going to end up in error. It's that simple, so you have to pray to God for that" (emphasis added).[38]

---

[38] For a transcript of the conference, see "Father Ripperger: Levels of Spiritual Warfare," WQPH, September 16, 2020, https://wqphradio.org/2020/09/fr-ripperger-levels-of-spiritual-warfare/.

Fr. Ripperger is correct, and if you are like me, you cannot claim that you have received a special grace; therefore, you must study the Faith deeply, which includes studying how to avoid adopting Modernism as a Catholic believer.

It is my hope that, in reading this section, you will grasp the severity and urgency of this matter because, as the majority of Catholics are laymen, it is vital that the Catholic faithful be on guard. Keep in mind the words of St. James, who wrote: "And whosoever shall keep the whole law, but offend in one point, is become guilty of all" (2:10).

Individual Experience and Religious Certitude

According to Pius X, the important difference between the Modernist as a philosopher or theologian and the Modernist as a believer boils down to the fact that Modernist intellectuals pontificate and theorize about religion, whereas average believers generally learn their faith through the practice thereof. Therefore, what "happens" in the life of the believer — think of our interaction with liturgical rites — has the greatest effect. Pius X refers to this as the "sphere of phenomena" (14).

For the Modernist philosopher, the object of faith is, in a sense, an objective thing to be studied and considered, even if this sort of philosopher does not believe religious truth to be objective in and of itself. The *believer*, however, does not concern himself with questions so academic and instead ascertains what he believes to be religious truth by way of *experience*. Again, as with all heresies, there is an aspect of truth in this claim.

Catholics enjoy what is called the *sensus Catholicus*, which can be called the "Catholic sense" in English. In essence, a Catholic has a certain "instinct" that is fostered over time and that results from catechesis and the life of grace received from the sacraments. Perhaps you have had this experience. You walk into a shop or a social setting and something feels "off," and upon further investigation, you look behind the counter and see a statue of a false god. Or perhaps someone sends you a citation from an alleged Marian apparition, and something about it is fishy; you can't identify anything objectively heretical in the message, but there is a certain *je ne sais quoi* about it. Upon further investigation, you discover a treatise on the writing from a good priest who breaks down the underlying theological error that illuminates the false apparition.

The point is that you knew *implicitly* that there was something wrong, even if the error was not *explicit*. This is where the problem arises with the Modernist as a believer; if his faith is muddled with philosophical error, he will not have the tools to avoid falling into further error. So, the *sensus Catholicus* is conflated with mere personal experience and private judgment. Therefore, when one is confronted with a salacious and tempting new doctrine, he can convince himself that he knows his Faith — even though he does not — and therefore, if he perceives it to be true, it must be, because it is reconcilable with what he believes to be Catholic teaching.

Pius X explains how believers are affected by Modernism:

> In *the religious sentiment* one must recognise a kind of intuition of the heart which puts man in immediate contact with the very reality of God, and infuses such a persuasion of God's existence and His action both within and without man as to excel greatly any scientific conviction. They assert, therefore, the existence of a real experience, and one of a kind that surpasses all rational experience.... It is this *experience* which, when a person acquires it, makes him properly and truly a believer. (14)

What Pius X is saying here is that absorbing Modernism leads believers to conclude that they will know the truth of religion in the fullest sense by experience, and that an experience that relates most strongly to how they *feel* about God will be the strongest proof for someone affected by Modernism. Again, there is a partial truth in this, as we can all have experiences of God, and at times in our spiritual lives, God will send us consolations that only we can understand and that are hard to explain to others. The kicker, however, as Pius X explains, is that believers plagued by Modernism appeal to a "real experience ... that surpasses all rational experience."

This is problematic because Catholicism is eminently reasonable, which means it is rational, and therefore believers should not look to experience beyond "rational experience" as a guide to religious truth. Even miracles are not beyond rational experience, as God intervenes in creation in ways that are in accord with the nature of the things He interacts with. For example, if God raises a man from the dead, either through the intercession of a saint or the direct action of Jesus Christ, who is God, this is a miracle, but it is not beyond rational experience. By raising someone from the dead, God merely restores a corpse to life, and being alive is perfectly reasonable for a human being. Likewise, when Christ turns water into wine, He merely changes the biological constitution of water, and wine is largely made up of water, as it is a liquid that comes from fruits that consist mainly of water.

Also, in the spiritual life, how can we assess whether our spiritual experience is in line with Catholic teaching if it surpasses rationality? What if a believer were to believe that God had told him to leave his wife and that this was confirmed by an experience that was intense and memorable? Obviously, God would never instruct someone to transgress the bonds of marriage, but if a believer comes to believe, by way of Modernist influence, that God speaks to us in ineffable ways in the inmost recesses of our hearts and that those experiences are necessarily of divine origin, then it is easy to see how one could become confused.

Certainly, if we hope to remain faithful Catholics, we must not appeal to experience over dogma, as Modernism would have us do. Yes, we can have strong religious experiences, and they can be edifying, but they must be evaluated in the light of sound, immutable teaching. Believers who have assimilated Modernist tendencies are likely to reject the immutability of Catholic dogma for all the reasons that have been explained thus far.

"Dearly beloved, believe not every spirit, but try the spirits if they be of God: because many false prophets are gone out into the world. By this is the spirit of God known. Every spirit which confesseth that Jesus Christ is come in the flesh, is of God: And every spirit that dissolveth Jesus, is not of God" (1 John 4:1–3). The traditional commentary on this passage written by St. John tells us that to "try the spirits" means to ensure that what is heard or felt in prayer is consistent with Catholic teaching and that a spirit that "confesseth that Jesus Christ is come in the flesh" does not refer to the Protestant notion of "faith alone" or a mere belief in Jesus as Lord. If it were enough to confess that Jesus is God in order for a spirit to be of divine origin, then we would have no grounds to condemn the heresy of Martin Luther. Once again, our experience is valid only if it is agreeable with the dogmatic teachings of the Church.

Phenomenology and Personalism

Remember that Pope Pius X referred to the realm of religious experience as understood in Modernism as the "sphere of phenomena," which could also be called the realm of experience. While it is true that we live in a sphere of phenomena, given that we have senses and we experience things, evaluating the truth solely or principally based on our interaction with phenomena is problematic because our perception of these experiences can be misunderstood. The perennial philosophical approach of Catholic theologians teaches that a thing consists of both essence and existence.

The essence of a thing can be described as its *quiddity*, which means what is particular about it that distinguishes it from other things; the essence of a thing, however, is distinguished from its accidents. Accidents are qualities or attributes of a thing that can change without altering what the thing is. For example, a human being is not an animal as a dog is an animal because a human being has a rational soul. And a human being could lose his arms, legs, eyes, and hair but still be a human being, even though certain accidents have been lost.

Existence is the fact that something *is*. In other words, essence is *what* something is, while existence is *that* it is. With modern philosophy, there was a shift to evaluating things primarily based on essence and not on existence, which has caused problems.

Phenomenology is a philosophical approach that focuses on the study of conscious experience or perception from the first-person point of view as a barometer of truth. The essence, or quiddity, of a thing is the primary mode of understanding the thing.

Contrariwise, in the Thomist and perennial approach, while understanding something by its essence is indeed paramount, this is not divorced from the objectivity of the existence of a thing. That a thing exists independent of our experience with it allows us to know the thing abstractly through our knowledge of the realm of existing things. Again, our sense perception can enlighten us and confirm for us what we understand in the abstract, but it is not the case that interaction with the essence of a thing is the primary focus for understanding.

For the phenomenologist, however, it is the individual who assesses external reality by seeing how it conforms to his experience of external things, rather than how the experience of the essence of things conforms to the objective reality of what a thing is by its existence. In essence, phenomenology attempts to return to "the things themselves," focusing on how phenomena present themselves to consciousness, aiming for a rigorous, yet rich, description of lived experience.

A central tenet of phenomenological thinking is what is called the *Lebenswelt*, a German word translated as "life-world." This term was introduced by the philosopher Edmund Husserl, who described the Lebenswelt as the realm of pure experience where things are understood before theoretical constructs are applied. In other words, it is an experiential mode of conceiving reality in which things are allegedly understood without the use of categories or definitions. It is also believed in this school of thought that the Lebenswelt changes with cultures and time periods. Husserl critiqued the objective scientific approach to reality and advocated a return to the subjective experience to understand phenomena through lived experience.

Husserl's work seems initially to have been a reaction against the subjectivist milieu of his time. He was a mathematician who believed in objective truth, but he fell prey to a certain subjectivity. His work heavily influenced his student Max Scheler, whose work heavily influenced Pope John Paul II. Scheler should not be considered a phenomenologist in the strict sense, and he was influential in the development of what is called personalism. Personalism is *not* phenomenology in a strict sense, but it should be considered an offshoot thereof.

John Paul II's doctoral dissertation was titled "Evaluation of the Possibility of Constructing a Christian Ethics on the Basis of the System of Max Scheler." In that work, John Paul II rejected many of Scheler's conclusions, though he still considered himself a personalist. In his work *Love and Responsibility*, first published in 1960, he proposed what he termed "the personalistic norm," for example.[39]

John Paul II did not reject Scheler's work wholesale; he was influenced by Scheler's personalism in his understanding of the person, love, and value. He sought to correct what he viewed as Scheler's errors by integrating these insights with a more robust Thomistic ontology and a Christian theological framework, ensuring that personalism did not lose sight of objective truth and the supernatural aspects of human existence. As will be shown, however, whatever his intentions, the flaws that can emanate from personalism showed up in John Paul's work over time.

In fairness to the Polish pope, he did study under the great Thomist Réginald Garrigou-Lagrange and focused on Thomism in his doctoral studies. Therefore, we cannot say that John Paul II did not understand Thomism. We will see, though, that on certain fundamental truths, he deviated from Aquinas substantially. We ought to keep in mind that having studied Thomism under a great teacher does not necessarily mean that John Paul II was a Thomist. Some commentators on John Paul's legacy object to criticisms about his aberrations from true Thomism

---

[39] "Personalism," Wikipedia, November 14, 2024, https://en.wikipedia.org/wiki/Personalism.

because of his background in Thomistic studies, but we should remember that virtually every priest and theologian for centuries would have been educated in a rigorous Thomism, yet many deviated from the path. It seems that John Paul II sought to fill in certain gaps in Thomistic thought, the thinking being that because St. Thomas was so objective, there needed to be more consideration of the subjective experience in relation to the objective. This is a noble endeavor, and I believe there is merit to this intention. Nonetheless, personalism was not an adequate approach to fill in those gaps.

Some would object to labeling John Paul II a phenomenologist, because he was a personalist, but many of the core concepts of the former are integral to the latter. There is continuity, even if there are differences. The difference is largely in where the focus lies, but the philosophical method is similar. Authors often use the terms interchangeably when discussing thinkers from each stream of thought.

In any event, Husserl's theory that the nature of things is known by observation was expanded on by Scheler, who proposed the theory that the value of things is known by feelings. As Husserl detached the essence of things from the things themselves, so Scheler detached the value of things from the things themselves, thereby also falling into subjectivism.

Scheler stressed the role of emotions and the intuitive grasp of human instinct as paramount in assessing ethics, which were referred to as "values." In essence, Scheler's approach to philosophy stressed the value of emotions in the human community, with an emphasis on the expression of love based on the dignity of the other person. Now, although there is value in this approach, it is also problematic. Pope John Paul II did *not* accept every concept taught by Husserl and Scheler, but the phenomenological and personalist style did color his approach to moral theology.

Theology of the Body

One area that illustrates for us the contrast between the historical Catholic approach and the approach adopted by John Paul II is how the reality of love is understood. We could say that the difference between the personalist or phenomenological approach to love and the historical Catholic understanding is that the former asserts that love determines ethics, whereas the latter asserts that ethics determine love. In other words, while we must consider the dignity and emotions of others to love them, we can love them properly only if we love what is objectively good and hate what is objectively bad, regardless of what implications this may have for another's experience or perception. Furthermore, love is an abstract concept, meaning it is objective and is not based on feelings or emotions.

In the personalist conception, man is first a loving being before he is ever a knowing being. This means that before there is self-knowledge and understanding, there is, according to personalism, love, which is seen in this approach as something realized in the unity of persons. To Scheler and, by extension, John Paul II, the person is a principle of agency who realizes himself as a person by loving. In other words, he knows himself by giving himself.

Following the personalist understanding of love, John Paul II stated that he based his "entire priesthood" on a "love for human love."[40]

This personalist or phenomenological approach adopted by John Paul II is evident in his Theology of the Body (TOB) teachings, which are immensely popular. French Catholic author Yves Semen authored an introduction to the French publication of TOB and wrote that TOB "can be seen as the culmination of all of Karol Wojtyla's [John Paul II's] philosophical and theological thought."[41] The pope began his work on this topic in response to Pope Paul VI's publication of *Humanae Vitae*, which upheld the Church's perennial teaching that contraception is impermissible for Catholics, and he was convinced that only a personalist morality, starting from subjectivity, would be a

---

[40] Jean-Paul II, *Entrez dans l'espérance* (Paris: Plon-Mame, 1994), 192.
[41] Yves Semen, introduction to Jean Paul II, *Théologie du Corps* (Paris: Le Cerf, 2014), 25.

valid response to the challenge posed by the ongoing sexual revolution. Before we continue, we should clarify that when we speak of "subjectivity" as a philosophical term in this context, we do not necessarily mean "relativism" or "subjectivism," which both assert that there is no absolute truth. The appeal to the subject in phenomenological and personalist thought alludes to a concentration on the "subject" — the human person — as the starting point for inquiry. In theory, one may start from the subject and maintain an objectively correct morality, but the opposite is also possible.

The personalist view of man is the Kantian view, which asserts that we should never consider man as a means but as an end. For Wojtyła, particularly in works such as *Love and Responsibility*, the Kantian principle is expanded into a theology of the body and a philosophy of action where love is described as the affirmation of the other as an end, not a means. This means that, in all personal relationships, one must act in a way that acknowledges and promotes the other's freedom and dignity. The authors of the Vatican II document *Gaudium et Spes* (*GS*) adopted this mentality; thus, we find in *GS* the statements that man is the "only creature on earth that God has willed for itself" (24), so that "everything on earth must be ordered to man as its center and summit" (12).

TOB is imbued with the same mentality and opines that true love entails total self-giving; this is consistent with another passage from *GS*, which states,: "Man, who is the only creature on earth which God willed for itself, cannot fully find himself except through a sincere gift of himself" (24). The logical conclusion of this is that man is fulfilled only in a "communion of persons," of which the union of man and woman is the first expression (12). John Paul II, before he was pope, was one of the authors of this document, so we must assume his philosophical approach was present throughout.

If man cannot fully find himself without giving of himself, then it stands to reason that he must fully give of himself. Now, there is truth to this, as we read, in the works of spiritual authors, of such things as "totally consecrating" ourselves to Jesus through Mary. The notion that man needs to "find himself," however, is ambiguous and open-ended to the point where numerous interpretations are possible.

Does this mean that man is lost? If so, where is he? What does it mean for man to "fully find himself"? Can he partially find himself? Does this mean giving oneself totally to God, or can we give ourselves fully to another person? Technically, we cannot give ourselves totally to another person because of the incommunicability of the human person. Also, we are commanded by Christ to love God in a total sense — with our whole heart, our whole soul, and so on — but our neighbor only to a lesser degree, namely, as ourselves (Matt. 22:37–39). Nonetheless, John Paul II acknowledged the incommunicability of the human person but still insisted that spousal love was the most complete form of love, which consists in the giving of the "inalienable and non-transferable 'I'."[42]

If we understand the notion of giving oneself with an interpretive key from John Paul II's work, we find that he asserts that spousal love — meaning the way couples demonstrate their love to one another, which includes the marital act — "fulfills the meaning of his being and existence."[43] He also wrote that "the revelation and discovery of the spousal meaning of the body explain the original happiness of man."[44] This is consistent with the personalist notion that man realizes himself by loving, which comes even before knowledge.

The idea that spousal love fulfills the meaning of being and existence is problematic if we consider the priesthood, for example. What does this mean for priests and religious who are not married? Even Jesus Christ was unmarried, but could we say that He did not give of Himself totally in a way that fulfills the meaning of being and existence? John Paul II did address this issue by describing the Holy Eucharist as a

---

[42] Karol Wojtyla, *Love and Responsibility* (Stock, 1978), 87–88.
[43] General Audience, January 16, 1980.
[44] General Audience, January 16, 1980.

"nuptial" sacrament, but it seems that this was his invention and an attempt to allow for the full realization of self for priests by associating the activity central to Holy Orders with spousal love.

Now, the personalism of TOB facilitates a major theological flaw at the heart of it — the very beginning, in fact — which colors the whole enterprise. To understand this, we must break down an important difference between the perennial approach of Thomism and personalism.

Thomism focuses more on the metaphysical structure of being, while personalism centers on the person's existential reality, which means focusing on lived experience. Thomism sees existence as an act that actualizes (makes a reality of) essence, whereas personalism emphasizes existence as the lived experience of the person, involving self-awareness, freedom, and relationality. Also, in Thomism, essence and existence are more distinctly treated, whereas personalism sees these as more dynamically integrated, especially in the context of human persons. Furthermore, Thomism tends to emphasize divine causation and the hierarchy of being, while personalism often explores how God's image is reflected in personal existence and community.

In one of his first TOB lectures, given in 1979, Pope John Paul II stated that "man became the 'image and likeness' of God not only through his own humanity, but also through the communion of persons which man and woman form right from the beginning."[45] This means that, in the mind of John Paul II, being made in the image and likeness of God is found in both his "humanity" and through "the communion" of male and female. We can see here the influence of personalism on his thinking. First, man did not "become" the image and likeness of God; he was created *in* the image and likeness of God: "And he said: Let us make man to our image and likeness" (Gen. 1:26). John Paul II's assertion is that the essence of humanity — "humanness," think quiddity — and the essence of male and female is what makes man *become* the image and likeness of God.

---

[45] General Audience, November 14, 1979.

Furthermore, the personalist reading of Genesis suggests that the image and likeness of God is found not only in the body but in the complementarity of the sexes. This interpretation is based on Genesis 1:27: "And God created man to his own image: to the image of God he created him: male and female he created them." The notion is that, since Scripture speaks of man's being created in God's image and then immediately follows this up with the mention of man's being made male and female, the two must be related. This is consistent with the personalist motif, given the centrality of the communal experience of essences as the realization of existence, and it is completely absent in Catholic tradition.

On this very topic — namely, the idea that the image and likeness of God is found in the reality of male and female — Thomas Aquinas says the opposite of Pope John Paul II. Replying to the objection that the image and likeness of God is found in the body, Thomas writes: "Therefore we must understand that when Scripture had said, 'to the image of God He created him,' it added, 'male and female He created them,' *not to imply that the image of God came through the distinction of sex*, but that the image of God belongs to both sexes, since it is in the mind, wherein there is no sexual distinction of sex" (emphasis added).[46]

The personalist view on essence and existence — namely, that existence is seen through the lived experience of a person and through his self-awareness — leads to an erroneous conclusion about the origin of man and image of God in man.

Furthermore, the notion that God's image is found in the distinction of male and female strikes at the heart of the divine simplicity. In God, everything is simple, a simplicity of infinite fullness, by reason of His infinite richness of being: "I am who I am" (Exod. 3:14). This fullness of being cannot support any composition, as this would entail the possibility of a decomposition, which is impossible in God. It is in this sense that God is said to be simple. But whereas there is simplicity

---

[46] *Summa Theologiae*, I, q. 93, art. 6, ad 2.

in God, the Creator introduces composition into the created, which is the mark of inherent limit in every creature, in its finitude. Therefore, we cannot suggest that the composition of male and female bodies is indicative of the image of God because this would suggest that a composition, which is not found in the divine simplicity, is where we find the image of God.

This flawed idea of the image of God being found in the body and fully expressed in the communion between two persons gives credence to the Modernist notion that spiritual truth is found totally in the experience of the human being. If being made in God's image is a bodily reality, then it stands to reason that we can best understand God through bodily experience, and the fulfillment of that expression would be found in the conjugal act, which is the "communion of persons," through sexual embrace. Another implication of this is that, since the nuptial embrace is the highest way of fulfilling our natures as being made in God's image, then marriage should be considered the highest sacrament, but the priesthood has always been understood as a higher calling. It is easy to understand why this is so because we do not need to be married in order to be saved, but we do need priests in order to be saved with the saving power of the sacraments. Furthermore, Scripture is clear that in Heaven there will be no marriage (Matt. 22:30), but a priest is a priest for eternity: "Thou art a priest for ever, according to the order of Melchisedech" (Heb. 7:17).

Also, given that John Paul II speaks of the highest reality of love being found in the communion of two persons, who, in their bodies, represent the image and likeness of God, this leads to the conclusion that the highest purpose of the union of man and woman is the nuptial embrace, which would necessarily give credence to the flawed modern notion that the love of spouses is the primary end of marriage. In fact, the procreation and raising of children is the primary end of marriage, and this is chronologically accomplished by the intimate union of spouses, but it is first only in time and not in intention or purpose. God created everything out of love; He intends that man and woman enter into participation in His creative act through an act of love and that they be for the child the reflection of His own creative love. Therein lies the beauty of the conjugal act lived in accordance with this divine plan. Therefore, the first end of marriage is the procreation and raising of children, which reflects God's creative love, and it is by an act of love between the spouses that this is accomplished. It is the opposite of the Kantian or personalist notion that man is the final end and not the means because we see in the perennial Catholic understanding that the coming together of man and woman is the means to the end of procreation, which is a reflection of God's creative love.

Thomistic Phenomenology and Personalism?

Given that John Paul II was also exposed to Thomism, he attempted to present his ideas with what has been called phenomenological Thomism or personalist Thomism. The attempted blending of the two is, in my opinion, in vain, and this is made evident by the fact the heart of the personalist TOB is strikingly opposed to the wisdom of Thomas Aquinas.

While Thomism relies on a deductive approach, starting from metaphysical and natural law principles to deduce moral norms, phenomenology starts with lived experience and then attempts to formulate moral insights from there. This contrasts with the more abstract, principle-driven approach of Thomism. It seems that John Paul II desired to integrate these two approaches, but it is difficult, if not practically impossible, to synthesize opposites into a comprehensive philosophy. In fact, we may recall that the synthesis of opposites or things opposed to one another is at the heart of Hegelianism.

This approach adopted by John Paul II may help to illustrate why he believed, along with Vatican II, that Tradition could be something given to us in the Deposit of Faith by the Apostles, while simultaneously progressing through the subjective experience of believers as an expression of their religious sentiments. In addition, the insights taken from the personalist belief found in TOB, that the full realization of man's being made in God's image is found in an intimate encounter with another human being, sheds light on John Paul II's assertion that not accepting the conciliar definition of Tradition — which is heavily based on the notion that Tradition is the distillation of shared experience — constitutes a risk of being a schismatic. We can see that, in the mind of John Paul II, since love is best described as an act of spousal communion that requires a total gift of self, it makes sense that he would believe any "holding back," even of intellectual ascent to a novel doctrinal proposition, would constitute a lack of "fullness" of communion with each other and the Church.

At any rate, Pope John Paul II's adoption of modern philosophy, which was heavily influenced by the problematic legacy of Kant and his intellectual disciples, colored his thought, and we cannot underestimate the massive influence that John Paul II has had on postconciliar Catholic thought.

I should also say that it is not technically heretical to be a phenomenologist or a personalist, so there is no accusation here that, because the Polish pope embraced that philosophy, this made all his theological assertions baseless or erroneous, as there are many correct insights in his large body of work. Given that this philosophical approach was born out of the modern philosophical milieu that has been shown to be strikingly antithetical to historical Catholic thought, however, I must also say that we should expect the adoption of personalism to facilitate an atmosphere that is more open to error or even heresy. Simply put, if we entertain philosophies that do not provide solid ground for the objective nature of Catholic doctrine, it should not surprise us if those philosophical approaches erode our ability to guard ourselves against adopting errors in the long run.

While it is technically possible to embrace a mode of thinking that does not fit well in the tradition of Catholic thought, it is ultimately unwise.

Finally, so as not to seem to have been unfair to John Paul II, I should mention that he came of age in Poland during a time of great political turmoil that would have impacted him significantly. When he was a young man in his twenties, Poland embraced the brutal communism that had spread from Russia, and he lived through the absolute horror of the Second World War. Under both the horror of communism and the merciless reality of mechanized warfare, people were slaughtered and dispensed with like animals of less worth than cattle. Furthermore, these historical realities brought with them a severe materialism as well as a strong atheistic worldview. So, in a sense, it is only natural that the zeitgeist of the age would have reacted to such realities with a philosophical approach that rejected the anti-human mentality and embraced an approach that was man-centered.

Which Personalist Is Correct?

John Paul II was hardly the only influential Catholic personalist; another major figure in the movement was Dietrich von Hildebrand. Personally, I view von Hildebrand as a heroic figure in the fight for Catholic tradition, and I am not alone in that. He was one of the original defenders of the Traditional Mass in light of the radical reforms to the liturgy, and he was a sharp critic of totalitarian regimes. Interestingly, he was not trained in Thomism, and his opinion of Scheler was strikingly different from John Paul II's; he was of the opinion that Scheler's work was more reconcilable with Catholic thought than John Paul II believed.

Now, both men are considered personalists, and both were strongly committed to the approach, yet they both came to *radically* different conclusions on fundamental problems of their eras that overlapped. Von Hildebrand viewed the New Mass as a catastrophe and was a sharp critic of the conciliar reforms, and, of course, John Paul II was not. Both men arrived at veritably opposite conclusions, although they both appealed to personalism as their philosophical foundation.

John Paul II encouraged the new liturgical spirit because of his emphasis on community as he understood it through the personalist lens, whereas von Hildebrand objected to the emphasis on communal worship realized in the New Mass because he believed this mentality diminished the intimate sacred experience realized in the more mystical presentation of the Traditional Mass.

Again, both men were animated by personalism, yet both believed radically different things and used personalism to express their conclusions.

Far be it from me to accuse von Hildebrand of being a subjectivist, but I believe this brief consideration of personalists with fundamentally different viewpoints on integral questions demonstrates how personalism is malleable to the philosophical emphasis of the particular philosopher. And herein lies the issue with personalism; however objective the individual personalist may be in his axiomatic presuppositions, his conclusions will largely depend on his personal emphasis.

While it is true that any approach could be abused, it is hard to make the case that this sort of thing could be accomplished with a perennial Scholastic or Thomistic approach. Thomists have always hotly debated disputed questions — that is a good thing — but it is difficult to see how something like what was seen in the vastly different conclusions of von Hildebrand and John Paul II could happen in a Thomistic framework.

For example, if we were to compare the New Mass and the Traditional Mass with the clear objectivity of Thomism, it would be systematic, analytical, and unemotional. While the effect on the human person would not be ignored, it would not be the primary focus. The Thomist would evaluate whether each rite is more or less sacred based on objective criteria, whereas the personalist would evaluate whether each rite was more or less *experienced* as sacred. Again, a personalist could defend the Traditional Mass as being more sacred than the other, but he could also do the opposite if he emphasized communal experience over personal experience in how he defined the sacred.

This milieu facilitates philosophy and theology that is in a constant state of flux, influenced by trends and emphases in streams of contemporary thought, which, because of the influence of Modernism, cannot guard against the Modernist emphasis on the evolution of ideas.

9

How Modernism Distorts the Relationship between Faith and Science

After dealing with the Modernist as a believer, Pius X moves to a topic that has become ever more relevant in the years subsequent to his pontificate — namely, the issue of faith and science. Now, the term "science" is not used in older literature, such as that of Pius X, to refer merely to *natural science*, such as biology, chemistry, and so on; rather, it refers generally to subjects of intellectual pursuit, including disciplines such as historical studies. Technically speaking, we still use the term "science" to refer to subjects not related to material sciences in academic settings, such as political science. In our day, however, when one refers to "science," he is most often referring to something belonging to the sciences of nature that deal with material things or processes.

The crux of the distinction between faith and science according to the Modernist system is a bifurcation between the two ways of understanding reality. Modernist thought tells us that the sciences are concerned with things that are material and objective, whereas knowing things by faith — the Modernist understanding of faith — is nothing more than the attempt to understand what is ultimately unknowable. Modernism asserts that "science is entirely concerned with the reality of phenomena, into which faith does not enter at all" (*Pascendi* 15).

This mentality is Cartesian, as it implies that the realities of spiritual and natural phenomena are separated by a division of reality into two zones that are independent of one another. This means that faith can never be the subject of a legitimate science, as it exists purely in the subjective realm of subconscious reality, and the study of created things exists in the realm of objective things. The consequences for this are obvious to anyone with sense — namely, that any attempt to label any religion as verifiably true is impossible, since by this logic we could trust only our knowledge of material things, which are more "real" than immaterial things.

This is a complete reversal of the order of knowledge according to the traditional systems of the great ancient philosophers and theologians, as it has been held since at least the time of Plato that the unchangeable spiritual essences or realities — commonly called Forms — are, in a sense, "more real" because they are not subject to change and therefore not subject to degradation. This means that unchangeable things are more proximate to the divine reality, which is subsistent in itself, as God is existence itself. In other words, the metaphysical is more real than the physical, which is explained by Christ when He says, "Heaven and earth shall pass, but my words shall not pass" (Matt. 24:35).

In classical thought, reality or being has been classified into three realms: eternity (God), aeviternity (angelic or spiritual), and the physical or corporeal (created beings with bodies subject to change). God is unchanging and is both the Creator and Sustainer of all things. Angels are created but do not have physical bodies; therefore, they have a beginning but no end and are not subject to change in the way material creatures are. Material beings, such as animals, exist within time and have both a beginning and an end. In addition, human beings are composites of body and soul, meaning we have a material body that is limited in space and time and a soul that is spiritual, which is created in time but not limited to space. This is why our bodies decay when we die, and our souls continue to exist, in that they have no end, but they do have a beginning. The union of the physical reality of human bodies with the aeviternity reality of the human soul will be accomplished at the resurrection of the dead, when our bodies will be reunited with our souls after the Second Coming of Christ.

Modernism confuses the relation between knowledge of creation (science) and knowledge of spiritual truth (faith) with an error that presupposes the realness of material things as more than the realness of spiritual or metaphysical things. So it is not only a bifurcation of two realms that is accomplished by Modernism but also a reversal in the hierarchy of being. Modernism wrongly asserts that because we can know the truth of material reality with repeatable material processes, this realm of reality must be more certain than the realm of metaphysical truth. The inherent flaw in this manner of thinking lies in the fact that there is a complete blindness to the obvious truth that the very contemplation of material things is a metaphysical activity and the act of contemplation exists independent of material things. Put another way, Modernism confuses the nature of causality.

The four causes, according to historical Catholic thought, are the *material cause* (what it is made of), the *formal cause* (what it is in its essence), the *efficient cause* (what made it happen), and the *final cause* (why it exists or what it is for). While it appears to the senses that the material cause comes first, it actually comes last. Consider a house. You would first encounter the house in its material form after it was constructed. The house began, however, as a thought or idea, which is metaphysical, in the mind of a builder and the mind is housed in the soul, which is also metaphysical. The builder then had to make a decision and act with his will, which is a metaphysical action, to move his material body to begin the process of designing and building. After that, he would follow the design and concept that represent the form of the house and come before the house, and he would eventually bring the metaphysical form of the house into material existence.

The material reality of the house is the culmination of a series of causes that precede its materiality. This is how all creation works. Although we cannot truly speak of a "before" in God, as God does not exist in time, it can be helpful to consider that creation came "after" God, and creation in its final form was complete "before" the creation of the world. Scripture speaks in a similar way in order to make this truth understandable for human beings, who live in time, "Before I formed thee in the bowels of thy mother, I knew thee" (Jer. 1:5).

All of this is to say that Modernism completely bungles the entire chronology and causal nature of creation by flipping the order on its head.

The consequence of the Modernist system in denying this wisdom of ancient and sound metaphysics is disastrous, as it discounts the objective knowledge — known through reason — of the unchanging metaphysical underpinnings of physical existence itself!

Applied specifically to religion, this turning upside down of reality in the mind of the Modernist makes any talk of the miraculous impossible. This is because miracles, given that they represent the supernatural action of God in nature, cannot be observed or evaluated if we follow Modernist logic because claims of the miraculous would be relegated to things of "faith," which constitutes a category of the unknown and therefore is ultimately unknowable. Thus, Pius X says, if it should be asked whether, according to Modernist thought, "Christ has wrought real miracles, and made real prophecies, whether He rose truly from the dead and ascended into heaven, the answer of agnostic science will be in the negative" (*Pascendi* 16).

The only justification for any talk of the miraculous according to the Modernist is that these miraculous "phenomena ... have been by faith transfigured and disfigured, they have been removed from the world of sense and translated to become material for the divine" (16). In essence, claims of miracles by religious people are basically legends or myths about events that are seen as important for people of "faith."

This is a fancy way of saying that there are no miracles but only religious sentiments that are actualized to the point that the *lived* faith of the believer becomes a miracle in the religious conscience. In other words, miracles are fantastical stories that manifest from religious psychology. In July 2021, at a weekly Angelus address, Pope Francis said that the true miracle recorded in the Gospel account of the multiplication of the loaves and fishes (Matt. 14:15–21) was the miracle of "sharing."[47]

Faith Subject to Science

Naturally, human beings place types of knowledge into hierarchies of reality, meaning that what is *more true* is regarded as being *more real*. For example, we make distinctions between history and legend. A classic example in the English-speaking world is the legend of Robin Hood, who was very likely a real person, but his story has been transfigured over time as a sort of symbolic allegory or myth that is representative of a greater story.

If a child asks you if "Robin Hood is a true story," you might reply, "Robin Hood was a real person, but, over time, much of the story has been made up and taken on different versions of the story." We understand implicitly that the story of Robin Hood may be a "true story" in the sense that it contains important moral lessons that speak to moral truths; we would never say that it is an *objectively historical* story but that it is a combination of fact and fiction.

This is how ancient *myths* are created, such as those of the great peoples of antiquity. Revealed religion, however, meaning the Bible and the Deposit of Faith, is not a myth or a legend, and, although ancient and filled with miraculous stories, is true both in its message and historicity. Of course, there are parts of the Bible that are clearly

[47] Pope Francis, Angelus, St. Peter's Square, Sunday, July 25, 2021.

not meant to be historical in the sense of recording a past event, as in the Apocalypse (book of Revelation), which, although it does pertain to what the end of the world will look like, also uses images that are symbolic and not necessarily literal.

Modernism makes the comprehension of revealed religion as objective and verifiable history very difficult because what is considered to be a matter of faith according to the Modernist conception is necessarily subject to scientific inquiry, which Modernism views as the only verifiable way to assess matters. If we follow this mentality, we run the risk of relegating the truth of the Catholic Faith and revelation to the realm of mythology and legend. In fact, this is exactly how the vast majority of academia views religion.

So, since faith must be subject to science, according to Modernism, the history of Christ is viewed more like the story of Robin Hood — in the same way that any talk of Robin Hood as a legend must be subject to objective history if the story is analyzed in the pursuit of any objectively verifiable truth. This mentality undoubtedly leads to heretical conclusions because every religious claim must be viewed apart from any divine reality, and even the experience of the believer who speaks of the miraculous must be viewed as a mere statement of faith in the way it is understood in Modernism. Consequently, religious claims are necessarily under the purview of material sciences according to Modernism, which leads Pius X to say, speaking as the Modernists would: "Let the believer leave the world if he will, but so long as he remains in it he must continue, whether he like it or not, to be subject to the laws, the observation, the judgments of science and of history" (17).

As a result, Pius X goes on: "It is therefore the right of philosophy and of science to form conclusions concerning the idea of God, to direct it in its evolution and to purify it of any extraneous elements which may become confused with it" (17). Of course, Pius X here refers to the *false* philosophy and science of the Modernists; this, in turn, means that any philosophical understanding of God must be erroneous as the very pursuit of philosophical knowledge has been in error since the start.

Theological discourse of this sort is rampant today, even among so-called conservatives, who take for granted the claims of the material sciences as being absolutes and therefore reinterpret the sacred history of salvation through the lens of the Cartesian errors that reflect the material sciences of Modernity.

Four severe condemnations of this manner of thinking come to mind, all written by Pius X in *Lamentabili Sane*, which accompanied *Pascendi*. The following statements are written in the positive and are condemned and proscribed:

- From the ecclesiastical judgments and censures passed against free and more scientific exegesis, one can conclude that the Faith the Church proposes contradicts history and that Catholic teaching cannot really be reconciled with the true origins of the Christian religion. (3)
- Since the Deposit of Faith contains only revealed truths, the Church has no right to pass judgment on the assertions of the human sciences. (5)
- Scientific progress demands that the concepts of Christian doctrine concerning God, creation, revelation, the Person of the Incarnate Word, and Redemption be re-adjusted. (64)
- Modern Catholicism can be reconciled with true science only if it is transformed into a non-dogmatic Christianity; that is to say, into a broad and liberal Protestantism. (65)

Think of the state of modern theological inquiry; can anyone honestly deny that these four condemned propositions do not animate the majority of research and scholarship in our day? How many times have you heard — or repeated yourself — that the book of Genesis is not reconcilable with "modern science" and therefore must be interpreted as poetry or allegory? Is there a mainstream Catholic scholar employed today who would not echo these sentiments?

On the contrary, modern Catholic scholars are seemingly embarrassed to profess the belief — held by virtually every single Catholic ancestor and pope before the postconciliar age — that the first three chapters of Genesis are true history, even if there is room for mystery where certain things are left unsaid. Instead, Catholic intellectual circles are filled with so-called scholars doing their best to prove — using changing and unsettled theories — that where the Bible says Adam was created specially by God, what is really meant is that a soul was infused into the first man who was born of a mother who was not human and had no soul.

The consequences of this thinking are ghastly. Adam would have suckled at the breast of an ape-like creature, and how he found Eve is anyone's guess. Therefore, the prefigurements of both Jesus and Mary existed in a world of soulless ape-like family members who would not have had reason or a human mind. This sort of horror story is *nothing* like the sacred history recounted in Genesis, yet to the Modernist — even the so-called conservative Modernist — this is the necessary interpretation of the Holy Bible. What a contradiction to what Pius X's direct predecessor, Leo XIII, wrote as a seeming afterthought in his encyclical on marriage, *Arcanum Divinae* (1880): "We record what is to all known, and cannot be doubted by any, that God, on the sixth day of creation, having made man from the slime of the earth, and having breathed into his face the breath of life, gave him a companion, whom He miraculously took from the side of Adam when he was locked in sleep" (5).

In addition, what does this say about the character of God? Again, even if we grant a sense of mystery to the first chapters of Genesis, the implications of the Modernist interpretation thereof make a plain reading of those chapters impossible. In reality, the evolutionary exegesis of Genesis does not match sacred history *in the slightest*. Thus, we are to believe that when Moses wrote that God created the world in six days, created Adam from the slime of the earth, and took Eve from his side, he really meant that God created the world over billions of years using a process of death and destruction, and that Adam was the offspring of an irrational animal, and that Eve did not really come from his side but was herself either the sister of Adam from the same nonhuman mother or the offspring of another transitionary hominid. Does this mean that Eve had no soul? The question is not absurd, as there is *no mention* of God's breathing a soul into Eve; therefore, if anyone uses an evolutionary key to interpret Genesis that is somehow reconciled — albeit impossibly — with the Creation story, he must profess something that is not found even allegorically in Scripture. Simply put, how is *any* of this tenable by an orthodox and believing Catholic?

Theistic evolutionists appeal to Genesis 2:7 to posit that Adam was a *Homo sapiens* who received his soul — which made him human: "And the Lord God formed man of the slime of the earth: and breathed into his face the breath of life, and man became a living soul."

What the Bible says is that Adam was formed specially by God and was *animated* — the word for "soul" in Latin is *anima* — when God breathed the "breath of life" into him. Theistic evolutionists reject this and propose that Adam was an animal who was born of another animal, and at a certain point, God breathed a soul into him. Of course, this is not present anywhere in Scripture and is a claim with no evidence. Now, let us suppose the theistic evolutionists are right. Well, how was Eve made a human then? We would have to believe by the evolutionary paradigm that she was an animal with no soul, and since Scripture does not speak of her being infused with a soul, we cannot say that she was.

Now, it may be opined that, since Adam was infused with a soul after his body was created by God, perhaps a similar thing happened to Eve — namely, she had an animal body and then a soul infused. Well, Scripture does not say that this did not happen, but Scripture also does not speak of evolution or prehuman hominids having souls infused into them to make them human. If a theistic evolutionist, by appealing to the fact that Adam had a soul breathed into him by God, were to opine that Eve started as a nonhuman hominid and then had a soul infused, we must view this as an extremely misguided reach based on a speculation that has no real foundation. It is one thing to speculate and "fill in the blanks" where Scripture is silent, but it is quite another to disregard the literal presentation in its entirety. Scripture tells us that Eve was made from Adam's side; then the first recorded activity of Eve is that she has a rational interaction with the Serpent and she sins, and it is not possible to sin without a human soul because animals cannot sin. So the theistic evolutionist must not only deny the literal meaning that Eve was born from Adam's side, which Pope Leo XIII said "cannot be doubted by any" but must also insert an event that is not recorded *at all*. The plain meaning of Scripture is that Adam's body was created and then God breathed into him "the breath of life" (Gen. 2:7).

In any event, following the evolutionary reading of Scripture, Adam married an animal with no soul, and, since she had no soul, she could not sin because animals cannot sin. This destroys the notion of Original Sin and the Fall. On the other hand, if we follow the basic metaphysical principle of sufficient causality — you can give what you have and cannot give what you do not have — the biblical narrative makes perfect sense; Adam was given his soul by God directly, and Eve was made from Adam, and therefore, her nature was animated because she was made from a human being.

Furthermore, the evolutionary interpretation seems to make God and Moses deceivers because what was written is *nothing* like what evolutionary thought would have us believe; this means that the Holy Bible led the vast majority of Catholics astray for *thousands* of years until a group of scholars applied a novel scientific hypothesis to sacred history that is not found in any Father, Doctor, Scholastic, theologian, saint, or pope before the second half of the twentieth century. This is Modernism par excellence: a novel interpretation of Scripture that is founded on modern philosophy that is subject to novel scientific musings that are based on an atheistic worldview and that render the historical character of Genesis impossible. This is a perfect example of subjecting faith — as Modernism understands it — to science, which Modernism views as the barometer of truth.

How can anything other than a Modernist exegesis be the foundation for this absurdity?

We will deal with the Modernist and the apologist when we consider a subsequent portion of *Pascendi*, but consider, for example, how in the realm of pro-life apologetics, the primary emphasis is almost always on proving that life begins at conception as a matter of "science." Of course, the good men and women who protect the unborn should not be accused of having assimilated Modernist principles. Nonetheless, it demonstrates that even with the best of intentions, there is an accepted emphasis on "science first" and "revelation second."

If we appeal primarily to the natural sciences to prove that human life begins at conception, while there may be some backing to this, it is a strategy that is necessarily limited, given the subjectivist nature of scientific interpretation. One could very well agree that what is called a human begins his journey to full humanity when he is conceived, but there is no room in natural science to prove the nature of a soul, and therefore the personhood of the zygote or embryo. Furthermore, the impression that nonbelievers might receive when spoken to with "science first" is that religious and moral truth is subject to the judgment of the sciences.

Ending this section on faith and science, Pius X, by quoting another predecessor, Pope Gregory IX, utterly eviscerates those who engage in the tactics of the Modernists: "Some among you, inflated like bladders with the spirit of vanity strive by profane novelties to cross the boundaries fixed by the Fathers, twisting the sense of the heavenly pages ... to the philosophical teaching of the rationalists, not for the profit of their hearer but to make a show of science ... these, seduced by strange and eccentric doctrines, make the head of the tail and force the queen to serve the servant."[48]

Given what we have learned in this section, is there any doubt that the majority of even conservative Catholic discourse and scholarship is riddled with the heretical tendencies of the Modernists?

---

[48] *Arcanum Divinae* 5.

10

How Modernism Uses Contradiction

Thus far, Pius X has focused primarily on the theological and philosophical underpinnings of Modernism so that the reader may well understand the "nuts and bolts" of the heresy. As it stands, we are approaching the halfway point of *Pascendi*, and in this second part of the encyclical, Pius X sees fit to expose the methods of the Modernists. It is all well and good to recognize Modernism as such, but given that these heretics have been so successful in recent decades, it would do us well to consider their methods.

The main ways in which Modernism is demonstrated in theological works is by the use of both truth and error or clarity and ambiguity in the same work and sometimes even on the same page.

Picking up where he left off in the previous section, where he castigates the Modernists with the words of Pope Gregory IX, Pius X states: "This becomes still clearer to anybody who studies the conduct of Modernists, which is in perfect harmony with their teachings." Their teachings consist of contradictions and confusion, as "they seem not infrequently to advocate now one doctrine now another so that one would be disposed to regard them as vague and doubtful" (18).

By this method, the Modernist can utter an erroneous statement or a statement that is adjacent to heresy while uttering truth in another statement. This is the tactic par excellence of the Modernist because it greatly weakens his opponent, who can, on one hand, express concern about an error or heresy that has been uttered, only to be confounded with an orthodox statement about the same or a similar subject that appears in the same document.

Joseph Ratzinger and Modernism

Before we continue, I believe it is necessary to inform you that we will discuss in this chapter and subsequent chapters how some of the work of Joseph Ratzinger (later Pope Benedict XVI) is indicative of Modernist tendencies. It is a difficult proposition for some to conceive of Ratzinger as being conciliatory toward the Modernist spirit, but his writings from his earlier years as a priest theologian suggest just that. It is not my intention here to disparage the name of Ratzinger or Benedict but only to point out that even in the work of a theologian deemed to be very conservative, even traditional by some, we find at least the shadow — if not the full form — of the Modernist mentality. Granted, Benedict did move more to the side of Tradition later in his life — he did a great thing for Tradition by recognizing the perennial rights of the Old Mass — but some of his reflections on the Council speak volumes, as do some of his other earlier statements.

That being said, I do not contend that Pope Benedict did not have supernatural faith, and I make no judgment on his intentions or his soul. I have spoken to many individuals who knew him personally, and I have only ever heard that he was pious, sincere, and a very good man. At the risk of seeming overly sensitive, I want to insist that it is not my intention to sully his reputation in the mind of any readers but only to demonstrate that the Modernist mentality is not only found in brazen heretics and progressives but has reached the deepest recesses of conservative Catholic thought. Also, we must remember that Pope Benedict came of age during the conciliar era, and many images can be easily found of him wearing a suit and tie, rather than a clerical suit or a cassock, which should demonstrate to us that he was not immune to "going with the times" as the myth of progress swept through the Church. The relevant citations from Ratzinger's work are mostly from his earlier years and are meant to demonstrate the Modernist trend as present throughout the majority of Catholic scholarship. I do believe that there are "two Ratzingers" — one more adjacent to Modernism in his youth, the other more conservative or traditional-leaning in his later years — and this will be discussed below. Finally, if we consider that the crisis in the Church has been raging since the time of Vatican II, it would be strange if somehow Joseph Ratzinger, who was the highest doctrinal authority under the pope in the Church, was somehow immune to the spirit of Modernism.

Contradiction and Confusion in Action

In any event, the use of contradiction is seen not only in the works of those whom the mainstream and conservative Catholic intelligentsia would label "Modernist" but also in the work of one Joseph Ratzinger. Before I present a citation that is sure to upset some traditional or conservative-minded Catholics who herald Ratzinger as a beacon of clarity and orthodoxy in a confusing era, please note that the scholar who presented this information was just that. The scholar is John Finnis, professor emeritus at the University of Notre Dame, a man who was made a Commander of the Order of the British Empire for his service to legal scholarship.[49] Before offering a critique of Ratzinger that is relevant to our discussion, he stated that he spent considerable time in the presence of Pope Benedict over the years and praised his "intellect, learning and holiness" as something he "can only envy."[50] Finnis

---

[49] Kevin Allen, "Professor Emeritus John Finnis Made a Commander of the Order of the British Empire," University of Notre Dame Law School, January 6, 2023, https://law.nd.edu/news-events/news/professor-john-finnis-2023-commander-order-british-empire/.

[50] John Finnis, "From the Heart Come Forth Words and Deeds That Defile"," Center for Ethics and Culture Conference, November 10, 2017, 14, https://law.nd.edu/assets/256941/cec_paper_10_nov_rev_online_pdf.pdf.

can hardly be called a jaded or hard-hearted critic of Ratzinger, and this, I believe, lends merit to his criticism, given that it cannot come from a place of malice.

What is interesting is that Finnis's critique is that he believes Pope Benedict's long post-synodal apostolic exhortation *Verbum Domini*, from 2010, fails to address widespread errors about the interpretation of Scripture that Finnis believes are in contradiction to paragraphs 18 and 19 of Vatican II's document on the Bible, *Dei Verbum*. Admittedly, paragraphs 18 and 19 of *Dei Verbum* are doctrinally sound and merely express the long-held belief that the Gospels were written by the Apostles or direct disciples of the Apostles and that the Gospels contain firsthand testimony or the scribing of what was seen firsthand. And the document says that this was all done under the inspiration of the Holy Ghost.

Recall, however, that Pope John Paul II, when writing against Archbishop Lefebvre, quoted the very same document for a definition of Tradition — a definition that seemed eerily similar to the Modernist definition. So it is interesting that Finnis alludes to *Dei Verbum* as a means to criticize the work of Pope Benedict, considering that that document is indicative of the Modernist spirit, considering it contains clear Catholic teaching and seemingly Modernist theology. Now, this does not mean that I accuse Finnis of Modernism; it is only an observation of how *Dei Verbum* matches Pius X's assertion that Modernist theology can present orthodoxy and dubious teaching concurrently. "They seem not infrequently to advocate now one doctrine now another so that one would be disposed to regard them as vague and doubtful" (18).

Finnis writes:

> In Pope Benedict's long follow-up post Synodal Apostolic Exhortation *Verbum Domini* in 2010, not a word was said about these radical, widespread, mainstream denials, or about *Dei Verbum* 18–19. And in his personal book *Jesus of Nazareth*, vol.

2 (later in 2010), at the decisive moment when Jesus appears to the apostles and disciples at supper on the evening of Easter Day, the author seems to concede to "most exegetes" that actually Jesus did not eat any fish (or anything else) and that "Luke is exaggerating here in his apologetic zeal" by claiming that he did.[51]

Now, does Pope Benedict explicitly state something contrary to Catholic teaching? No, he does not. But does he leave the door open for a Modernist interpretation? Yes, he does. One could come away thinking that Benedict gives credence to the notion that Luke is "exaggerating" when he states that the resurrected Christ ate a piece of fish with the Apostles. In plain English, this would mean that Christ *did not* eat a piece of fish and that the Gospel of Luke contains something that is simply not true. Now, the contrary argument could be that Benedict is merely relating what "most exegetes" believe and not what he believes, but Finnis — again, an admirer of Benedict — addresses this as well, stating: "So: does Joseph Ratzinger agree with 'most exegetes'? He leaves us to believe so.... Thus the opinion of 'most exegetes' holds the field."[52]

What does this mean? Well, Finnis, an obvious proponent of Vatican II and a great admirer of Pope Benedict, shows in his work that Benedict is at least open to or leaves open the possibility that Luke's Gospel contradicts the real history in question, and Benedict seems to contradict the teaching of *Dei Verbum*, a document that is not immune to Modernist-leaning theology when approaching the topic of Tradition.

What is even more fascinating for the purpose of this work is that Benedict himself heralded *Dei Verbum* as a *break* with the Church's long-standing Tradition regarding the Holy Scriptures. Referring to

---

[51] Finnis, "From the Heart," 14.
[52] Finnis, "From the Heart," 16.

the original schema prepared for Vatican II on the Bible, a text that was unceremoniously thrown out at the beginning of the Council after years of preparation, he said:

> The [original schema] was utterly the product of the anti-modernist mentality that had taken shape about the turn of the century.... The text was written in a spirit of condemnation and negation, which had a frigid and offensive tone to many of the fathers. And this despite the fact that the contents of the text were new to no one, it was exactly like dozens of textbooks familiar to the bishops from their seminary days, and in some cases their former professors were actually responsible for the text presented to them.... The real question behind the discussion can be put this way: Was the intellectual position of anti-modernism, the policy of exclusiveness and condemnation and defence, leading to an almost neurotic denial of all that was new to be continued, or would the Church after it had taken all the necessary precautions to defend the Faith turn over a new leaf and move on into a new and positive encounter with its own origins, and with its brothers and with the world today?[53]

So, Ratzinger characterized the preconciliar perspective on Sacred Scripture as being personified by the spirit of *anti-Modernism*, and he viewed this as negative! Now, that Ratzinger believed the original document was too "anti-Modernist" does not necessarily prove that he believed the new document should be "pro-Modernist," but we would do well to read between the lines in Ratzinger's statement. Let us grant that there could be a spirit of anti-Modernism that is unhelpful; fair enough. Ratzinger, however, seems to juxtapose the notion of being

---

[53] Quoted from Joseph Ratzinger's book *Theological Highlights of Vatican II* in a talk called "Ecumenism: The Original Sin of the New Mass," given by John Vennari at the 2014 Angelus Press Conference.

anti-Modernist with the possibility of the Church's turning over a "new leaf ... a new and positive encounter with its own origins, and with its brothers and with the world today." This means that the Church might move on from anti-Modernism — which he does not adequately define but only describes in psychological terms — and rediscover her "origins," which is reminiscent of the Modernist tendency to go back to the primitive era of the Church to reevaluate; and, he suggests that this might happen with an "encounter" with its "brothers" and the "world today."

This seems to be not unlike the Modernist tendency to combine an inquiry or evaluation of the primitive Church with Modern thought (the "world today") and the experience of believers. In other words, it is a reevaluation of religion with modern methods, which would include modern historical methods and philosophical methods. This seems consistent with Pius X's statement about how Modernism requires a reevaluation of the history of religion with modern methods: "Guided by the theory that faith must be subject to science, they continuously and openly criticise the Church because of her sheer obstinacy in refusing to submit and accommodate her dogmas to the opinions of philosophy; while they, on their side, after having blotted out the *old theology*, endeavour to introduce a *new theology* which shall follow the vagaries of their philosophers" (18, emphasis added).

The way Ratzinger writes of the original schema is very much in line with what Pius X explains. Ratzinger sharply criticizes the perennial position of Catholic theology and describes a resistance to novel positions as "an almost neurotic denial," which is an even sharper way to say "obstinate." Ratzinger laments the prevailing theology of the Church because it does not adapt to the modern world, criticizes the inherited theological tradition with strong language, and clamors for the introduction of a new approach, just as Pius X described.

Ratzinger went on to rejoice at the fact that the anti-anti-Modernist approach was accepted by the bulk of the Council Fathers and that the two main arguments used to defend this position "rested on the intention of Pope John XXIII that the texts should be pastoral and their theology, ecumenical."[54]

This is an amazing admission and demonstrates the futility of appealing to Vatican II as a bulwark of Tradition when even the likes of Ratzinger — no lightweight! — heralded the new orientation of the Council, which was distinctly in *contradiction* to the anti-Modernist doctrine of the Church laid out by Pope Pius X.

We would do well to consider that when the term "ecumenical" is used in the context of the conciliar era, it almost always refers to the notion of appealing to Protestants. So, is Ratzinger pleased that *Dei Verbum* fulfilled the desires of Pope John XXIII for a theology that was advantageous for Protestant acceptance?

If we return to Benedict's statements about the Gospel of Luke in *Jesus of Nazareth*, which defenders call a "personal work" of Benedict and not a magisterial work, we would do well to call to mind the following words of Pius X: "When they write history they make no mention of the divinity of Christ, but when they are in the pulpit they profess it clearly; again, when they write history they pay no heed to the Fathers and the Councils, but when they catechise the people, they cite them respectfully" (18).

So Pius X sees it as a problem that the "old theology" is usurped by the "new theology," but is this not at the heart of the conciliar age? What school of theology did Ratzinger and the others belong to if not the school of the *Nouvelle Théologie?* The New Theology will be addressed in a subsequent chapter.

One gets the impression in our day that if we do not conform to the novel theological dispositions so common in academia, we are somehow in a position wherein we must defend our insistence on holding fast to the Tradition. In another letter from Pius X, called *Notre Charge Apostolique*, written in 1910, we find the following statement from the pope: "Indeed, the true friends of the people are neither revolutionaries

---

[54] Quoted in John Vennari, "Ecumenism."

nor innovators: they are traditionalists." Now, this letter was addressed to the French bishops and pertained mainly to political matters, but the sentiment is clear: a desire for innovation in the realm of Catholic thought is dangerous and is to be avoided. If one is only a true friend of the people by holding fast to Tradition, then it stands to reason that the enemies of the people are *not traditionalists*.

11

The Modernist as Theologian

At this point, we arrive at Pius X's treatment of the Modernist as theologian, and it is my opinion that the encyclical "switches gears" from the philosophical to the theological and the practical. *Pascendi* contains almost sixty paragraphs (in the official English translation), but this section, which begins at paragraph 19, feels almost like the halfway point of the document. Up until this point, Pope St. Pius X has labored extensively to lay the philosophical groundwork necessary for the reader to understand the foundation of Modernist thinking — if what Modernists do can be called "thinking." Before Modernism becomes a heresy in religion, it must first be a heresy in thought; hence the lengths Pius X goes to in order to tease out the Modernist intellectual framework.

Thus, Pius X explains how the Modernist becomes a theologian. Before we consider the pope's wisdom on the matter, let us look at why it is puzzling to think that a Modernist could be a theologian in any real sense. A theologian necessarily contemplates and studies the things of God, as the word "theology" means "the logic of God." So, if Modernists are relativists in their conception of God — which they necessarily are, at least to some degree, on account of their principles of agnosticism and immanence — then we cannot expect a Modernist theologian ever to present truths of religion in a clear, concise manner.

You have likely noticed this if you have ever compared the theological writings of the saints and popes of old with the writings of modern theologians and popes. Take, for example, the document called *Dignitas Infinita*, released on April 4, 2024, by Cardinal Víctor Manuel Fernández, with the approval of Pope Francis, and compare it with *Pascendi*. The modern document, which is *longer* than *Pascendi*, is riddled with grave error, if not outright heresy!

Many astute commentators, such as Dr. Peter Kwasniewski and Dr. Edward Feser, have pointed out the inherent problem in *Dignitas Infinita*, which is that it begins with the presupposition that humans have infinite dignity just because they exist. This is in contradiction to the teaching of Pope Pius XII, for example, who wrote in *Mediator Dei* (1947): "Let the faithful, therefore, consider to what a high dignity they are raised by the sacrament of baptism" (104). It stands to reason that man cannot be elevated in dignity if he already possesses infinite dignity; therefore, either Cardinal Fernández and Pope Francis are correct or Pius XII was correct. Of course Pius XII was correct, and we know he was correct because what he said concurred with everything the Church had previously taught on the subject and was in perfect accord with human reason. Therefore, the modern document is in grave error, if not heretical in the explicit sense.

Pius X's encyclical was one of the longest encyclicals ever released by a pope, and it was that long only because of the profound complexity of Modernism, which necessitated a lengthy and detailed exposition. But, in our age of Modernism, it seems that everything that comes out of Rome is almost as long as a manuscript that a novelist would write. This is because, when you speak with clarity and precision, you do not need to say much, but when you are imprecise and unclear, you must create the impression of sophistication in the mind of the reader with verbosity in order to present your ideas as profound. Modern theology and philosophy are therefore extremely hard to read and understand,

and that is their greatest "asset": no one can really understand what is being said; therefore, those who read it can be easily confused. The consequences of this should be obvious to all.

How Modernist Theologians Follow Modernist Philosophical Principles

Following the lead of Modernist philosophy, Modernist theologians also subject matters of faith to the authority of science, which Pius X calls "the conciliation of faith with science." Now, this does not mean that Modernists seek to view faith through the lens of reason, as sound reason would tell us that material and natural sciences cannot properly judge supernatural and spiritual reality; instead, they exalt natural scientific inquiry to a place of primacy. Pius X describes a process that leads to what he calls "theological immanence": "The process is an extremely simple one. The philosopher has declared: *The principle of faith is immanent*; the believer has added: *This principle is God*; and the theologian draws the conclusion: *God is immanent in man*. Thus we have *theological immanence*" (19).

What the pope is saying here is that since Modernism requires that faith be subject to science — knowledge of the created world — the Modernist must look for the truth of divine things in the creature, which is to say, *in* man. And because Modernism relegates religious truth to the realm of immanence and symbolism, it is clear that any study of divine realities (theology) would be a study of the immanent experience of the religious sense in believers — a sense that can be represented only in a symbolic sense to the external world. Furthermore, since all pursuits have an end in mind — we don't start "going somewhere" without somewhere to go — Modernist theologians must necessarily look to the immanent nature of God in the subconscious and experience of believers, and therefore, theology is nothing more than the study of the experiences believers have with their religious sense.

This renders theology into a form of psychology and renders it impossible to study theology in any objective sense, as no two experiences and symbolic representations thereof will be the same. The consequences of this are seen in the modern infatuation with ecumenism. Since, according to Modernism, religion is subjective and not objective, we have no ground to stand on if we compare one religion with another; therefore, all religions must in some way be representations of the same ineffable truth that we merely approximate with our symbolic representations. The cathedral is one example of religious architecture, the mosque another, the synagogue another, and the ashram yet another. None is truer than another, and none can be called "false" in the absolute sense, even if a Modernist believes subjectively that one better represents the divine in a way that is more representative of the collective experience of the immanent religious sense in man.

In a practical sense, we would expect the influence of this thinking to lead to things such as interreligious activity, which Popes John Paul II and Benedict both took part in at Assisi, Italy, where they prayed with leaders of false religions for world peace. Or we might expect someone truly steeped in this spirit to do something like build an ecumenical house of religion, like the Abrahamic Family House in Abu Dhabi, which was built with the blessing of Pope Francis and where members of the three "Abrahamic" faiths — Christianity, Judaism, and Islam — meet for religious ceremonies.

How Sacraments and Liturgy Are Affected

The consequence of such thinking is that a theologian influenced by Modernism begins to view religion as largely symbolic of religious sentiment. In other words, symbols, being mere representations that are necessarily incomplete, are not wholly important given their inherent inadequacy. So believers ought not to put too much emphasis on religious formulas — dogmas, liturgy, prayers, and so forth — as all are subject to change or *evolve* as the collective religious subconsciousness of humanity progresses toward the unknowable divine reality. "Modernists fall into the gravest errors" when it comes to their understanding of sacraments (*Pascendi* 21) because, for them, sacraments are nothing more than signs and symbols that satisfy man's innate desire to express his religious sense. Therefore, we should not expect the leaders of the Church, if they have been influenced by Modernism, to concern themselves too much with the safeguarding of sacramental formulas and the associated forms of worship. In fact, we should expect to see the opposite.

We have seen this in the Church in spades since the Second Vatican Council. Catholics used to worship in a particular liturgical form that was largely unchanged for centuries, but the popes and theologians since the Council deemed it necessary to change perennial formulas of worship and prayer to adapt to the needs of *modernity*. This is because it is believed that modern man is different qualitatively from premodern man, and therefore, he must worship in a way that moves with the times and the ways of the world, lest he get stuck in some out-of-touch and outdated religious formula that has lost its efficacy. It should come as no surprise to traditionally minded Catholics that they are met with scorn by so many prelates when they express their devotion to the Old Rites and old formulas because to go "backward" is to deny the fundamental doctrines of immanence and evolution that are entrenched in the Modernist system. So a traditional Catholic who is orthodox in his belief *and* practice is really a heretic to the Modernist, who rejects the unchanging nature of Tradition in the first place.

Because of the principle of agnosticism that is at the heart of the heresy, Modernist theology must reject the notion that the sacraments were definitively instituted by Christ in a verifiable and historical way. This leads Modernists to reject the idea that sacramental and liturgical formulas should be permanent or relatively unchanging because they know that these formulas and rubrics express what is believed; but Modernism requires an evolution of what is believed, so the formulas cannot stay the same. Furthermore, because they believe in a continual evolution of religion in the hearts of believers, an evolution that is then expressed, they believe that liturgical and sacramental formulas *must* change with time. This does not mean that Modernists reject the notion that Christ did, in some way, institute the sacraments, but they believe this happened "mediately," which means that Christ somehow instituted the sacraments and the liturgies *through* believers. Pius X explains it this way:

> All Christian consciences were, they affirm, in a manner virtually included in the conscience of Christ as the plant is included in the seed. But as the shoots live the life of the seed, so, too, all Christians are to be said to live the life of Christ. But the life of Christ is according to faith, and so, too, is the life of Christians. And since this life produced, in the course of ages, both the Church and the Sacraments, it is quite right to say that their origin is from Christ and is divine. In the same way they prove that the Scriptures and the dogmas are divine. And thus Modernistic theology may be said to be complete. (20)

So, in some mysterious way, the religious sense of believers is united to Christ in the same way that phones connect to a 5G tower. Thus, the collective and shared religious experience is, over time, manifested in symbols that become sacraments in the hearts of believers; and although they effect no substantial change in the soul, they do effect a profound change in the religious experience of believers. This religious experience is shared and handed down over time and becomes the "tradition" of Modernist religion. It is worth calling to mind the modern notion of Sacred Tradition found in the conciliar document *Dei Verbum* that was discussed in chapter 7: "[Tradition comes from the] contemplation and study of believers who ponder these things in their hearts ... from the intimate sense of spiritual realities which they experience." Again, the irony is that a definition of Tradition — though seemingly Modernist to the core — was used against the founder of a society of priests who chose Pius X as its patron.

At any rate, given that Modernists believe God is immanent in man, they can sincerely say that sacraments — as they understand them — do come from Christ in some way and that these symbolic sacraments are of divine origin. It is not hard to see why Pius X defined Modernism as the "synthesis of all heresies," as we can spot in just this section at least three major heresies that have afflicted the Church over the centuries. First, the seeming inclusion of man in the "conscience of Christ" seems either to divinize man in a pantheistic way or to lower Christ to the realm of man in a way that could deny His divinity. Second, to relegate the sacraments to the realm of mere symbolism — even if sacraments are, in fact, symbolic in a sense — is to view sacraments and all rituals the way Protestants view them; in a Protestant communion service, there is, of course, no real Eucharist, but the Protestant believes that God's presence is made manifest through the faith of the congregation in the symbolic representation of the Last Supper by the leader of the assembly and the devotion of the people. Third, since Modernist religion can only be *internal* and known through knowledge, we also have the spirit of *Gnosticism*, in which it is through experience in the mind, *gnosis*, that one achieves a state of spiritual perfection.

Modernism, as it should be evident, is an immensely damaging heresy, and it affects virtually every aspect of the Catholic Faith. We could end the book here and be content to have investigated and exposed a truly vicious heresy. But Modernism, being the synthesis of all heresies, provides us with more to consider.

12

How Modernism Destroys a True Understanding of History

Earlier in the book, I mentioned that the historical-critical method was commonly abused in liberal Protestant biblical scholarship and how this trend influenced Modernist theology. In this chapter, we will consider the depravity of thought that results from the Modernist conception and complete reimagination of history. For Modernism, it is vital to rewrite history with the mentality that inspires the heresy, especially with the principles of agnosticism and evolution. The agnostic tendency inspires Modernists to doubt what is in the historical record if it does not match current trends in the historical sciences, and the evolutionary tendency inspires a view of history that requires a long march from the primitive to the more evolved. What is fascinating, or tragically daft, is that the inherent agnosticism encourages Modernist scholars to do the opposite of what you would expect a good historian to do.

The study of history is a bit like being a detective, in the sense that you look for testimonies, clues, and evidence that helps you to put together the pieces of a puzzle. Any good detective knows that a testimony of an event that comes from someone who saw the event or was very close to those who did is likely the most reliable. If a detective was trying to figure out who murdered someone many decades ago, he would jump at the chance to read the journal of someone who witnessed the murder. He would have to be out of his mind to disregard what was written in the journal and instead look for more current claims about the murder and assess the journal in light of the supposed evidence that is many years removed from the source. Nevertheless, Modernist historians are like the detective who ignores the most proximate testimony because it is not the most current, and they judge claims from very ancient times based on ideas from their era because they believe that what is more modern must necessarily be more sophisticated. This demonstrates their commitment to the evolutionary principle, in that progress from the lower to the higher is a law of nature, and therefore even knowledge from the modern day about ancient times must be more accurate than ancient records because scholarship necessarily *evolves*.

This trend is seen not only in Catholic theology and philosophy inspired by Modernism but throughout academia as a whole. How did this happen?

The Destruction of True Education

One of the greatest misconceptions of modern intellectual life is that the different disciplines of scholarship can exist independently. The mathematician exists in his realm, the musician in his, the litterateur in his, and the biologist in his. Disciplines do not mingle; therefore, those with an affinity for this or that area of study become entrenched and isolated in their "bubble" and often come to view other domains as unimportant or even inferior.

It is no secret that, in our postmodern world, the materialist disciplines are consistently heralded with the highest degree of esteem. And it is often the case that those with an affinity for the natural sciences or STEM fields are viewed as being more intelligent than the average person. Of course, during the Covid period, we saw the result of such thinking on full display as medical doctors and virologists were looked at like divinely inspired oracles. Many such examples could be brought up.

In any event, this trend in society writ large is reflective of the trends in academia that began long ago with the Enlightenment and that began to flourish in the Catholic Church with the advent of Modernism. Since time immemorial, a truly Catholic form of education was classical and holistic. Taking the best of what the Hellenist tradition had to offer, Catholic-run educational institutions inspired the development of the whole person, neglecting neither mind, body, nor soul. This meant that Catholic scholars did not specialize in only one discipline but were educated in all major disciplines. The most excellent example of this is St. Thomas Aquinas, who, while known mainly for his theological work, was also expertly trained in the natural sciences, philosophy, and literature. He even wrote breathtaking hymns and poetry such as the "Adoro Te Devote" and the "Pange Lingua." Of course, Aquinas stands out due to his unmatchable genius, but he was not unique in the sense of being formed differently than his companions. Furthermore, his mentor was St. Albert the Great, who is known as perhaps the greatest natural scientist of the medieval period. St. Albert wrote extensively on natural science, logic, rhetoric, mathematics, astronomy, ethics, economics, politics, and metaphysics. He was canonized by Pope Pius XI in 1931 and made a Doctor of the Church.

Clearly, when we consider Aquinas and his master, we see that, far from hindering excellence in academic pursuits, a well-rounded education with instruction in all areas of study only enhances overall intelligence. If a scholar from a premodern period were to walk into a modern university, he would be baffled to find that campuses were sectioned off into different disciplines, with students of modern languages never darkening the doorstep of the mathematics faculty, and vice versa. Now, this does not mean that the great thinkers of the past viewed all realms of study as equal. On the contrary, theology has always been called the "queen of the sciences," which is to say the highest form of knowledge, as knowledge of God is the highest and most perfect thing one could study. And because theology was always seen as the summit of all knowledge, all other academic pursuits were viewed in light of this hierarchy of order. So the ancient scholar who would study the natural world would study it with the understanding that creation would speak to the glory of God by way of the order God established in the natural world.

Modernists, however, are fully entrenched in the modern heresy of education that pits one discipline against another and arranges disciplines in contrived hierarchies with material and natural disciplines always rising to the top. The Modernist understanding of knowledge insists that matters of faith be subject to the claims of ever-changing and increasingly godless natural sciences. This represents a complete inversion of the hierarchy of knowledge, and all intellectual disciplines suffer as a result. This means that, in the mind of Modernists, divine truth must be subject to natural truth or the experience of "phenomena," which, in essence, puts the divine reality at the mercy or subjugation of natural reality. It represents nothing more than the Luciferian inversion of the hierarchy of order, in which the creature subjugates the Creator. In essence, it leads to the conclusion that God is not God, but man is a god.[55] As the Serpent said to Eve, "You shall become like gods" (Gen. 3:5).

It is important to keep all this in mind as we consider what Pius X explains about how Modernists view historical science. According to Pius X, historians permeated with the Modernist mentality propose

---

[55] There does exist a sound doctrinal position in the Church that man is divinized, commonly called the process of *theosis*, wherein, due to his participation in the divine nature by Baptism and the other sacraments, man becomes like God or becomes divine through participation with the Divine. This still requires God to be supreme and "above" man and creation, however, so that man can be elevated through participation in the Divinity, which subsists in Itself and does not depend on man's participation in order to be divine.

that they engage in the science of history without reference to philosophy or theology: "Some Modernists, devoted to historical studies, seem to be greatly afraid of being taken for philosophers. About philosophy, they tell you, they know nothing whatever" (*Pascendi* 30).

The reason they purport to separate their historical research and opinions from metaphysical sciences is so that they may feign pure objectivity. As Pius X so astutely explains, however, "the truth is that their history and their criticism are saturated with their philosophy, and that their historico-critical conclusions are the natural fruit of their philosophical principles" (30).

The notion that one can be purely objective or rational in the realm of human sciences — in the Modernist system, they believe history is purely scientific[56] — is necessarily a philosophical or metaphysical claim: to say that historical sciences *must* be approached in a purely rational manner is to say that history is a purely rational enterprise, which is a philosophical claim in itself. Therefore, there is a contradiction at the very root of the Modernist understanding of history. It is like when the materialist atheist claims that there can be no such thing as absolute truth or objective morality, not realizing that he has made an absolute claim about truth or an objective claim about morality. Those who think like this are like a man who stands on a branch and severs the branch from the tree. The consequences are obvious; he will fall to his death.

Likewise, the Modernist pursuit of a purely rational history — as if metaphysical or divine principles do not factor into history — is doomed to failure, or at least doomed to suffer from the total rejection of divine intervention in history; this is to say that the Creator is not part of the history of His creation. The practical consequence of

---

[56] One must keep in mind that the word "science" does not pertain solely to the natural sciences and that many sciences — which is to say, systems of knowledge — exist in their own right. For example, we speak of social science and even library science and do not mean that these pursuits are matters best discussed with biology, chemistry, or physics.

this manner of thinking is that God is, at *most*, like a watchmaker who designs the watch, sets the mechanisms in motion, and then leaves the watch to tick on its own; or that there is no God in practicality and that history is merely a matter of natural phenomena that take place without any metaphysical principles or direction. The first conception leads to nothing more than Deism — God exists but is absent from human life; and the second conception leads to either atheism or pantheism — reality exists, but reality is all there is, and it is not dependent on the Creator, who is above or somehow independent of His creation.

Modernist historians act this way because of the three principles inherent in their philosophy — namely, agnosticism, transfiguration, and disfiguration.

"*Agnosticism*," Pope Pius X says, "tells us that history, like every other science, deals entirely with phenomena, and the consequence is that God, and every intervention of God in human affairs, is to be relegated to the domain of faith as belonging to it alone." As a result, "in things where a double element, the divine and the human, mingles, in Christ, for example, or the Church, or the sacraments, or the many other objects of the same kind, a division must be made and the human element assigned to history while the divine will go to faith" (30).

In other words, there is "objective" history, which concerns events that have taken place, and there is "religious" history, which concerns the religious perception of what those events mean for believers. It is a fancy way of saying that miracles are not real, unless by "miracle" you mean the personification of the impulse of personal piety that can transform people connected to the same story. This leads to a distinction in Modernist thought between the Christ of history and the Christ of faith, discussed briefly in chapter 6. It is not just that Christ is divided into a historical and a religious person, however, but every element of the Catholic Faith is affected. This includes the sacraments, sacred writings, and so on. *Everything* must be divided and reevaluated through the lens of modern historical methods, and nothing is safe.

Because of this, Modernism must deny the divinity of Christ in the way that Catholicism holds Him to be divine. Because Modernism cheats with vocabulary, though, a Modernist *can* say that Christ is divine but *not* mean that He is God in the true sense. Divinity, in Modernism, is more of a description than a definition. A Modernist can say Christ is divine because, according to the heresy, to be divine means to be expressive of or representative of the divine impulse that is found in the religious subconscious. So Christ can be called divine in the same way that one may see the Buddha or some other ancient sage as divine. Pius X says: "They [Modernists] proclaim that Christ, according to what they call His *real* history, was not God and never did anything divine, and that as man He did and said only what they, judging from the time in which he lived, can admit Him to have said or done" (30). The key here is that Modernists will allow Christ to have *really* said only what modern philosophy and historical methods *allow*. And, since modern methods do not account for the miraculous, due to an inherent materialism, this means that Christ must be reassessed and every supernatural claim must be rejected. This leads to, as Pius X says, "a double Christ: a real Christ, and a Christ, the one of faith, who never really existed; a Christ who has lived at a given time and in a given place, and a Christ who has never lived outside the pious meditations of the believer" (31).

This historical approach is the unholy offspring of the Cartesian bifurcation of reality that arbitrarily splits reality into internal and external realms, as you may recall from our discussion of Descartes at the outset of the book. Remember that Descartes was so committed to the separation of the interior (metaphysical) world and the exterior (physical) world that he locked himself in a box until he was convinced that because he was thinking, he must exist. Again, the consequence of this is that "reality," as Cartesian philosophy sees it, begins on the "inside," and the "outside" is real only insofar as it is perceived by the individual. If you have ever heard cockamamie hypotheses such as the idea that we might exist in a "simulation," meaning that the physical world is really an illusion that we just perceive as real through our minds, you have heard of a Cartesian theory, even if it is a ridiculous or unserious one.

I remember that in my first year as a religion teacher in a Catholic high school, I was given a selection of resources to use to teach grade-nine students. The textbook I was presented with was called *Jesus of History, Christ of Faith*, a standard text used across the board in the Catholic school system in the province of Ontario. As you can imagine, the book asserted that there was a "real" Jesus, who was a historical person, and the "Christ of faith," who was ultimately the result of religious belief. The book was not new, either, and had been in use for decades. Ontario is a province of around fifteen million people, with about 30 to 35 percent of students attending Catholic schools. How many millions of Catholic students in this one province alone have been taught the Modernist conception of Christ and, by extension, history as a whole?

Now, I imagine it is easy for the reader to conceive of the most egregious of Modernists adopting the belief that there are "two Christs" — one of history and one of religion — but remember, it is *principles* of Modernism that warrant such a conclusion. If a scholar or a prelate is committed to agnosticism, immanence, and evolution, there is the danger of coming to this Modernist conclusion about Christ.

This Modernist historical approach is *not* something that happens only in the most obviously liberal circles; it is present in Catholic biblical thought as a whole, and conservative scholarship is not immune. In the next chapter, we will discuss in more detail how Modernists relegate the first books of the Bible to the realm of mythology or pious fiction, but it is worth considering in this context of Modernist historicism what the Modernist vivisection of history has led to in how Catholics consider Adam as a historical person. Truly, the modern — Modernist — obsession with *evolution* has done to Adam, the first prefigurement of Christ, what Modernists have done to the fulfillment of that prefigurement, the *New Adam*.

The Modernists tell us that we must subject the truths of faith to the claims of modern science. So, if we play their game, we must subject the story of the beginning of history and the creation of man to the claims of modern evolutionary sciences. It is worth noting that evolutionists come in many forms, and many of them are in stark disagreement with one another. Furthermore, evolutionary science — at least as a science that seeks to explain the facts of unseen ages dogmatically — is, by nature, very *unscientific*, considering the fact that an evolutionist, no matter how much he loves Darwin, cannot *observe* anything that has happened in the past. He can only *infer*, which is to say, make an educated guess or an assumption. Of course, this does not mean that there aren't evolutionists who are of goodwill and thoughtful in their approach to history. Nonetheless, the holes in the evolutionary method itself should be considered, and we must discuss the consequences of believing the evolutionary narrative about the origins of man and how this shapes our understanding of religion. If Modernists begin with the beginning of history and start with fundamental errors in both religious and nonreligious history, we can only expect them to compound those errors over time; like a ship that begins even slightly off course, they will end up very far from the destination of truth when all is said and done.

Adam of History, Adam of Faith

The following paragraphs demonstrate how a Modernist historian would necessarily view Genesis:

> If it is true that man evolved from an apelike hominid, then it could simply *not* be true that the first chapters of Genesis have *any* historical merit in the *objective* sense. Adam being created out of the slime or clay of the earth is a far cry from a soulless apelike hominid birthing a human son who would have necessarily embarked on an improbable adventure wherein he survived the primitive wilderness, surrounded by soulless

animalistic hominids. Or perhaps the contention is that the human race had evolved over eons of time, and there was a race of humans who had no souls, and at a certain point, God decided to infuse a soul into Adam. Then, at some point, Adam takes a wife who is called Eve in the Bible, but, of course, she does not come from his side in the *objective* sense, and like Adam, must have been some other soul-infused human being.

At a certain point no one really knows — because, of course, the Bible relates *religious* truth and not "truth" truth — Eve encounters the Serpent. But the Serpent is not really the Serpent because snakes don't talk or communicate with humans. So perhaps the religious impulse of believers prompted a collectivized narrative that transmits a primordial fear of reptiles due to an ancestral memory of our hominid ancestors who huddled in trees during the terrifying ages of gigantic lizards roaming the earth. And because there is no *objective* Garden of Eden, there must also be no *objective* tree with a forbidden fruit; so the Garden is really a place of interior — Cartesian — tranquility wherein the first humans lived without the stresses of materialism and the anxiety of conflict; and the tree of the knowledge of good and evil is simply a metaphor for self-awareness. This is what the "Sacred Author" — whoever that is but certainly not Moses! — meant when he wrote of the Serpent warning Adam and Eve of their "eyes being opened" (see Gen 3:5). The opening of their eyes to the knowledge of good and evil is just a poetical rendering of the journey that one makes from infancy to adulthood whence a man loses that primordial innocence he once had when young and carefree.

"And when they heard the voice of the Lord God walking in paradise in the afternoon air, Adam and his wife hid themselves from the face of the Lord God, amidst the trees of paradise" (Gen. 3:8). After their encounter with the metaphorical Serpent, Adam and Eve were prompted by an inner "voice" that was divine — perhaps their conscience — and they ran from the prospect of facing this inner turmoil, which threatened to turn the warm afternoon of the paradise of innocence into a dark night of the soul.

We then read in Genesis that God calls upon Adam, and Adam expresses to God his shame for having been naked and afraid. Now, of course, because the *objective* Adam grew up around completely naked hominids who would have had no sexual morals or taboos resembling anything like those of civilized humans, we cannot accept the traditional view that Adam's realization of being nude was indicative of the beginnings of the rebellion of the flesh in fallen man as being "historical."

Furthermore, when Eve is told that her sufferings in childbearing would be severe and that her husband would rule over her (see Gen. 3:16), we have a religious explanation that amounts to a completely understandable evolutionary truth. It will cause Eve pain to bring forth children because of the cranial capacity of fully evolved hominids, and, because of their brain size relative to body size, human infants are more dependent on their mothers than other mammals are. These two factors combine to make women wholly dependent on their male companions to care for them, due to the physical trauma of bearing children and the necessity to be provided for by men, who are free to do so because they are not bearing children.

So the entire account of the Creation and Fall bears little or no resemblance to *objective* history and is merely a mythology that best represents the prompting of the inspired religious impulse of believers. Thus, we can speak of an "Adam of history" and an "Adam of faith."

The historical Adam was more like a character in a science-fiction story who became fully conscious out of a race of apelike siblings and cousins, who struggled for survival and fathered a race of people. And the Adam of faith was an idealized son of God who was *transfigured* into a religious character as an exemplar of why man needs to find his salvation in the New Adam, whom he finds within himself.

Of course, this may all sound insane to the reader, but this narrative I have just presented is *exactly* what many so-called conservatives believe about the Creation story. How could they believe otherwise? If they accept the historical narrative proposed by the materialist-atheist world of evolutionary theory as *objectively true*, then *of course* they cannot accept Genesis 1–3 as real history. So we necessarily have an Adam of history and an Adam of faith. And, of course, no Father of the Church, no Doctor of the Church, no theologian or other saint of the past had any exegetical commentary on the first chapters of Genesis that sound *anything* like this, but we ought to accept this science-fiction narrative over the understanding of upwards of six thousand years — including the Old Covenant period — of prophets, saints, and popes. Furthermore, the feast of St. Adam and St. Eve was traditionally celebrated on December 24, the Vigil of Christmas. The reason for this is that Christ is the New Adam, and therefore, it makes sense to celebrate the feast of the First Adam just as the New Adam arrives. It is based on the notion that Adam was real, not just "real" in the religious sense, and he prefigured the Christ to come. Was the Church, for *centuries*, celebrating the feast of an imaginary person? If Adam was largely imaginary, or only a representative of a vague historical beginning of the human race, then what does Christ fulfill?

This confusion is due to the Modernist subjection of faith to modern science. This is all too acceptable to the Modernist mentality because, according to them: "In the Sacred Books there are many passages referring to science or history where manifest errors are to be found. But the subject of these books is not science or history but religion and morals. In them history and science serve only as a species of covering to enable the religious and moral experiences wrapped up in them to penetrate more readily among the masses" (*Pascendi* 36).

But remember, if you question this approach in the mixed company of "conservative" Catholic intellectuals, you might seem like a "fundamentalist." I should add that this Modernist evolution creation narrative I have weaved together was made possible because, for a year or two, I listened to hundreds of hours of Jordan Peterson lectures, and what I have written is more or less exactly how he explains Genesis 1–3. Peterson has done many good things and helped many people, but his theological musings are Modernist and even Gnostic. It should also be noted that the "conservative" Catholic who's who of the Catholic mainstream constantly express how enamored they are with Peterson's wisdom and insight into religion.

One might ask, "Why would Modernists go to all this work to reconcile Genesis with the evolutionary narrative?" Pius X gives us the answer: "It is next for the historian to ... examine carefully the circumstances and conditions affecting the Church during the different periods, the conserving force she has put forth, the needs both internal and external that have stimulated her to progress, the obstacles she has had to encounter, in a word everything that helps to determine the manner in which the laws of *evolution* have been fulfilled in her" (33, emphasis added).

And Modernists see no issue with the fact that what they view as *objective* history is completely irreconcilable in any obvious way with the *subjective* history of *faith* because "the masses understood science and history as they are expressed in these books, and it is clear that had science and history been expressed in a more perfect form this would have proved rather a hindrance than a help" (36). Thus, the enlightened Modernist is here to enlighten us simple "fundamentalists" on the real truth of Scripture and why modern man is now equipped to understand the truth of materialist evolutionary science, for which the simpleton saints, Doctors, and Fathers of the past simply weren't ready.

With the Modernist historian, we have ultimately neither religious history nor nonreligious history but a fabrication based on a philosophical presumption that all historical narratives were necessarily tainted and therefore the Modernist critic must rescue the process with an approach not "tainted" by philosophy or religion. But, of course, the whole endeavor is riddled with bad philosophy and is a contradiction in terms because Modernism is based on philosophical errors from two hundred to three hundred years ago, and Modernists should now reject those ideas because history and science have "evolved."

Ultimately, Modernist historians — and, by extension, many modern biblical scholars — are engaging not in the science of history but in philosophy. They begin with *a priori* assumptions about reality and the supposed evolutionary progress of history, and what results is a narrative about how history ought to have been and not about what really happened. Pius X does not mince words when speaking about the Modernist approach to history:

> From beginning to end everything in it is *a priori*, and *a priori* in a way that reeks of heresy. These men are certainly to be pitied, and of them the Apostle might well say: *They became vain in their thoughts … professing themselves to be wise they became fools* (Rom. 1:21–22); but, at the same time, they excite just indignation when they accuse the Church of torturing the texts, arranging and confusing them after its own fashion.... In this they are accusing the Church of something for which their own conscience plainly reproaches them. (33)

Modernist history is a monstrosity that completely reimagines the entire historical record because of a commitment to heretical beliefs that lead to the most disastrous conclusions. Sadly, as we will discuss in the next chapter, what results from this mentality is a complete *butchering* of the Bible.

13

How Modernism Butchers Sacred Scripture

As was covered in the last chapter, the Modernist historical method necessarily leads to a prejudicial butchering of sacred history as well as profane history. And, as was stated earlier, the origins of Modernist biblical scholarship are found in the post-Enlightenment liberal Protestantism that was adopted by many Catholic scholars and was condemned strongly by Pope Pius IX and the First Vatican Council. Nonetheless, the spirit of this heretical orientation morphed — evolved — and was repackaged by the Modernists, who found a way of skirting the condemnations of Pius IX and Vatican I. The liberal scholars of the nineteenth century adopted the terminology and expressions of the liberal Protestants, and because of this, we may say that they "overplayed" their hand; thus, a new approach was needed to continue the spread of heresy. It was no longer sufficient simply to parrot the now-condemned terminology and methodology used by adherents of the historical-critical method; therefore, the Modernists did what they do best; they cheated with words.

In this chapter, we will discuss how biblical theology in recent years, by following the Modernist approach, has adopted the tendencies of

Modernism, even if what is done isn't explicitly called "the 'Modernist Method,'" or "Modernist Biblical Theology" by those who employ such methods. Simply put, Modernism has done a number on how Catholic theologians and prelates handle the Bible, and we will investigate how this happens and what has been done.

Relativism about History

Rather than simply denying, for example, the perennial dogmas concerning the historicity and divine inspiration of the Scriptures, Modernists applied their relativistic understanding of history and inspiration to the Scriptures.

For the sane and rational Catholic, history is an objective thing, whether we speak of sacred history or the documented history of ages past. For example, we may read about Alexander the Great in the annals of history recorded by an author from antiquity, and we may read about the same man in the first chapter of the first book of Maccabees. That Alexander appears in a "religious" book of the Bible does not change the fact that he was a real person and real facts are presented about him. As it happens, it does not seem that modern historians have many disagreements with what the Bible states about Alexander, as what is written about him is general information that sets a backdrop for what takes place in the book of Maccabees.

In any event, Modernists do not operate with this commonsense approach to history or sacred history, given that they are plagued with the bifurcation of reality inherent in the Cartesian method so vital to their philosophy. There can be no truly *objective* history for Modernists; for them, all historical claims are tainted because what is transmitted by one person as fact is merely the expression of an *experience* of something external that was then internalized. In the Modernist framework, one cannot trust anyone's claims about history, or any fact, for that matter, because no two experiences will be the same.

If we also consider that Modernists are convinced that divine realities are understood by *immanence*, and therefore relative to the individual perception thereof, we cannot even speak of the divine inspiration of sacred history in the way that Catholics have always understood the concept.

"According to the principles of the Modernists they [the Scriptures] may be rightly described as a collection of *experiences*, not indeed of the kind that may come to anybody, but those extraordinary and striking ones which have happened in any religion. And this is precisely what they teach about our books of the Old and New Testament" (*Pascendi* 22).

Modernists even view the past through the lens of *experience* because "although experience is something belonging to the present, still it may derive its material from the past and the future alike, inasmuch as the believer by memory *lives* the past over again after the manner of *the present*, and lives the future already by anticipation" (22). In essence, the "truth" of historical events is measured by its relation to the *living history* — living tradition? — of the believer. So the Resurrection, for example, does not need to be a legitimate historical event that took place the way it was described in the Gospels but is historical only insofar as it represents what the believers of the time *experienced* in how they perceived the death and Resurrection of Christ. The same could be said of any miraculous event in the Old or New Testament.

Where "Conservative" Scholarship Goes Wrong

While it is rare today to find a theologian who will deny in principle that Jesus objectively rose from the dead, it is quite common to find even "conservative" theologians who will deny that the first eleven chapters of Genesis have any real historical merit. This is because, for Modernists and Neomodernists alike, faith *must* be subject to science, as has been well established in *Pascendi* and in this book. Since the modern materialist scientific narrative completely rejects any possibility of the special creation of Adam and Eve or the universal flood at the time of Noah, modern theologians must essentially mythologize the beginnings of Scripture following the methods of the Modernists. To avoid being condemned as heretics, however, they do not explicitly deny that the first chapters of the Bible are "inspired" or historical in a sense, even though, in effect, they do deny it.

To do this, they resort to a type of trickery and recategorize the Creation and flood stories in Genesis as a type of allegory or poetry. "It isn't that Genesis is completely unhistorical," they say. "It's just that, for the sacred authors,[57] history did not mean the same thing for them that it does for us, so they wrote their history in a poetical or allegorical way." This allows theologians afflicted with Modernism to allow for some sort of inspired historicity in Genesis without affirming that Genesis is historical in the objective sense, which was always believed. Concerning this, Pius X states: "Inspiration, they reply, is distinguished only by its vehemence from that impulse which stimulates the believer to reveal the faith that is in him by words or writing. It is something like what happens in poetical inspiration, of which it has been said: There is God in us, and when he stirreth he sets us afire. And it is precisely in this sense that God is said to be the origin of the inspiration of the Sacred Books" (22).

Now, this method is effective because it *is* true that accounts of sacred history can be poetical and allegorical while also being historical. Who can deny that the sacred history in Genesis is not written like a modern history textbook? To expect Holy Writ to be written in a fashion acceptable to modern historical sciences, however, is again to subject the truths of faith to the methods of modern science, which is a condemnable error. Scripture is layered with meaning and significance and can be true in the literal sense while also being prophetic or allegorical.

When we read that the Serpent conversed with Eve (Gen. 3), we need not throw out the historical truth of that fateful event because

---

[57] They will never name Moses as the principal author of Genesis, even though this has been long established as a fact in Tradition and was reaffirmed by the Pontifical Biblical Commission under Pius X.

God did not deem it necessary to provide us with diagrams or documentary evidence of how Satan could take the form of a Serpent and how the Serpent could communicate with a human being. We are, of course, dealing with the inspired account that provides an illustration for us of an encounter between human beings and the preternatural being who fell from Heaven. Should we expect there to be no mystery or awe-inspired wonder in that event?

Even the Modernist, if he is not a complete pantheist, would accept the creation *ex nihilo* of the universe as a miracle performed by God, yet in the inspired history that explains how this creation took place and what immediately followed, he rejects the supernatural and preternatural events simply because they are supernatural and preternatural! This is why Modernism ultimately leads to de facto materialism and results in practical atheism, as all divine intervention in history must necessarily be explained by natural or psychological causes.

The consequences of this manner of thinking are tremendous. For, if there is no real Garden of Eden and no real dialogue with the Devil, then there can be no real Fall of Man and therefore no real Original Sin. Perhaps a Modernist may begrudgingly accept the infallible dogma of Original Sin, but it is difficult to see how it could be understood in a Catholic way. If the sacred history of Genesis is nothing more than an inspired — in the Modernist sense — fable or fairy story, then the Fall of Man is nothing more than a doctrinal expression of the inherent weakness of human beings who "fall short" due to their yet-to-be perfected nature and who therefore cry out to God for redemption. Modernists may well admit that human beings have fallen in some vague sense, but the account of the Fall did not literally happen the way it is expressed in Genesis.

Furthermore, it must be understood that the Modernist rejection of the historicity of Genesis results in grave consequences in Christology, which is to say, the truth of who Christ is. If there is no real Old Adam, then Christ can be the New Adam only in a metaphorical sense, in that He represents a perfected man who best embodied the immanent truth of the divine reality. This principle of "embodiment" allows the Modernist to speak of the Incarnation; for him, Christ is God incarnate because God is alive in Christ. Again, Modernists can say Catholic things while believing heretical things and slide under the condemnations of the Church in an era of ineffective churchmen who allow the chaos to continue.

Furthermore, the necessity of the Crucifixion as the propitiatory sacrifice in order to satisfy the justice of God is also called into question. If anything, the Crucifixion in the mind of the Modernist is nothing more than an egregious act of violence by a spiritually blind civilization that could not recognize the immanent divinity of Christ. In other words, Christ did not need to die for the sins of men the way Catholics have always understood it; instead, He died because the Jews who crucified Him were ignorant of the divine dignity that Christ personified as an exemplar for men to follow.

All that business about Christ fulfilling various prophecies in the Old Testament and being sacrificed as the Lamb of God is ultimately, for the Modernist, the result of pious impulse over time by "sacred authors" who amalgamate the experiential traditions of believers, who together create a cohesive narrative. "For they are ready to admit, nay, to proclaim that Christ Himself manifestly erred in determining the time when the coming of the Kingdom of God was to take place, and they tell us that we must not be surprised at this since even Christ was subject to the laws of life!" (*Pascendi* 36).

In addition, the rejection of the historicity of the first chapters of Genesis relegates the infallible dogma of the Immaculate Conception to the realm of metaphor. While a Catholic believes that Mary was conceived without Original Sin as a necessary fact, a Modernist may believe that to speak of the Blessed Mother as immaculately conceived is merely a poetic device. In other words, the cult of the Virgin Mary, so important to Catholics for reasons of piety and devotion, necessitates an exaltation of her divine maternity due to her participation in the life of Christ. In this way, the Modernist can say that Mary was conceived without sin but only in the sense that he can say that Christ was divine, meaning that the religious sentiment that leads to a collective veneration of Mary as sinless necessitates a dogmatic expression that best represents that communicated impulse that has resulted from the piety of believers.

Modernist biblical scholarship, therefore, not only attacks the dogmatic truth of the Bible but attacks *dogma itself*:

> After this what is to become of the dogmas of the Church? The dogmas brim over with flagrant contradictions, but what matter[s] that since, apart from the fact that vital logic accepts them, they are not repugnant to symbolical truth. Are we not dealing with the infinite, and has not the infinite an infinite variety of aspects? In short, to maintain and defend these theories they do not hesitate to declare that the noblest homage that can be paid to the Infinite is to make it the object of contradictory propositions! But when they justify even contradiction, what is it that they will refuse to justify? (36)

> But it is all mere juggling of words. For if we take the Bible, according to the tenets of agnosticism, to be a human work, made by men for men, but allowing the theologian to proclaim that it is divine by immanence, what room is there left in it for inspiration? General inspiration in the Modernist sense it is easy to find, but of inspiration in the Catholic sense there is not a trace. (22)

Modernist Biblical Scholarship Is Still the Norm

I should add that in recent decades there has arisen a style of biblical scholarship that is not wholly Modernist in the most egregious sense but is still imbued with certain aspects of Modernism. Again, we look to a young Fr. Ratzinger for evidence of this.

Speaking to the German bishops on the eve of the Second Vatican Council, Fr. Ratzinger spoke of how modern theologians might understand the notion of inerrancy and inspiration in light of the fact that many moderns believe the Scriptures contain errors in matters of fact. He said:

> According to a practically irrefutable consensus of historians there *definitely are mistakes and errors in the Bible* [emphasis added] in profane matters of no relevance for what *Scripture* properly *intends to affirm*.... *Scripture* is and remains inerrant and beyond doubt in *everything that it properly intends to affirm*, but this is not necessarily so in that which accompanies the affirmation and is not part of it. As a result ... the inerrancy of Scripture has to be limited to its *vere enuntiata* [what is really affirmed]. Otherwise historical reason will be led into what is really an inescapable conflict.[58]

Typical of Ratzinger's wordy German style, the commonsense meaning of what he said is lost in the shadows of the eloquence with which he says it. He makes a number of striking claims. First, he claims there is "practically irrefutable consensus" that there "definitely are mistakes and errors in the Bible." Now, he says this with the caveat that he is referring merely to what he believes to be obvious historical or biographical problems, but that doesn't save this statement when we consider what the Church had perennially taught. Pope Leo XIII was *extremely* clear that what Ratzinger proposed would be impossible. He wrote in *Providentissimus Deus* in 1893: "For all the books which the Church receives as sacred and canonical, are written wholly and entirely, with all their parts, at the dictation of the Holy Ghost; *and so far is it from being possible that any error can co-exist with inspiration*" (20, emphasis added). Furthermore, Leo XIII wrote in the same document:

---

[58] This quotation from Ratzinger's address to the German bishops is cited in Aaron Pidel, S.J., "Joseph Ratzinger on Biblical Inerrancy," *Nova et Vetera* 12, no. 1, English ed. (Winter 2014): 314, https://stpaulcenter.com/14-nv-12-1-pidel/.

For the system of those who, in order to rid themselves of these difficulties [supposed historical inaccuracies], do not hesitate to concede that divine inspiration regards the things of faith and morals, and nothing beyond, because (as they wrongly think) in a question of the truth or falsehood of a passage, we should consider not so much what God has said as the reason and purpose which He had in mind in saying it — this system cannot be tolerated. (20)

To his credit, Pius X echoes the wisdom of his predecessor in no uncertain terms in *Pascendi*, blasting the notion that *any error whatsoever* could exist in Scripture, stating that to propose such an idea would be to attribute *dishonesty to God*: "We, Venerable Brethren, for whom there is but one and only one truth, and who hold that the Sacred Books, written under the inspiration of the Holy Ghost, have God for their author (Conc. Vat., *De Revel.*, c. 2) declare that this is equivalent to attributing to God Himself the lie of utility or officious lie." Continuing, he adds: "We say with St. Augustine: *In an authority so high, admit but one officious lie, and there will not remain a single passage of those apparently difficult to practise or to believe, which on the same most pernicious rule may not be explained as a lie uttered by the author wilfully and to serve a purpose* (Epist. 28). *And thus it will come about, the holy Doctor continues, that everybody will believe and refuse to believe what he likes or dislikes*" (36).

Are Leo XIII and Pius X not plainly condemning what Ratzinger proposed? Granted, Ratzinger was much more careful in his presentation, but the substance is the same. Ratzinger does not say in his statement that the Bible is inerrant only in matters of faith and morals, but he does say, "*Scripture* is and remains inerrant and beyond doubt in *everything that it properly intends to affirm*, but this is not necessarily so in that which accompanies the affirmation and is not part of it." Is there really a qualitative difference between what Leo XIII calls impossible, what Pius X compares to accusing God of lying, and what

Ratzinger suggests? Ratzinger's insinuation is that Scripture is without error, but only where Scripture intends to be without error, which is another way of saying that Scripture *does* contain errors. These distinctions between what modern theologians may believe the authors of Scripture intended to affirm and what they did not intend to affirm are completely arbitrary.

Furthermore, this mentality also fits the Modernist notion that matters of faith must be subject to modern science. When Ratzinger speaks of a consensus of historians who believe that the Bible has historical errors, he must surely be referring to historians of the middle part of the last century, unless we are to believe that, for thousands of years, the stewards of the Old Testament Scriptures and the New Testament Scriptures persisted in claims of inerrancy even though it was believed by practically all scholars that the Scriptures themselves were historically dubious. Also, does it seem odd to the reader, as it does to me, that we should expect scholars in 1950 to have a better grasp of ancient history than the inspired authors of the Old and New Testaments? Again, this renders the notion of inspiration completely arbitrary; inspiration comes and goes and touches some things and not others, but we are still to believe that the totality of the Bible in what it affirms as true is, in fact, true, even though the Bible contains statements that are not true.

It is truly characteristic of the modern educated man to educate himself out of common sense.

While Ratzinger may have been convinced that a simple belief in the inerrancy of Scripture outside of some arbitrary confine would create an "inescapable conflict," I would beg to differ, as would men such as St. Jerome, who gave us the Latin Church's official translation of the Bible — the Vulgate.

The Church has always endorsed the Latin Vulgate, edited, compiled, and translated by St. Jerome. St. Jerome (347–420) was born in the Roman province of Dalmatia, in the area we know today as Bosnia. He spent much of his formation as a Christian in Rome, Gaul,

Constantinople, and Antioch. Finally, he spent the rest of his days as an ascetic living in a monastery he founded near Bethlehem. Christian traditions relate how he often prayed and studied in the very cave where Our Lord was born. Because of his continual education and immersion in all the major language centers of biblical literature and the early Church, St. Jerome was uniquely qualified in his ability to translate the Scriptures accurately. More importantly, he was a master theologian, lived a life steeped in the mind of the Church, and attained great holiness.

As far as I can tell, this great, saintly scholar of the Church — who had unmatchable expertise, given his experience and formation — was not convinced that the Bible contained obvious historical and factual errors.

It is true that some things in Scripture are hard to understand. It is also true that copying or translations may be done poorly. As with all matters of faith, we have the great saints to look to for wisdom. In correspondence with St. Jerome, St. Augustine said the following: "I have learned to pay such honour and reverence as to believe most firmly that *none of their writers has fallen into any error.* And if in these Books I meet anything which seems contrary to truth, I shall not hesitate to conclude either that the text is faulty, or that the translator has not expressed the meaning of the passage, or that I myself do not understand."[59] Yet, if we were to follow Ratzinger's insistence that the Bible is only inerrant in certain respects and not in others, then we would jettison the wisdom of great saints such as Jerome and Augustine. Ultimately, to reject the great witness of these saints and adopt the Modernist mentality would be to accept a system of biblical scholarship that Leo XIII said "cannot be tolerated."

Augustine and the Literal Meaning of Genesis

Foreseeing a certain objection, it seems wise to address St. Augustine's opinion on Genesis, as he held that the mention of six days of creation

---

[59] Quoted in *Providentissimus Deus* 21.

in Genesis did not necessarily mean six literal days. St. Augustine had no command of Hebrew or Greek, and by his own admission, he encountered difficulties when trying to learn these languages. Perhaps he was like some people who have a difficult time with math (like me) or other disciplines. So, he accomplished his work in Latin, but he also necessarily relied on Latin translations of the Bible. Augustine relied on the *Vetus Latina* (Old Latin) translation of the Bible, which had some inaccuracies compared with the later, more accurate Vulgate by St. Jerome. This translation, particularly of Genesis, led Augustine to interpret "day" in a manner that did not necessarily bind him to a strict twenty-four-hour period. His understanding was that God created everything simultaneously, and the "days" were a literary device to communicate this to human understanding.

Now, Augustine did *not* believe that a literary device was used in Genesis instead of a literal explanation because he was under the impression that the men of ancient times could not understand the natural sciences like moderns — a belief that Modernists hold. On the contrary, Augustine also had philosophical reasons for his interpretation, influenced by Neoplatonism, where ideas of time and eternity were seen differently. He believed that God's creation was an instantaneous act from an eternal perspective; thus, the "days" could symbolize different aspects or stages of creation rather than actual time periods. Far from believing that the days in Genesis could be seen as many thousands or millions of years, he believed there were no time periods because creation happened in an instant. In fact, in *The City of God*, he wrote, "They are deceived, too, by those highly mendacious documents which profess to give the history of (man as) many thousand years, though, reckoning by the sacred writings, we find that not 6000 years have yet passed."[60]

---

[60] *The City of God*, bk. 12, chap. 10, trans. Marcus Dods, in *Nicene and Post-Nicene Fathers*, First Series, vol. 2. ed. Philip Schaff (Buffalo, NY: Christian Literature, 1887), revised and edited for New Advent by Kevin Knight, http://www.newadvent.org/fathers/1201.htm.

In any event, we must consider what led him, besides his philosophical approach, to take the days of creation as nonliteral. He did this because of his understanding of Sirach 18:1, which states, "He that liveth for ever created all things together." Augustine believed that this meant that God created all things at once, or "together," which provided an interpretive key when he read Genesis 2:4 in the translation he used, which stated: "This is the book of the creation of heaven and earth, when the day was made, God made heaven and earth, and every green thing of the field."[61] Now, for Augustine, the phrase "when the day was made" was proof that creation took place in an instant. In the Hebrew, however, the phrase is בְּיוֹם (bə yō·wm), which means "in the day that," which is an idiomatic expression meaning "when," as in the phrase "when God had created the heavens and the earth and every green thing of the field."[62]

As was mentioned, St. Jerome provided the Church with the official Latin translation — the Latin Vulgate — which corrected this inaccuracy. St. Jerome faithfully translated the passage, and the English translation in the Douay-Rheims Bible is faithful to Jerome's translation; it states: "These are the generations of the heaven and the earth, when they were created, *in the day that* the Lord God made the heaven and the earth: And every plant of the field"[63] (Gen. 2:4–5, emphasis added).

---

[61] In Latin it is written: *Hic est liber creaturae coeli et terrae, cum factus est dies, fecit Deus coelum et terram, et omne viride agri.* Joseph Gedney, "St. Augustine Rediscovered: A Defense of the Literal Interpretation of St. Augustine's Writings on the Sacred History of Genesis," The Kolbe Center for the Study of Creation, December 14, 2018, https://kolbecenter.org/st-augustine-rediscovered-a-defense-of-the-literal-interpretation-of-st-augustines-writings-on-the-sacred-history-of-genesis/.

[62] "St. Augustine Rediscovered."

[63] Gedney, "St. Augustine Rediscovered." The Latin from the Vulgate is written as: "Istae generationes caeli et terrae, quando creatae sunt, in die quo fecit Dominus Deus caelum et terram: et omne virgultum agri antequam oreretur in terra, omnemque herbam regionis priusquam germinaret."

Considering this important discrepancy amended by St. Jerome, we must return to the verse in Sirach that seems to present Creation as instantaneous, as Augustine believed. Commenting on Sirach 18:1, Cornelius à Lapide, arguably the most renowned biblical commentator in Church history, explained that when it says God created all things "together," it means that God "created all things in their entirety, that is, all things categorically, with no exception."[64] So, the word "together" does not modify "[He] created" but "all things." Lapide added: "Whence in place of together in the Greek text of Ecclesiasticus, we read κοινῇ, *koinei*, 'in general.'"[65]

In addition, Augustine wrote a work called *The Literal Meaning of Genesis*, wherein he stated: "The narrative indeed in these books is not cast in the figurative kind of language you find in the Song of Songs, but quite simply tells of things that happened, as in the books of the Kingdoms and others like them."[66] Furthermore, he objected to those who believed that Genesis constituted some sort of allegory or poetic tale: "Let nobody assume that what I have said about [the nonliteral interpretation of the days of creation] ... that none of this can be said strictly and properly, but that it all belongs to a kind of figurative and allegorical understanding."[67]

And even though Augustine had a mystical approach to understanding the way "days" was used in Genesis, he stated, "We can have no hesitation in believing the fact" that Genesis records *what* happened and *how* it happened.[68]

In summary, Augustine's belief in nonliteral days was based on an inaccurate translation, and he reconciled a seeming discrepancy by considering the nature of time and the timelessness of God; therefore, he philosophized in a way to *vindicate* the literal meaning of Genesis

[64] Gedney, "St. Augustine Rediscovered."
[65] Gedney, "St. Augustine Rediscovered."
[66] Gedney, "St. Augustine Rediscovered."
[67] Gedney, "St. Augustine Rediscovered."
[68] Gedney, "St. Augustine Rediscovered."

and not to deny it. His approach was the *complete* opposite of Modernists, who see what they believe are discrepancies in the Bible and then explain away the literal meaning. In reality, Augustine was extremely holy, and therefore humble, so he believed, rightly, that if there was an apparent contradiction, it was necessarily the result of a faulty text, a mistranslation, or a limit in his own intelligence. Modernists would do well to consult Augustine's work in full and to seek to imitate his humility.

The Pestilence of Modernist Biblical Scholarship

Pius X summarized all that is wrong with Modernist biblical scholarship in no uncertain terms:

> To hear them talk about their works on the Sacred Books, in which they have been able to discover so much that is defective, one would imagine that before them nobody ever even glanced through the pages of Scripture, whereas the truth is that a whole multitude of Doctors, infinitely superior to them in genius, in erudition, in sanctity, have sifted the Sacred Books in every way, and so far from finding imperfections in them, have thanked God more and more the deeper they have gone into them, for His divine bounty in having vouchsafed to speak thus to men. Unfortunately, these great Doctors did not enjoy the same aids to study that are possessed by the Modernists for their guide and rule — a philosophy borrowed from the negation of God, and a criterion which consists of themselves. (34).

He even went so far as to say that anyone who embraces or employs the Modernist abuse of historical criticism of the Bible "places himself in opposition to Catholic faith" and compared the method to a "pestilence in the air which penetrates everywhere and spreads the contagion" (34).

Throughout these last few chapters, we have concentrated with Pius X on the egregious harm that Modernists do to history and sacred history. We have seen that the Modernist method has *not* fallen out of fashion, and this is typified by Ratzinger's troubling statements. You would be hard-pressed today to find a "conservative" theologian or apologist who does not herald Ratzinger as something like a Church Father of the twentieth century. If Ratzinger is "conservative," and he proposed a theory that renders the Bible de facto errant, then one can only imagine the standards of biblical scholarship in universities and seminaries worldwide. Modernism is literally everywhere.

And to think, if Catholics simply held fast to Tradition and stood firm against the atheistic sciences of modernity, they could pray with simple faith a prayer said by so many millions of Catholics and avoid this calamity entirely: "I believe these and all the truths which the Holy Catholic Church teaches because Thou hast revealed them who canst neither deceive nor be deceived."

14

Modernist Reform: The Confusion of Vatican II

It is now necessary to discuss Modernism and its influence on the Second Vatican Council and the subsequent reforms. In *Pascendi*, Pius X's discussion of the Modernist as reformer is profound. His treatment of Modernist reform is so filled with insight that it would be impossible to discuss it in view of Vatican II in one chapter. So I have divided the analysis into four chapters.

This chapter will lay the groundwork for a discussion on Vatican II's novel theological statements in light of what Pope Pius X wrote. The next will discuss the novel theological orientation behind Modernist reform. The third will discuss Modernist reform in action, and the fourth will discuss the Modernist reforms of worship.

Doubtless, there are innumerable opinions about Vatican II; therefore, in order to present a reasonable position on the Council in the context of Pius X's work, it is necessary to consider the theological atmosphere of the Council, as well as the interpretive understandings of the liberal and Modernist — or at least Modernist-adjacent — theologians who led the charge during and after the Council. Also, given that some readers may be concerned that the teachings of an ecumenical council could be questioned, this will be addressed.

I should add that it is *not* the intention of this chapter or the next to comb through the documents of Vatican II in great detail, as this would be another work entirely. Instead, I will consider certain aspects of the Vatican II question and provide, I hope, sufficient evidence to allow a Catholic conscientiously to object to, or at least question, the statements of Vatican II in some instances, as well as the reforms that followed. I will present a reasonable position that explains a Traditional conception of what happened with Vatican II and show that there is good reason to apply *Pascendi*'s warnings about Modernist reform to the conciliar paradigm.

Pius X's Prophecy

The following paragraph from *Pascendi*, which will be presented in full due to its profundity and abundance, should strike us as a prophecy of what would befall the Catholic Church in the 1960s and the years that followed:

> It remains for Us now to say a few words about the Modernist as reformer. From all that has preceded, some idea may be gained of the reforming mania which possesses them: in all Catholicism there is absolutely nothing on which it does not fasten. Reform of philosophy, especially in the seminaries: the scholastic philosophy is to be relegated to the history of philosophy among obsolete systems, and the young men are to be taught modern philosophy which alone is true and suited to the times in which we live. Reform of theology; rational theology is to have modern philosophy for its foundation, and positive theology is to be founded on the history of dogma. As for history, it must be for the future written and taught only according to their modern methods and principles. Dogmas and their evolution are to be harmonized with science and history. In the Catechism no dogmas are to be inserted except those that have been duly reformed and are within the capacity of the people. Regarding worship, the number of external devotions is to be

reduced, or at least steps must be taken to prevent their further increase, though, indeed, some of the admirers of symbolism are disposed to be more indulgent on this head. Ecclesiastical government requires to be reformed in all its branches, but especially in its disciplinary and dogmatic parts. Its spirit with the public conscience, which is not wholly for democracy; a share in ecclesiastical government should therefore be given to the lower ranks of the clergy, and even to the laity, and authority should be decentralised. The Roman Congregations, and especially the index and the Holy Office, are to be reformed. The ecclesiastical authority must change its line of conduct in the social and political world; while keeping outside political and social organization, it must adapt itself to those which exist in order to penetrate them with its spirit. With regard to morals, they adopt the principle of the Americanists, that the active virtues are more important than the passive, both in the estimation in which they must be held and in the exercise of them. The clergy are asked to return to their ancient lowliness and poverty, and in their ideas and action to be guided by the principles of Modernism; and there are some who, echoing the teaching of their Protestant masters, would like the suppression of ecclesiastical celibacy. What is there left in the Church which is not to be reformed according to their principles? (38)

What the holy pope lays out for us here is the ultimate goal of the Modernist revolution in the Church: nothing other than a complete overhaul of all things. Everything from the nature of how priests are formed, to the types of catechisms that are promulgated, to changes in liturgical rituals, a change in the conception of virtues, the removal of the Index of Forbidden Books, reforms in Church law and discipline, and so on.

Now, ask yourself: Is there anything that Pius X mentions here that has not taken place in recent decades in the Church? And, if these prophesied calamities occurred, when did they begin in earnest? Of course, any astute observer of Catholic affairs over the past few decades knows full well that virtually everything, to the letter, that Pius X warned of, has, in fact, taken place, and the fountainhead for this complete overhaul of the Catholic Church was, of course, the Second Vatican Council.

Compare and contrast Pius X's warnings about Modernist reform with important statements of the two popes who oversaw Vatican II, John XXIII and Paul VI.

In his opening address of the Council, Pope John stated:

> In calling this vast assembly of bishops [I intend] to assert the [Church's] magisterium ... in order that this magisterium ... might be presented in exceptional form to all men throughout the world.... The salient point of this Council is not ... a discussion of one article or another of the fundamental doctrine of the Church which has repeatedly been taught by the Fathers and by ancient and modern theologians, and which is presumed to be well known and familiar to all. For this a Council was not necessary. But ... the Christian, Catholic and apostolic spirit of the whole world expects a step forward toward a doctrinal penetration and a formation of consciousness in ... conformity with authentic doctrine which, however, should be studied and expounded through methods of research and ... the literary forms of modern thought.... The Catholic Church, raising the torch of religious truth by means of the Ecumenical Council, desires to show herself to be the loving mother of all, benign, patient, full of mercy and goodness toward the brethren who are separated from her.[69]

During the Last General Meeting of the Second Vatican Council, on December 7, 1965, Paul VI stated:

---

[69] Cited in Michael Baker, "What's Wrong with the Novus Ordo," *Super Flumina*, June 3, 2018, https://www.superflumina.org/novus-ordo-its-problems.html.

The Council devoted its attention not so much to divine truths but rather, and principally, to the Church.... This secular religious society, which is the Church, has endeavoured to carry out an act of *reflection about herself, to know herself better, to define herself better* and, in consequence, to set aright what she feels and what she commands.... The Council ... has been deeply committed to the study of the modern world. *Never before perhaps, so much as on this occasion, has the Church felt the need to know, to draw near to, to understand, to penetrate, serve and evangelize the society in which she lives; and to get to grips with it, almost to run after it, in its rapid and continuous change....* Yes, the Church of the Council has been concerned, not just with herself ... but with man — man as he really is today: living man, man all wrapped up in himself, man who makes himself not only the centre of his every interest but dares to claim that he is the principle and explanation of all reality.... We call upon those who term themselves modern humanists, and who have renounced the transcendent value of the highest realities, to give the Council credit at least for one quality and to recognize our own *new type of humanism*: we, too, in fact, we more than any others, honour mankind.... *The modern world's values were not only respected but honoured,* its efforts approved, its aspirations purified and blessed.... The modern mind, accustomed to assessing everything in terms of usefulness, will readily admit that the Council's value is great if only because everything has been referred to human usefulness. *Hence no one should ever say that a religion like the Catholic religion is without use,* seeing that when it has its greatest self-awareness and effectiveness, as it has in council, it declares itself entirely on the side of man and in his service. (emphasis added)[70]

[70] Baker, "What's Wrong."

Even a cursory glance by the uninitiated will see that the Council began with an ambiguity of purpose, as Pope John XXIII clearly expressed that refinement of Catholic doctrine was not the intention, but the intention for the Council itself was really an open question. And Paul VI was unambiguous about his opinion that Vatican II was all about "modernity" and "newness," even presenting the Church as running after the "rapid and continuous change" of the world, as if this were a good thing. And what, pray tell, are the "modern world's values" that should be "respected and honoured"?

In addition, Paul VI tells us that Vatican II was a psychological event, wherein the Church participated in self-reflection and came to know herself better. This assertion would be almost laughable, if it was not so pitiable, given the identity crisis that so many Catholics and prelates have undergone in recent decades.

Furthermore, Paul VI's utterance about the usefulness of the Catholic religion was straight out of the Modernist playbook. Pius X exposed the notion that the Church showed her vitality and usefulness by always changing and adapting to present trends and challenges as a distinctly Modernist thought. According to Pius X, Modernism asserts that the Church is guided by a spirit of change and development as she accepts different things from different times so she can stay relevant and useful to the men of different eras *on their terms* (*Pascendi* 35). This insinuation is, of course, that the Church must change because the opinions of men change, and not that men must conform themselves to the timeless truth and wisdom the Church represents and gives to the world.

From just the opening and closing statements of Popes John XXIII and Paul VI, we gain astonishing insights into the nature of the Council. It is obvious from the two popes who oversaw the Council that the purpose was not to define doctrine, which was completely out of the ordinary as far as Councils are concerned, but to open up the Church to the world and to adapt to the whims and streams of modern thinking. Some may object and claim that Vatican II is not to be blamed for the crisis in the Church because things were not perfect before the Council, and therefore, if there is a crisis, it cannot be blamed on the Council. While it is true that there were problems before the Council — hence, the conciliar revolution! — this objection is shortsighted. It is like saying, "We cannot blame the invasion on the fact that we took down the walls that protected the city, for there were already internal disputes within it and the enemy was already trying to break down the walls." Granted, theological rot was growing before the Council, and had been for some time; thus the necessity for Pius X to write *Pascendi*. But it cannot be denied by any reasonable person that Vatican II demonstrated a great shift in theological language and precision and that it precipitated — if not caused — a complete overhaul that facilitated the instantiation of the Modernist reforms of which Pius X warned. In fairness to the strongest proponents of the Council, they usually do not deny that Vatican II was a monumental shift — which we will discuss in earnest — but suggest that a monumental shift was needed. Well, history would argue otherwise, as the crisis in the Church has reached epic proportions to the point where one wonders if the Gates of Hell have not already prevailed. Of course, we do not deny the promise of Our Lord that this would not happen, but the situation is dire, to say the least.

Worthwhile Considerations about Vatican II

I do expect that some readers may believe that it is not possible to blame the Second Vatican Council, as if the texts themselves were objectively erroneous or harmful. What would be required to prove that the texts of Vatican II are riddled with positive — which is to say, explicit — errors, would be a different work wherein we would comb through the texts of the Council and assess the different arguments for and against the various positions. That is not the purpose of this work;[71] as was said at

---

[71] If you would like to read helpful materials on Vatican II from the Traditional perspective, I can recommend three books: (1) *The Great Facade*, by Chris Ferrara and Tom Woods, (2) *Prometheus*, by Fr. Alvaro Calderon, and (3) *The Second Vatican Council: An Unwritten Story*, by Roberto de Mattei.

the outset of the chapter, we are at present attempting to understand the Modernist spirit and the teachings of Pius X so that we may recognize the source of this crisis in all its forms. That said, it should also be noted that Modernism as a spirit or tendency can be transmitted in documents or approaches that are not explicitly heretical. Modernism is as much an attitude as it is a heresy. This is because Modernism is based on the principles of agnosticism, vital immanence, and evolution, which constitute presuppositions about the nature of reality, history, and religion.

Adopting the principle of agnosticism inserts into the mind an axiomatic doubt; adopting the principle of vital immanence results in a psychologization of religion; and the mindset that all things must evolve creates in the mind an expectation of continual development. It is possible for one not to adopt condemned heretical positions explicitly while being permeated by those principles. A Modernist may write or propose something that does not express an objective heresy but represents the mentality that undergirds Modernism. An example would be the statement in *Gaudium et Spes* discussed in an earlier chapter that considered John Paul II's Theology of the Body: "Man, who is the only creature on earth which God willed for itself, cannot fully find himself except through a sincere gift of himself." It would be hard to argue that this statement presents an explicit heresy, even if it is undergirded by erroneous or unhelpful philosophy, but it is also an incomprehensible statement if examined logically, as it presupposes that man is lost in the first place and needs to "find himself," which is vague if not meaningless. Furthermore, the spirit of the statement is that man must search for himself by giving himself to others, which is to suggest that he will "find himself" by engaging in intimate experiences with others, and in these experiences he will, presumably, find the truth when he finds himself. This infuses in the reader who tries to understand it the personalist mentality of beginning with the subjective before proceeding to the objective; and as has been discussed at length earlier, this manner of thinking is consistent with the errors of modern philosophy that provide the foundation for Modernism as a whole. In this way, we can see that Modernism is a mentality or an attitude that can be heretical or erroneous in spirit, even if not in explicit statements.

When assessing the Modernist spirit and its influence on Vatican II, we would also do well to take the words of the progressives at the Council at face value, considering that what has resulted from the Council has been a continual onslaught of progressive — Modernist — reform. Commenting on the fundamental shift that took place at the Council, a young Fr. Ratzinger said in 1967: "Now, *after the refusals of the last hundred years*, the Council has taken the initiative to start the process of accepting this positive encounter to coordinate the Church and the modern world.... The fight of the Conciliar Fathers over *Schema XIII* [*Gaudium et Spes*] can be nothing but the beginning of a movement that continues" (emphasis added).[72]

Joseph Ratzinger was *no lightweight* at Vatican II and the time that followed, and that he was made the head of the Congregation for the Doctrine of the Faith as a cardinal speaks volumes. We are not dealing with some "fringe" theologian writing on some blog or posting on social media. No, Ratzinger was a darling of the Council and the conciliar era, and he was very clear that Vatican II represented some sort of "movement" of synthesis between modernity and the Church. Now, we must assume that Ratzinger, writing as a theologian, did not mean that the Church should synthesize with the arbitrary advancements of modernity, such as cable television and cellular phone technology. Given that he was commenting on a major Council document, we rightfully conclude that he meant a conciliation between *modern thought* — philosophy and science — and the Church.

What is modern philosophy if not a continual footnote to Hegel, Kant, and Descartes? What could a coordination — synthesis? — of the Church and the modern world be other than a mingling of two

---

[72] Joseph Ratzinger, *Problemi e risultati del Concilio Vaticano II*, 1967 quoted in Atila Since Guimarães, *In the Murky Waters of Vatican II*, 3rd ed. (Los Angeles: Tradition in Action, 2008), 103.

opposing forces? The Church, timeless and unchanging in her vital substance, and the modern world, so obsessed with evolution and progress and a radical rethinking of every institution; how can these two things "coordinate"? Is there a quintessentially modern manner of thinking that is not at root Modernist, or at least liberal?

Furthermore, what "refusals" is Ratzinger referring to? Well, in the hundred years prior to 1967, we can look to three major papal figures who wrote voraciously against Liberalism and Modernism. Pius IX gave us his *Syllabus of Errors*, Pius X gave us *Pascendi*, and Leo XIII gave us his significant corpus of anti-liberal work. Of course, Pius IX and Pius X gave us many more works and did many more things, but the two works mentioned are likely the most well known. Under these popes, the Church *refused* to act in a conciliatory manner with Modernism and Liberalism. Shouldn't we view this as a good thing? Shouldn't Ratzinger also view this as a good thing? Instead, it seems that Ratzinger was of the mindset that, casting aside the refusals of these great popes, to dance with the devil of modernity was somehow not a bad thing.

One of the major architects of the progressive reforms at the Council, Cardinal Léon-Joseph Suenens, spoke in distinctly Modernist terms about the Council upon its conclusion: "For his part, Pope Paul VI wrote these far-reaching words that engage the future: The Council's decrees, more than a point of arrival, are a point of departure toward new goals. The Spirit and the renewing wind of the Council must continue to penetrate deeply into the life of the Church. *The germs of life sown by the Council in Church soil must reach their full maturity*" (emphasis added).[73]

What could be more Modernist in spirit and tendency than the notion of "germs of life" needing time to mature into something new? Is the notion of vitality — vital immanence — not at the heart of the

---

[73] L.J. Suenens, *Discorse ufficiale d'apertura*, in V.A., *L'Avvenire della Chiesa*, 46, quoted in Guimarães, *Murky Waters*, 99.

Modernist concept of religion? For Modernists, the proof of religion is that it "lives," which is to say, it *changes*. If it is believed that Vatican II was the beginning, or the beginning of the beginning, of a fundamental change in the Church, then the notion of a seed needing time to reach "full maturity" is perfectly apt. If it was only a seed planted at the Council, then the proponents of the Council can say, "Oh, Vatican II needs more time to mature, because the acorn is far from being the oak tree." Thus, this notion of the immanent vitality of the theological shift at Vatican II is the perfect Modernist plot. Anything and everything can be attributed to Vatican II, and it can change on a whim because, of course, the reforms, the reforms of the reforms, and the reforms of the reforms of the reforms are but signs of the *living Spirit of the Council* that has not yet reached maturity. It is worth noting that Suenens was integral in the promulgation of the Charismatic Renewal in the Church, and he was also famous for saying, "Vatican II is the French Revolution in the Church."

While it may not be technically heretical in the strictest sense to say what Suenens and Paul VI said, it is also true that such a mentality must necessarily be imbued with the heretical spirit of the heresy of Modernism. The belief that Vatican II was a "point of departure" is to say plainly that the Church at Vatican II was "leaving" some location and going toward another. Where was she leaving from, and where is she going? Is she going toward a Chardinian "Omega Point"? And, if the Church departed from some location with Vatican II, what did she leave behind?

John Paul II's New Springtime

This mentality is consistent with claims made by various theologians, including Pope John Paul II, who looked at Vatican II as some sort of "rebirth" of the Church, almost as if the Holy Ghost finally moved in a way that could spread the Gospel in a new and dynamic manner. Pope John Paul II, speaking to a group of movements and communities, said: "The movements and new communities, providential expressions of the new springtime brought forth by the Spirit with the Second Vatican Council, announce the power of God's love which in overcoming divisions and barriers of every kind, renews the face of the earth to build the civilization of love."[74]

So, the "Spirit" — one assumes the Holy Spirit — brought forth a new springtime with Vatican II. Really? Does this match reality *at all*? Sure, there has been *numerical* growth in the Church since 1965, based on the growth of Catholic populations as a whole, but there has been a stark *relative* decline when we consider the continual downturn in orthodoxy and practice among baptized Catholics. If it is a springtime, then we would imagine we would see things budding forth with new life, and for the days to be longer and the sun to be hotter, leading to a summer of abundance. Of course, we have not seen this, at least not outside the Traditional movement — with rare exceptions, such as in Africa[75] — but we have seen the opposite in almost *every place in the world*. Perhaps some who are involved in movements such as the Charismatic Renewal are tempted to believe that their experience is indicative of a larger trend, but it certainly is not. In addition, even this notion that there could be a "new springtime" is a problematic way of viewing the Church and her maturity. To suggest that a council ushered in a new "season" of Church life is suggestive of a cyclical nature of death and rebirth in the Church, which is reminiscent of a pantheistic mentality.

It should be noted that the pope saw great significance in the coming of a new millennium as if there was some sort of spiritual key to

---

[74] Homily, May 31, 1998.
[75] Even the African situation is not an infallible sign of growth since Vatican II, as many African nations that were formerly majority Catholic have seen massive amounts of people leave for Protestant sects, which are growing exponentially in Africa. Also, it was ironically Archbishop Lefebvre who was arguably the most integral bishop in Africa and who laid the groundwork for the Church in Africa — at least in French-speaking Africa, which is the largest contingency of Catholics — which has fared better than the Church on other continents.

the changing of centuries. While I will not accuse John Paul II of the heresy of millenarianism — a heresy that ascribed different millennia of the Church to Persons of the Trinity (thousand-year periods for the Father, the Son, and the Holy Ghost) — this notion that the Holy Spirit ushered in great renewal through the Council that was becoming realized at the new millennium is troubling.

John Paul II also spoke of a "new Advent" in his encyclical letter *Redemptor Hominis* (1979): "We also are in a certain way in a season of a new Advent, a season of expectation" (1). In the same document, he called the Catholic Church "the Church of the new Advent" (20). What is the Church of the new Advent? Is it the "people of God," or the "Conciliar Church," or the "Mystical Body of Christ"? Of course, there can be no new Advent any more than there can be a New Incarnation, and taken at face value, that claim — without the benefit of the doubt or context — would be blasphemous. To suggest there is a "new Advent, a season of expectation" in the literal sense would mean that a new Christ was coming. Now, I do not believe the pope believed this in the literal sense, but the analogy is troubling if understood in the Modernist context that governs our times. And it is consistent with this unfettered obsession with "novelty" and "departure" that was incarnated through the "Spirit of Vatican II."

John Paul II was only following in the footsteps of Pope John XXIII, who prayed at the outset of the Council for a "new Pentecost." So, you see, with Vatican II, everything is "new," and everything is the "Spirit," and everything is "new in the Spirit," but nothing remotely resembling these calls for a rebirth or regrowth ever came true.

The Robber Council of Pistoia

If we return to the notion of departure, we must ask ourselves a question: How can we say that the Church departed from her previous location at Vatican II and now seeks a fullness of maturity in the growing tree of the Council without saying, at least implicitly, that the Church was *not* mature before the Council? Or perhaps the Church was mature, but she needed to be pruned down to her very roots to grow again because, over the centuries, she had accrued numerous accretions that hindered her ability to transmit the *true doctrine* first received from Christ. This pruning would mean going back to the "early Church" as a place of pure doctrine and essentially "starting fresh." If we were to agree with this notion, then we would be in danger of adhering to what Pius XII condemned in *Mediator Dei* (1947) — a document concerned with the problem of liturgical reform — when he wrote: "This way of acting bids fair to revive the exaggerated and senseless antiquarianism to which the illegal Council of Pistoia gave rise" (64). The Synod of Pistoia was a robber council, which is to say, a council that operated without permission from the pope and that sought to instantiate reforms and teachings that a number of liberal bishops desired. It was condemned by Pope Pius VI in 1794.

The synod was convened in 1786 in Pistoia, a city northwest of Florence. It was presided over by Bishop Scipio de Ricci, who was the bishop of Pistoia and Prato. An animating spirit of the synod was the Gallican movement, which sought to transfer much of the Holy See's authority to local bishops and national churches. Furthermore, Enlightenment rationalism and Jansenism — a heresy that downplayed the need for sacramental Confession and adopted Protestant mentalities about the nature of grace — were also instrumental in the spirit of the synod.

The synod sought extreme innovations in governance and desired massive changes in a variety of areas, including monastic discipline, sacramental theology, and liturgical rubrics. The participants in the synod sought to distinguish between "what is necessary or useful to retain the faithful in spirit, from that which is useless or too burdensome for the liberty of the sons of the New Covenant to endure."[76] In other words, they wanted to rid the Church of disciplines and rubrics

---

[76] Peter Kwasniewski, "Does Pius VI's 'Auctorem Fidei' Support Paul VI's Novus Ordo?," in Peter A. Kwasniewski, *The Road from Hyperpapalism to Catholicism* (Waterloo, Ontario: Arouca Press, 2022), 84.

that were not in keeping with the "liberty" of Christians; they wanted to simplify things and water them down. Does this sound familiar?

One author wrote on this subject, "The acts of Pistoia anticipate the thinking of the theologians of the *Nouvelle Théologie* responsible for the calamities that followed the Second Vatican Council." The synod was condemned by Pius VI's bull *Auctorem Fidei*, wherein he wrote that the acts of the synod were "confusing, destroying... utterly overturning [sound Christian doctrine] by introducing troublesome novelties under the guise of a sham reform."[77]

All sorts of analogies may be given to support the defense of all things Vatican II, especially that it represented a "going back to the sources" or a "pruning of dead wood" from the Church. Modernists and conciliar defenders may point to references in the Gospel wherein Christ speaks of pruning vines (John 15:2) or that a seed must die before it may bear fruit (John 12:25). The suggestion of the Modernist mentality, however, is not that Christ must die once and for all — which is the meaning of His discourse on the wheat seed dying in order to bear fruit — but that there must be *continual* death and rebirth of the Church! This notion is Cabalistic and pantheistic, as it presupposes continual cycles of death and renewal as a sign of the vitality of a spiritual organism; it is a cyclical birth and rebirth that comes and goes with the passing of time.

Again, the purpose here is not to comb through the documents of Vatican II and test the technicalities of the claims of the most dubious passages but, instead, to assess the spirit of the thing and test that spirit against that of Modernism. I think as we assess the claims of Pius X about Modernist reforms, there will be no doubt that whatever Vatican II may have taught — heretical or otherwise — it *cannot* be denied that the Modernist mentality was incarnated by and through the Council.

---

[77] Quoted in "Pius VI and the Synod of Pistoia," *Unam Sanctam Catholicam*, April 15, 2023, https://unamsanctamcatholicam.blogspot.com/2019/07/pius-vi-and-synod-of-pistoia.html.

Dogmatic Nature of Vatican II

Now, if we return to the direction envisioned for the Council by the popes, we will remember that Vatican II was meant not to define dogma, as John XXIII stated, and Paul VI was clear that modern "values" — philosophy — were at the heart of the Council, and, there was mention of continuous change, ecumenism, and so forth. Of course, the ambiguity, the call to ecumenism, the commitment to change, and the influence of modern philosophy all call to mind the whole Modernist enterprise, which we have discussed at length. So we are in no position to deny that Modernism was present in Vatican II. The question is: If that is so, what is the dogmatic nature of the Council? In other words, since it was a valid Council, does this mean Catholics must ascribe to Modernism to some degree? In order to answer this, we must consider the dogmatic nature of Vatican II.

While it is true that Vatican II defined no dogmas, it is also true that it contained many presentations of dogmas that had been defined in the past. On January 12, 1966, Pope St. Paul VI said in an audience: "Given the Council's pastoral character, it avoided pronouncing, in an extraordinary manner, dogmas endowed with the note of infallibility."

For this reason and others, Vatican II has been called pastoral, but this does not mean that doctrines are not expounded at various places therein. Where Vatican II speaks of the Trinity, for example, we understand that the dogma of the Trinity is a defined dogma, and therefore, there are dogmatic statements in the Council.

But there are novelties in the conciliar documents — this has been admitted by competent authorities — and Catholics are not required to assent to novel doctrinal statements that are unclear and even in contradiction to perennial Church teaching. In a practical sense, however, we *know* that since the Council, it has been the predominant opinion that not assenting to the whole of Vatican II is not only problematic but could even be "schismatic." Remember that Pope John Paul II used a troubling definition of Tradition from *Dei Verbum* when writing against Archbishop Lefebvre, and he believed a misunderstanding of this novelty was the *root of schism*.

It is not the case that questioning certain parts of Vatican II is impermissible, though. Archbishop Guido Pozzo, in his capacity with the *Ecclesia Dei* Commission which oversaw traditional orders such as the Priestly Fraternity of St. Peter and the Society of Saint Pius X, said about *Nostra Aetate*, the Vatican II document that speaks about other world religions: "*Nostra Aetate* does not have any dogmatic authority, and thus one cannot demand from anyone to recognize this declaration as being dogmatic."[78] This is but one example, but its purpose is to demonstrate that while it is true that Vatican II contains references to many doctrines — and those are surely binding on Catholics — it is also true that certain things are *not binding* when they represent undefined novelties or pastoral recommendations that are ambiguous.

Again, we recall John Paul II's assertion that Archbishop Lefebvre had entered a schismatic path because he alleged that Lefebvre did "not take sufficiently into account the living character of Tradition ... the Second Vatican Council clearly taught."[79] No new dogmas were defined at Vatican II — the Council where everything was "new" — yet Lefebvre, due to his supposed misunderstanding of something from Vatican II, had therefore entered into a schism due to that error. How is this possible? If Vatican II did not define anything new — which is what we are supposed to believe — then it stands to reason that if someone were simply to stick to all prior presentations of Church teaching, he would be fine.

---

[78] Maike Hickson, "Abp. Pozzo on SSPX: Disputed Vatican II Documents Are Non-Doctrinal," OnePeterFive, August 9, 2016, https://onepeterfive.com/abp-pozzo-on-sspx-disputed-vatican-ii-documents-are-non-doctrinal/.

[79] *Ecclesia Dei* 4.

How could it be possible that Lefebvre — or any other Catholic — could have an incomplete understanding of the so-called living Tradition if nothing new about that doctrine was defined? This would be like saying, "I have taught you nothing new definitively, but because you do not adhere to my teachings that are not definitive, you are not in accord with my definitive teachings."

If something were taught in a nondefinitive way about Tradition — or any doctrine — through the Council documents, this would be in the realm of nondefinitive teaching, and that would mean that a Catholic would not be bound to assent if he had grave reason to withhold such assent. At the very least, it would be impossible to say that someone could enter into a *schism* due to a dispute about a novel dogmatic formula that is *not binding or infallible*.

Also, if we are to take Archbishop Pozzo's statement at face value, then what interpretive key can we use to decide which documents of Vatican II are binding and which are not? Isn't the whole Council "pastoral" and buttressed by a commitment to modern philosophy?

The way doctrine is presented is no trivial matter. If we hearken back to the issue of nominalism that began largely with William of Ockham, we must admit that *words matter*, and it is not sufficient to say that a sentence or definition means something that it seemingly doesn't and to expect full assent to that presentation when it is problematic.

The Church has always taken great care to express her teachings in Councils very clearly and with great precision. Vatican II, however, is novel in this respect as the documents are presented without definitions or anathemas and in a verbose manner that lends itself to multiple interpretations. In some places, it is the *emphasis* that leads to confusion; in other places, it is the *absence* of qualifying distinctions or context that is problematic.

While one may *prefer* the way the teachings of the Church were presented in the Council, we *cannot* say that Catholics are *bound* to the conciliar presentation of a doctrine, unless what was presented was, in fact, a novel definition — that is, a new dogma.

Now, the Modernist spirit is at the heart of this because, due to its Hegelian influence, Modernism requires ideas and beliefs to be in conflict, as this facilitates the thesis-antithesis-synthesis method. Simply put, *confusion* is expected in Modernism because confusion leads to conflict. It is not a defect in Vatican II that they facilitate confusing interpretations or even warring interpretations; this is inherent in the Modernist system. Because Vatican II defined nothing, and because the various documents are of different dogmatic values — which the average Catholic will never understand or investigate — then we can expect never-ending debates and conversations about the "true meaning" of Vatican II, which will never be properly understood. This process results in continual change and piles confusion on top of confusion to the point where we all just lived through a *Synod on Synodality*, which was a series of meetings about meetings. This Modernist spirit has led us to a place of clownish absurdity, and the faithful are left more confused with each passing pontificate.

What Should We Believe?

Of course, this confusion about what we should or should not believe when it comes to Vatican II is profound; thus, it is helpful to consider what Catholics are required to believe when theological statements from the various organs of the Magisterium are disputed or doubtful.

Dr. John Joy, an expert theologian on the subject of disputed questions of dogmatic infallibility, writes:

> This religious submission of will and intellect, which is normally due to the teaching of the authentic magisterium, is a genuine interior assent of the mind, which has the character of opinion rather than knowledge, since the doctrine is to be accepted as true though with the awareness that it could possibly be false. This assent may legitimately be withheld in certain cases, although to do so merely on the basis of one's own private judgment would be rash and dangerous. However,

assent must be withheld when the teaching in question clearly conflicts with any irreformable doctrine of the Church, i.e., a doctrine that has been taught infallibly.[80]

It is worth adding that conscientious objectors to various ambiguities and novelties emanating from Vatican II are not doing so based on "private judgment." There are plenty of formidable and established theological minds in our day, such as Bishop Athanasius Schneider and the late Bishop Vitus Huonder, who have expressed their views about Vatican II in the proper way, knowing full well that they dissent from the mainstream interpretation that is common among churchmen. They do this by carefully presenting arguments based on prior presentations of Church teaching that seem to contrast with what has been taught in and since Vatican II in some instances. It is worth noting that Lefebvre acted similarly during his life, having submitted his disputes to Rome under the form of *dubia* and in numerous private meetings with popes and cardinals.

Again, it is not the intention to dissect a large selection of statements from Vatican II and evaluate whether they present positive errors or heresies rather than merely a Modernist spirit, but we would do well to consider one assertion from Vatican II that plainly seems to be an error. The conciliar document *Dignitatis Humanae* states: "This Vatican Council declares that the human person has a right to religious freedom. This freedom means that all men are to be immune from coercion on the part of individuals or of social groups and of any human power, in such wise that no one is to be forced to act in a manner contrary to his own beliefs, whether privately or publicly, whether alone or in association with others, within due limits" (20). The same document also states: "The freedom or immunity from coercion in matters religious which is the endowment of persons as individuals is also to be

---

[80] Dr. John Joy, S.T.D., "Disputed Questions on Papal Infallibility — Part 1," *OnePeterFive*, August 5, 2022, https://onepeterfive.com/disputed-questions-on-papal-infallibility-part-1/#_ftnref27.

recognized as their right when they act in community. Religious communities are entitled to teach and give witness to their faith publicly in speech and writing without hindrance" (4). And, this freedom is based on the "dignity of the human person" (3), which sounds all too personalist and phenomenological.

These are remarkable statements that, after our study of the doctrines of the Modernists, are in keeping with the Modernist penchant for ecumenism and an indifference to truth.

Notice that the document does not say "tolerance" but "freedom," and this freedom to practice *any religion you want* and even to practice it *publicly* and to *teach it* to others is called a "right." Call to mind earlier in the book when we considered the errors of William of Ockham and noted that he professed a belief that the Church and the State should be separated to the point where the State did not need to answer to the Church. This was an error because it presupposed that the State was not beholden to the authority of the Church, which is the arbiter of Truth. Also, remember that the vast corpus of the eighteenth- and nineteenth-century popes and Pius X taught solemnly *against* the religious liberty proposed in Vatican II. Explicitly, Pope Pius IX condemned the modern notion of religious liberty as a "right" numerous times in his *Syllabus of Errors*. He condemned the notion that every man is "free" to practice whatever religion he wants; he condemned the idea that Catholicism should not be the religion of the State; he condemned the proposition that believers of false religions should have the right to practice their religion publicly; and he condemned the notion that allowing the spreading of false religion could not harm society.[81]

---

[81] Pope Pius IX, *Syllabus of Errors*:

Proposition 15: "Every man is free to embrace and profess that religion which, guided by the light of reason, he shall consider true." (Condemned.)

Proposition 77: "In the present day it is no longer expedient that the Catholic religion should be held as the only religion of the State, to the exclusion of all other forms of worship." (Condemned.)

In at least two encyclicals, *Libertas Praestantissimum* and *Immortale Dei*, Pope Leo XIII reiterated the same teachings. In any event, the Vatican II document *Dignitatis Humanae* is plainly in contradiction to the perennial teaching of the Church, and only a fit of mental gymnastics can attempt to see it otherwise.

Commenting on this very issue, Bishop Athanasius Schneider stated:

> But how can this be? How is it possible that from the end of the eighteenth century until the mid-twentieth century, till the death of Pope Pius XII, so many popes were wrong? It would have been rather an exotic period in Church history. Well, yes, but what came before them? *When did the break with the previous teaching happen?* At what moment did this exotic element appear? Well, there is no such moment. It's impossible to point to another moment in history when a break similar to the one that happened on the issue of religious freedom during the Second Vatican Council would have occurred.... There is a strict continuity of teaching on the question of religious freedom, beginning with the Church Fathers of the third and fourth centuries after Christ and ending with Pius XII. We can speak here of a continuous development in the proper sense of the word.[82]

> Proposition 78: "Hence it has been wisely decided by law, in some Catholic countries, that persons coming to reside therein shall enjoy the public exercise of their own peculiar worship." (Condemned.)
>
> Proposition 79: "Moreover, it is false that the civil liberty of every form of worship, and the full power given to all of openly and publicly manifesting any and all of their ideas whatsoever by word of mouth, through the press, or in any other way, conduces more easily to corrupt the morals and minds of the people, and to propagate the pest of indifferentism." (Condemned.)

[82] Bishop Athanasius Schneider and Pawel Lisicki, *The Springtime That Never Came* (Manchester, NH: Sophia Institute Press, 2021), 4–47.

If we follow the perennial teachings of the Church, we cannot come to any other conclusion than the fact that Vatican II is in error on this topic, whatever justifications may be attempted by its proponents.

All of this is to say that the problem of Vatican II is far from simple, and Catholics have every right to question some of the teachings therein.

Although not exhaustive, these preliminary remarks on the Council should show that one can find issues in the Council and even reject some of its more obscure and even erroneous statements while in no way rejecting the teachings of the Church in the proper sense.

Lastly, we would do well to briefly consider various Constitutions from the Fourth Lateran Council (1215), a council that proclaimed many things infallibly, unlike Vatican II.

- "Lest too great a variety of religious orders leads to grave confusion in God's church, we strictly forbid anyone henceforth to found a new religious order."
- "All bishops should wear outer garments of linen in public and in church."
- "It sometimes happens that by mistake Christians join with Jewish or Saracen women, and Jews or Saracens with Christian women. In order that the offence of such a damnable mixing may not spread further, under the excuse of a mistake of this kind, we decree that such persons of either sex, in every christian province and at all times, are to be distinguished in public from other people by the character of their dress."

So, if we are to take the Constitutions of Lateran IV at face value and with no context given to the setting or the intention of the proclamations, then we might conclude that the Jesuits, Opus Dei, the Priestly Fraternity of St. Peter, and the Holy Ghost Fathers (Spiritans) are in contravention of an ecumenical council, given the fact that they are religious orders or societies of priests that emerged after 1215. Furthermore, if your local bishop does not wear outer garments of linen *in public*, let alone in a church, he is also in defiance of an ecumenical council. And any suggestion that Jews or Saracens (Muslims) should be able to dress like Gentiles is but another example of outright defiance of an ecumenical council.

Granted, these constitutions are disciplinary and not presented as matters of faith and morals. But that is exactly the point: not everything proclaimed in a council is infallible, especially when infallibility is not invoked, as it wasn't in Vatican II.

Clearly, even an ecumenical council can proclaim things in a given context and such proclamations are not binding under pain of sin in perpetuity; at the same time, there can be dogmatic pronouncements of a council that do bind in perpetuity. Given the fact that Vatican II was adamantly not concerned with definitions or proclamations or infallible definitions, we ought to give the benefit of the doubt to conscientious Catholics who object to ill-defined or expressed novelties in the Council that seemingly contradict or sharply contrast with previously defined doctrines.

15

The New Theology behind the New Springtime

The phenomenology and personalism adopted by John Paul II, Vatican II, and others is not the only revolution in Catholic thought that resulted from the adoption of modern philosophical principles. The New Theology, or *Nouvelle Théologie*, emerged in the twentieth century, and its proponents view it as the victorious school of thought at Vatican II. Bishop Robert Barron stated in a podcast that the "great texts of Vatican II ... represent the victory of the Nouvelle Théologie stream over the more conservative stream."[83] This is an astonishing admission, and Bishop Barron is nothing if not an intellectual heavyweight and, I believe, a sincere man who wants to do what is best for the Church. Nonetheless, this is a brazen statement, considering he made these remarks in the context of how the New Theology triumphed over the perennial — which he calls conservative — theology that preceded the Council. If true, then we cannot but view this as a sort of revolution or radical change in direction that took place at Vatican II, and since

---

[83] Bishop Robert Barron, "Understanding the Post–Vatican II Church," *Word on Fire Show*, October 7, 2019, https://www.youtube.com/watch?v=ZLy188DgyEI.

the crisis in the Church has only intensified since then, we must take an honest look at the roots of the New Theology to evaluate its effect properly.

The Reform of Philosophy

In paragraph 38 in *Pascendi* — which I have called a prophecy — where Pius X explains what Modernist reform would look like, he states that Modernist reform would lead to "reform of philosophy, especially in the seminaries: the scholastic philosophy is to be relegated to the history of philosophy among obsolete systems, and the young men are to be taught modern philosophy which alone is true and suited to the times in which we live."

Philosophy has been called the "handmaid of theology" due to the symbiotic relationship of philosophy and theology. Before any theological assertion can be made or proven, certain terms must be established that adequately reflect what is being expressed. It is for this reason that the Church has always concerned herself with the philosophical sciences. In fact, it was not always the case that theology and philosophy were seen as separate sciences. In older works, you will find theology referred to as "Christian philosophy," for example. This is because philosophy, concerned as it is with metaphysical principles, must ultimately concern itself with the question of God and divine things. If a philosopher is to engage in questions of morality, he cannot do so in earnest if he does not have a sound moral system or principles. In order to have sound moral principles, his principles must be grounded in something that offers the basis for such a system.

A philosopher cannot conclude that action X is moral and action Y is immoral if he does not hold to a standard that governs the morality of actions. So he must appeal to a metaphysical principle that is unchanging and by which he can judge the morality of actions in light of what he knows to be true about morality. The perennial philosophical tradition adopted by the Church did not make arbitrary distinctions between philosophy and theology, and God or divine realities permeated their works. Plato spoke of his Forms, Aristotle spoke of the Prime Mover, and Confucius spoke of Heaven. It should be noted that in antiquity there was a battle of ideas between the philosophers whose ideas were adopted by the Church and those who held antithetical ideas. In the dialogues of Socrates, for example, we can see the philosopher battling the Sophists, who espoused ideas similar to many of the trends common in modern philosophy, such as relativism and nominalism.

The Church Fathers took the best of what learned men had to offer in antiquity and baptized any pre-Christian idea that could be used as a help for theological science. Augustine used platonic language masterfully in his *Confessions* and *The City of God* to express the reasonableness of Christianity, for example. Clear and precise philosophical language was paramount in the Church's battles with heresies as she understood that the Devil really is *in the details* and thus a surgical use of language and terms was necessary to avoid the proliferation of errors, even if they seemed small. Over time, the theologians and scholars of the Church refined and perfected their use of philosophical terms in theology, culminating with the philosophical and theological school that is called Scholastic. The most revered and praised Scholastic Doctor is, of course, Thomas Aquinas.

It is often overlooked that theology is a *science*, and therefore, like any science, some methods are more or less reliable or infallible and can be utilized. For the Modernist, however, theology is based on the principles of agnosticism, evolutionism, and vital immanence; therefore, Modernist theologizing is an exercise of continually groping for truth in the darkness of religious ineffability.

Since Modernists begin with doubt and experience, theology for them can never really be *scientific*. When something is truly a science, we can expect that an infallible *method* will be discovered or refined. In mathematics, we know that certain ways of doing arithmetic will *always* work, assuming we do the calculations properly. This is why the Church has heralded on numerous occasions the method of Thomas Aquinas, or Scholasticism. Sure, a Thomist could be wrong, as a mathematician could be wrong, but the method is not in error. Furthermore, if anything is a science, there will come a point when no improvement in method is possible. We will never figure out a better way of doing arithmetical equations than by following the order of operations. In a similar way, we have been gifted with Scholasticism, which provides a sure, trustworthy tool for discerning philosophical and theological truths. We should rejoice in this, as it is a sign that God has guided the Church into all truth, and we can trust her saints and theologians.

St. Thomas used the Scholastic method and took the accumulated wisdom of Aristotle, Plato, and Augustine and other Church Fathers and purified the wisdom of antiquity. Leo XIII's 1879 encyclical on the restoration of Christian philosophy, *Aeterni Patris*, proclaims: "Among the Scholastic Doctors, the chief and master of all towers Thomas Aquinas, who, as Cajetan observes, because 'he most venerated the ancient doctors of the Church, in a certain way seems to have inherited the intellect of all'" (17). In this way, Leo XIII suggests that Thomas Aquinas demonstrates a grasp and understanding of philosophy and theology that is unmatched. He adds:

> The doctrines of those illustrious men, like the scattered members of a body, Thomas collected together and cemented, distributed in wonderful order, and so increased with important additions that he is rightly and deservedly esteemed the special bulwark and glory of the Catholic faith. With his spirit at once humble and swift, his memory ready and tenacious, his life spotless throughout, a lover of truth for its own sake, richly endowed with human and divine science, like the sun he heated the world with the warmth of his virtues and filled it with the splendor of his teaching. Philosophy has no part which he did not touch finely at once and thoroughly; on the laws of reasoning, on God and incorporeal substances, on man and other sensible things, on human actions and their principles, he reasoned in such a manner that in him there is wanting neither

a full array of questions, nor an apt disposal of the various parts, nor the best method of proceeding, nor soundness of principles or strength of argument, nor clearness and elegance of style, nor a facility for explaining what is abstruse. (17)

This is but a small selection of the praise that Leo XIII heaped on Aquinas, and Pope Leo was hardly the first pope to do so. In the same encyclical, Leo references the praise that numerous other popes have expressed for St. Thomas and the fact that Thomism was the theological and philosophical basis for the teachings of many important ecumenical councils:

> The ecumenical councils, also, where blossoms the flower of all earthly wisdom, have always been careful to hold Thomas Aquinas in singular honor. In the Councils of Lyons, Vienna, Florence, and the Vatican one might almost say that Thomas took part and presided over the deliberations and decrees of the Fathers, contending against the errors of the Greeks, of heretics and rationalists, with invincible force and with the happiest results. But the chief and special glory of Thomas, one which he has shared with none of the Catholic Doctors, is that the Fathers of Trent made it part of the order of conclave to lay upon the altar, together with sacred Scripture and the decrees of the supreme Pontiffs, the Summa of Thomas Aquinas, whence to seek counsel, reason, and inspiration. (22)

It is hard to imagine greater praise being heaped on a theologian. While we would not say that Thomas is infallible, or that there is "no salvation outside Thomism," we *cannot* say that Thomism has not been deemed indispensable for a variety of reasons by some of the greatest popes and councils in the history of the Church. Simply put, St. Thomas was a gift from God, and there is hardly a theologian in Church history who has been so vital in the intellectual life of the Church. This is to take nothing away from the great theologians who came before Thomas, as Thomas himself only purified and magnified the truth of their teachings all the more.

Modernism abhors Thomas Aquinas and Scholasticism in general, mainly because with Thomas and Scholasticism there is no "wiggle room." Something is either true or false, clear or unclear, and the subjectivism of Modernist theology and Modern philosophy cannot survive in the atmosphere of unrelenting exactitude of Thomism.

For this reason, Pius X wrote of the Modernists: "For scholastic philosophy and theology they have only ridicule and contempt. Whether it is ignorance or fear, or both, that inspires this conduct in them, certain it is that the passion for novelty is always united in them with hatred of scholasticism, and there is *no surer sign that a man is on the way to Modernism than when he begins to show his dislike for this system*" (42, emphasis added).

Buttressing his claim, Pius X referenced a proposition common to modern thought that was condemned by Pius IX in the *Syllabus of Errors*. The following assertion was condemned: "The method and principles which have served the doctors of scholasticism when treating theology no longer correspond with the exigencies of our time or the progress of science" (13).

While Pius IX was writing against Liberalism, Pius X saw fit to repeat the same condemnation in his work on Modernism; this makes sense because Modernism is the synthesis of all heresies and would thus have a liberal element. Also inherent in the condemned statement is the notion that knowledge is in a constant state of progress — evolution — which is a foundational principle of Modernism.

Furthermore, Pius X *reaffirmed* Leo XIII's insistence in *Aeterni Patris* that Thomism be the theological North Star of the Church, adding:

> We will and ordain that scholastic philosophy be made the basis of the sacred sciences.... And let it be clearly understood above all things that the scholastic philosophy We prescribe is that which the Angelic Doctor has bequeathed to us, and We,

therefore, declare that all the ordinances of Our Predecessor on this subject continue fully in force, and, as far as may be necessary, We do decree anew, and confirm, and ordain that they be by all strictly observed. In seminaries where they may have been neglected let the Bishops impose them and require their observance, and let this apply also to the Superiors of religious institutions. Further let Professors remember that they *cannot set St. Thomas aside, especially in metaphysical questions, without grave detriment.* (*Pascendi* 45, emphasis added)

Assessing Ratzinger's Early Work in Light of Pius X's Warnings

Unfortunately, the express will of the popes that Aquinas be at the center of priestly formation seemed to fall out of fashion, and this had an impact on even the brightest minds, such as a young Joseph Ratzinger. There are various opinions about why this happened, but I think the strongest opinion has to do with the massive societal changes that took place because of the two World Wars and the rise of totalitarian systems in the twentieth century. Communism took hold in a huge portion of the world, including a number of nations that were majority Catholic. This made traditional seminary formation difficult, given the fact that Catholic institutions were either suppressed or heavily surveilled, and, of course, communists don't appreciate perennial Catholic thought.

Also, even in nations that did not become communist, such as most of western Europe, the devastation from the wars ushered in expansive changes to social institutions. Public education, which was not Catholic, became the norm, and with it came all the trappings of Modernity, including modern philosophy. Furthermore, there was a heavy insistence on the primacy of the natural sciences because the mechanization of war redirected untold resources into the development of technology. This created an atmosphere that heralded materialism and modern thought, and combined with the fact that the

Church herself lost so many good men and priests due to the carnage, the effect of what happened cannot be quantified. Therefore, given how this happened, we ought to extend a little understanding and acknowledge that it was hardly the fault of the youth who inherited the situation. Nonetheless, it did happen, and the young men who entered the priesthood were often malformed in philosophy, or at least formed without the necessary bulwark to protect their minds from the traps set before them.

Although it has already been said in this book that Ratzinger had many virtues and that he was always known to be kind and sincerely pious, this is still worth repeating. Furthermore, the reason I have chosen to show that Modernism seemingly influenced Ratzinger is that it is vital to show that the plague of Modernism has affected not only obvious liberals and dissidents. Surely it would be far easier to sift through the works of the worst offenders and prove that Modernism is present in their thinking, but what would this prove other than the fact that obvious dissidents are dissidents?

For example, we could go through the works of infamous priests and theologians of our day — perhaps many come to mind — and easily show how bad their statements are. But this would do no more than provide a catalogue of the errors uttered by certain priests whom no one expects to be orthodox. It is arguably more vital to show that even in the works of priests who are seemingly unaffected by heretical trends, there may be things to worry about. This is paramount because the doctrinal and liturgical crisis in the Church is so vast that we must come to terms with the fact that Modernism is *everywhere*, even in areas we might least expect.

In any event, consider the aforementioned words of great popes on the centrality and necessity of Aquinas with the sentiments of a young Joseph Ratzinger. He shared the following with his biographer Peter Seewald when speaking about his attitude at the time of the Council: "[I was] of the opinion that scholastic theology, as it had been firmly settled, is no longer a means fit to bring the faith into the language of the time."[84] Contrast this statement with the statement of St. Pius that I included at the outset of this section when explaining how Modernists view Scholasticism: "The scholastic philosophy is to be relegated to the history of philosophy among obsolete systems, and the young men are to be taught modern philosophy which alone is true and suited to the times in which we live."

In another place, Ratzinger said:

> Well, I didn't want to operate only in a stagnant and closed philosophy, but in a philosophy understood as a question — what is man, really? — and particularly to enter into the new, contemporary philosophy. In this sense I was modern and critical. Reading Steinbüchel was very important to me, because he ... gave a comprehensive overview of contemporary philosophy which I sought to understand and *inhabit*. Unfortunately, I could not go as deeply into philosophy as I wanted, but just as I had my questions, my doubts, and didn't simply want to learn and take on a closed system, I also wanted to understand the theological thinkers of the Middle Ages and modernity *anew* and proceed from this. This is where personalism, which was in the air at the time, particularly struck me, and seemed to be the right starting point of both philosophical and theological thought.[85] (emphasis added)

The young Ratzinger, as hyperintelligent as he may have been, was clearly enamored of modern philosophy, which, as has been clear in

---

[84] Translated from the original German by journalist Dr. Maike Hickson, quoted in her article "The Great Influence of Joseph Ratzinger in the Revolutionary Upheaval of the Second Vatican Council," first published at *Rorate Caeli* in December 2020, https://rorate-caeli.blogspot.com/2020/12/rorate-exclusivenew-biography-describes.html?m=1.

[85] Pope Benedict and Peter Seewald, *Last Testament: In His Own Words* trans. Jacob Phillips (London: Bloomsbury Continuum, 2016), 75–76.

this book, is the unholy offspring of the subjectivist, nominalist, and agnostic thinkers of the Enlightenment period.

In Ratzinger's own words, we find a theologian who wanted everything to do with modern philosophy and who seemed to have imbibed the trend that it was time to move on from Scholasticism. And what he did understand of the different schools (which he says was not much, although he was likely being humble)? He wanted to understand them "anew" and proceed with novelty.

In his 1997 autobiography, *Milestones: Memoirs 1927–1977*, Ratzinger expresses why he has seemingly soured on Thomism and Scholasticism. After expressing his love for Augustine and Jewish philosopher Martin Buber, Ratzinger writes: "By contrast, I had difficulties in penetrating the thought of Thomas Aquinas, whose crystal-clear logic seemed to be too closed in on itself, too impersonal and ready-made."[86]

Do Ratzinger's sentiments about Scholasticism not match Pius's distillation of the Modernist anti-Scholasticism perfectly?

To be fair to Ratzinger, the fact that he disliked Thomas and Scholasticism as a young priest does *not* mean he was necessarily a Modernist for that fact alone, and some have opined that an uninspired neo-Scholasticism that was common before the Council was to be blamed. At the time of Vatican II, there was a trend in theology that more or less reduced Thomism to a series of manuals and rote knowledge. Now, there is nothing wrong with a theological manual, but when students are required to memorize Thomas Aquinas without learning to think like him, the purpose of Scholasticism has been missed. Archbishop Lefebvre, who could not have heralded Thomas Aquinas any more than he did, lamented the downturn in how Thomism was taught. Nonetheless, a watered-down or uninspiring Thomistic milieu does

---

[86] Joseph Ratzinger, *Milestones: Memoirs 1927–1977* (San Francisco: Ignatius Press, 2010), 44, quoted in "The Memories of a Destructive Mind: Part 1" first published in *Si Si No No*, no. 31 (March 1999), https://www.sspxasia.com/Documents/SiSiNoNo/1999_March/The_Memories_of_a_Destructive_Mind.htm.

not justify a rejection of Thomas or of Scholastic thought. This would be like saying, "Because priests have been saying the Latin Mass in an uninspired way and because the faithful don't really understand what is going on, we must move on from this and discover something new." And that is exactly what happened in the realm of liturgy, and we are still suffering the consequences. The response to a crisis in Thomism, as we will see when we consider the end of Pius X's encyclical, is a return to *true Thomism*, which inspired so many popes and councils.

In any event, a rejection of the "crystal-clear logic" of Thomas is troublesome, especially given the perennial adulation given to him by the great popes before the Council. Ratzinger was far from unintelligent, and it is regrettable that he did not demonstrate the same zeal for Scholasticism that he did for modern philosophy. We can only speculate, but with an intellect like his, Ratzinger could have been a leader in Thomistic thought, and that would have been invaluable to the Church.

In any event, it is recorded in Seewald's biography of Raztinger that one of Ratzinger's professors considered "the young theologian to be a Modernist."[87] Now, some believe that this accusation was unfair and that the professor demonstrated an animus toward Ratzinger. This may be true, but given what we have seen from the young Ratzinger when evaluated in the light of *Pascendi*, we cannot disregard the assertion.

Two Ratzingers?

Some may object and suggest that there are "two Ratzingers," which is to say, a young, theologically immature Ratzinger and an older, wiser Pope Benedict. I do not doubt that Ratzinger leaned more toward the conservative side of the aisle with age and that he did a great thing by liberating the Traditional Latin Mass. Of course, this was very positive for so many, and as more and more Catholics have come into contact with the Old Mass, their spiritual lives have been greatly enriched. It

---

[87] Quoted in Hickson, "Great Influence."

must also be acknowledged that Ratzinger himself *rejected* the notion that he went from progressive to conservative. When asked if he had any regrets about his association with notably Modernist theologians such as Karl Rahner and Hans Küng during the 1960s, he stated: "Absolutely not. I did not change; they changed."[88]

Küng and Rahner were true liberals or Modernists, and Küng was officially disciplined by Pope John Paul II in 1979. In their earlier years they were associated with a young Joseph Ratzinger, but due to theological differences, Ratzinger stopped his official association with them, and Küng especially expressed vehement dissatisfaction with Ratzinger. We could say that the likes of Küng and Rahner went deeper into the Modernist pit, but this does not change the fact that young Ratzinger and his — at one time — like-minded colleagues had already demonstrated that novel theological tendencies had influenced them. They were all part of the Concilium theological association, founded in 1965, but eventually Ratzinger resigned from the group, along with other theologians, such as Henri de Lubac, and started the Communio theological association in 1972. The theologians from both groups were influential during Vatican II. Two of Ratzinger's confreres, influential conciliar theologians Yves Congar and Henri de Lubac were "under the suspicion of heresy" on the eve of the Council.[89] It is fascinating, or maybe alarming, that so many involved with both groups were at one point suspected of heresy. I, for one, would be troubled if a significant number of my professional confreres had been flagged for heretical tendencies.

As has been noted in this book, Ratzinger is indicative of the zeitgeist that gripped the Church during and after the Council, and he is

---

[88] Quoted in Oliver Putz, "I Did Not Change; They Did! Joseph Ratzinger, Karl Rahner and the Second Vatican Council," Academia, accessed January 15, 2025, , https://www.academia.edu/470398/_I_did_not_change_they_did_Joseph_Ratzinger_Karl_Rahner_and_the_Second_Vatican_Council.

[89] Quoted in Hickson, "Great Influence."

hardly the only example. He was a darling of the progressive school of theologians and was heartily promoted by the German bishops as a rising star of philosophy. He was, by his own admission, not a Thomist or a Scholastic. And in our day, he is regarded as one of the more *conservative* theologians of the conciliar non-Thomistic movement.

He is not an isolated case but signifies a trend of progressive — dare I say, Modernist — theologians who have exercised a great influence on the Church since the Council.

Ratzinger was a first-rate intellectual in the sense that he possessed great intellectual powers and was prolific in his publications, and no one can deny that, throughout his writings, there are numerous passages of genius, especially when he writes on music and aesthetics. But when we consider the corpus of his work, we can note a distinct lack of clarity and Scholastic thought, and along with solid Catholic insight, we can find passages that reveal why he would have been suspected of Modernism.

The young Ratzinger demonstrated all the characteristics of the Modernist aversion to Scholasticism, which Pius X warned of in no uncertain terms, and his career as the head of the Congregation of the Doctrine of the Faith (CDF) and as pope seem to demonstrate in him that modern philosophical tendency always to question, always to seek to redefine, always to find "new ways" to speak the truth to the world in the language of the world. As one bishop wrote, Ratzinger "seems to have suffered the malady of all those philosophers who, elevating becoming above being, unceasing doubt above certitude, the quest above possession,"[90] thereby demonstrate the tendencies of evolution (becoming), agnosticism (doubt), and immanence (the continual spiritual quest).

---

[90] Bishop Bernard Tissier de Mallerais, "Faith Imperiled by Reason: Benedict XVI's Hermeneutics," trans. C. Wilson from *La Sel de Terre* 69 (Summer 2009), https://www.sspxasia.com/Countries/Philippines/OLVC/Articles/Faith-Imperiled-by-Reason.pdf.

Amazingly, Ratzinger was considered an arch-liberal by traditionalists before he became pope. One of the greatest books written on Vatican II and the conciliar era, *The Great Facade*, by Christopher Ferrara and Thomas Woods, picks apart numerous statements by Ratzinger when he was head of the CDF. The first edition of the book was published in 2002, with a second edition published in 2015 after Pope Benedict's papacy had come to an end and after he had done much good for Tradition. In a chapter devoted to Ratzinger's document *Dominus Iesus*, which was heralded by the Catholic mainstream as a "new *Syllabus*" — an allusion to Pius IX's *Syllabus of Errors* — Ferrara and Woods wrote:

> Is DI [*Dominus Iesus*] a roadmap out of the postconciliar crisis? Is it, like the *Syllabus*, a major corrective measure that will shore up Catholic orthodoxy in a time of peril to the Faith? Unfortunately, the suggestion that DI is a new *Syllabus* does not correspond to reality.... It is none other than DI's principal author, Cardinal Ratzinger, who has assured us that "there can be no return to the *Syllabus*" and that the documents of Vatican II are a "countersyllabus," whose aim is to attempt "an official reconciliation" with an era whose institutions are now founded on the very errors the *Syllabus* condemns.[91]

What a difference in tone a couple of decades makes when we consider how Ratzinger is perceived. It was common traditionalist thought just twenty years ago that Cardinal Ratzinger was a liberal, if not a Modernist, and that he sought to formalize the very heresies and errors condemned by preconciliar popes!

At the outset of the second edition, noting the seeming tectonic shift from Cardinal Ratzinger the liberal and Modernist to Pope Benedict XVI, the pope who liberated the Latin Mass and became the darling

---

[91] Christopher Ferrara and Thomas Woods, *The Great Facade: The Regime of Novelty in the Catholic Church from Vatican II to the Francis Revolution* (Brooklyn, NY: Angelico Press, 2015), 252.

of conservatives, Ferrara noted the shift that took place under Benedict, most notably with his liberation of the Traditional Mass in 2007. He said: "With *Summorum* [the document that was published with the liberation of the Latin Mass] and a few other acts of papal governance, Benedict XVI would favourably alter the ecclesial landscape in a way traditionalists could only have dreamed of.... The hallmark of what can now be called the Benedictine Respite was Benedict's valiant attempt to loosen the grip of the postconciliar regime of novelty."[92]

Now, I agree with Ferrara that, under Benedict, there was a type of "respite," as he calls it, but the fact that it was a respite and not a restoration is further evidence that the rot that festered in the Church since the Council — much of that time with Ratzinger in high positions — was too deep.

In any event, Ratzinger's habit of never-ending questioning and searching seemed to lead him closer to the traditional thought of the Church as he aged, but his legacy of progressive and Modernist thought has been significant. Not only was he influential during the Council, but from 1982 to 2013, he was first the leading theologian in the Church under John Paul II and then the pope himself. Numerous priests and theologians have been formed with a strong Ratzingerian influence, and that influence was from an admittedly non-Scholastic place.

Though Ratzinger uttered numerous genius statements, his work is also filled with utterances that would have been condemned in the preconciliar era or at least put under heavy suspicion by orthodox prelates. This sort of thing is to be expected if we consider that Pius X warned that where the influence of Modernism takes root, "in their books you find some things which might well be expressed by a Catholic, but in the next page you find other things which might have been dictated by a rationalist" (*Pascendi* 18).

Many believe that Ratzinger is a saint, and given the fact that every conciliar pope has been or is in the process of being canonized, I

---

[92] Ferrara and Woods, *Great Facade*, 306.

expect he will be as well. Whatever his personal holiness or piety may have been — and I do not opine on that here — we cannot ignore that Pius X's warning about Modernist reform of philosophy and theology was largely unheeded during Ratzinger's tenure, even if he did some objectively good things during his pontificate.

It should be noted that in this consideration of what happens when Scholasticism is ignored or rejected, typified by Ratzinger's work, we haven't even touched on the plethora of outright liberal theologians who have held high offices in the Church since the Council and the many who were chairs of Catholic universities and seminaries. If Ratzinger rejected Scholasticism and was still conservative to some degree, what can be said about the majority of clerics who were formed in a distinctly non-Scholastic manner and were outright liberals?

While there may be pockets of Scholastic revival here and there, I think we can all agree that the Scholastic method — heralded as *necessary* by so many popes — has been largely ignored or forgotten. If Ratzinger-Benedict is the closest thing we have to a traditionalist hero since Vatican II, we should not, therefore, expect anything other than an almost complete takeover by Modernist philosophical and theological principles from root to fruit, even among conservatives.

Nouvelle Théologie Condemned

The late great Catholic writer John Vennari wrote an article that first appeared in 1998 called "A Short Catechism on the New Theology."[93] In it, Vennari showed that the New Theology was seen almost unanimously before the Council as suspect and even outright heretical. He wrote, "Because it was recognized as resurgent modernism, it was kept under a lid by the Vatican and was condemned by Pope

---

[93] Vennari's article first appeared in *Catholic Family News* but has since been republished in numerous places online. For this book, I have used the electronic version of his article, accessed at Catholic Apologetics Information, http://www.catholicapologetics.info/modernproblems/modernism/newtheo.htm.

Pius XII in *Humani Generis*." Presenting a study of the document *Humani Generis* would require another book as long as this one, but as providence would have it, we do not have to comb through Pius XII's work in great length to find out what he thinks about the New Theology. On September 17, 1946, Pope Pius XII spoke to the electors of the Society of Jesus at their General Congregation called to elect a new superior general. In his address, he spoke of his concerns about trends in modern thought that had infiltrated the Jesuits, who had been the guardians of orthodoxy for so many centuries. Among other things, he told them:

> That which is immutable, let no one disturb it or change it. Much has been said, but not enough after due consideration, about the *"Nouvelle Théologie"*, which, because of its characteristic of moving along with everything in a state of perpetual motion, will always be on the road to somewhere but will never arrive anywhere. If one thought that one had to agree with an idea like that, what would become of Catholic dogmas, which must never change? What would happen to the unity and stability of faith?[94]

Fr. David Greenstock, a prolific and highly respected Thomist of the preconciliar era, wrote of the New Theology: "The main contention of the partisans of this new movement is that theology, to remain alive, must move with the times ... [and that] ... traditional theology is out of touch with reality."[95]

---

[94] Pope Pius XII's Address to the Jesuits (September 17, 1946), https://rorate-caeli.blogspot.com/2014/02/let-what-is-certain-and-firm-be.html.

[95] David L. Greenstock, "Thomism and the New Theology," *Thomist* 13 (1950), Internet Archive, https://archive.org/stream/ThomismAndTheNewTheologyGreenstock/Thomism%20and%20the%20New%20Theology%20%28Greenstock%29_djvu.txt, quoted in Vennari, "A Short Catechism on the New Theology."

Greenstock showed that at the heart of the New Theology is a mentality that is utterly unhistorical:

> According to such teachers traditional theology, with its foundations in Aristotelianism, has lost during the centuries which followed St. Thomas, a mass of notions, ideas, and even methods of expounding the faith which were well known to the Fathers of the Church, some of which have been taken over by the leaders of contemporary non-Catholic thought. Such ideas and methods must be recovered if any approach is to be made to the modern world, and they must be incorporated into theology, even if that means rejecting Aristotelianism or even Thomism as we understand it today.[96]

The assertion here is that the progenitors of the New Theology held the opinion that "true Thomism" has been lost and that, with a fanatical adherence to a narrow school of thought, the Church's theologians have ignored the great richness of Catholic thought that is found in the Fathers. And, because of this, the Church cannot relate to "modern man," who understands things better with modern philosophy.

Well, that is quite the assertion, isn't it?

All of those popes and councils who exalted Thomas and the Scholastic method were, according to the New Theologians, woefully ignorant of a massive profundity of Catholic thought, somehow lost to history. And it is, of course, up to the New Theologians to discover this thought *anew* for us and to synthesize it with modern philosophy. What an indictment of the greatest saints and Scholastics and popes!

Listen to how Fr. Greenstock describes the New Theology's approach to Divine Revelation:

> When God speaks to man and communicates to him divine mysteries it is the fact which is revealed, and *not the logical*

---

[96] Greenstock, "Thomism and the New Theology."

proposition in which that fact is presented to us. Consequently, very different philosophical systems can and indeed should be used to express that divine revelation and to explain it to the people for whom it is intended, who are *not all theologians by any means*. The supernatural virtue of faith which is given to us by God in order that we may believe the truths which He has revealed is essentially a vital thing, part, that is to say, of our lives, and as such it can not be separated from the age in which we live. Only in a very secondary way is it concerned with those formal propositions under whose form the faith is presented to us. *Faith will thus give birth to theology*, because the truths of faith are expressed in words and concepts taken from philosophical systems, but since those philosophies will naturally tend to evolve according to the needs of the times it follows that theology too will be in a *state of constant evolution*. However, the real progress in the development of revealed truth is to be found, not in the use of philosophical terms or logical propositions and reasonings, but in an *ever-growing penetration into the truths of faith by a deeper and more vital Christian life*. Since the life of the individual as a Christian and a member of the Mystical Body can not be separated from the age in which he lives, it will be natural and even necessary to adopt the terms and the concepts familiar to modern thought in order to express the truths of faith in such a way that they will be intelligible and attractive to those outside the true Church who are *groping their way* towards the knowledge and the love of God. (emphasis added)[97]

Simply put, this is nothing more than the Modernism condemned by Pius X that has been discussed in this book. As an aside, the New Theologians are also comedians if they believe that the New Theology

---

[97] Greenstock, "Thomism and the New Theology."

is for those who "are not all theologians," because the only people who could understand this are theologians.

For the New Theology, the assertions in the Bible are not logical; theology is the result of a faith experience; theology will therefore be in a constant state of evolution; believers and theologians will understand religion more deeply as they live their religion more vitally and grope toward the truth. At what point, one might ask the New Theologians, can we say that enough groping has taken place before we find the truth? Perhaps the New Theologians should stop groping in the dark and instead live in the light of the mountain of theological brilliance that the greatest minds in history have given us.

Furthermore, this mentality makes it seem as if true faith is "earned" after years of searching, which is out of step with the fact that some of the greatest saints in history have been very young or even children. St. Dominic Savio, who famously uttered, "Death, but not sin!" was merely a child, yet he demonstrated *heroic* sanctity. Did he somehow skip the process of groping around for an evolving faith inspired by the methods of modern academics? What about St. Lucy, who died around the age of twenty almost seventeen hundred years ago? Did she also fast-track her arduous search for true faith just in time to be martyred? In fact, little pious children often have the simplest and most unshakeable faith, and they are never disciples of the New Theology.

In any event, the New Theology has always been a theology for academics. Fr. Réginald Garrigou-Lagrange — arguably the greatest Thomist, if not theologian, of the twentieth century — encapsulated this problem in his devastating takedown of the New Theology, called "Where Is the New Theology Leading Us?" He wrote:

> Moreover, no new definition of truth is offered in the new definition of theology: "*Theology is no more than a spirituality or religious experience which found its intellectual expression.*" And so follow assertions such as: "If theology can help us to understand spirituality, spirituality will, in the best of cases,

cause our theological categories to burst, and we shall be obliged to formulate different types of theology.... For each great spirituality corresponded to a great theology." Does this mean that two theologies can be true, even if their main theses are contradictory and opposite? The answer will be no if one keeps to the traditional definition of truth. The answer will be yes if one adopts the new definition of truth, conceived not in relation to being and to immutable laws, but relative to different religious experiences. *These definitions seek only to reconcile us to Modernism.*[98]

Garrigou-Lagrange, a man whose intellect towers above the minions of the "new springtime" like a tree over a sapling, sees in the New Theology nothing more than Modernism.

In the same article, he references several positions *condemned* by the Holy Office in 1924, one of them reminiscent of something one might expect of any postconciliar theologian: "Even after Faith has been received, *man ought not to rest in the dogmas of religion, and hold fast to them fixedly and immovably,* but always solicitous to remain moving ahead toward a deeper truth and even *evolving into new notions,* and even correcting that which he believes."[99] Consider this condemnation in light of Ratzinger's mentality from his younger years as a priest: "[I was] of the opinion that scholastic theology, as it had been firmly settled, is no longer a means fit to bring the faith into the language of the time." And: "Well, I didn't want to operate only in a stagnant and closed philosophy, but in a philosophy understood as a — what is

---

[98] Fr. Réginald Garrigou-Lagrange, O.P, "Where Is the New Theology Leading Us?" trans. Suzanne M. Rini, *Catholic Family News*, August 1988. The article first appeared in the prestigious Roman theological journal *Angelicum* in 1946. A PDF copy is available online at https://www.scribd.com/document/353425559/Where-is-the-New-Theology-Leading-Us-Garrigou-Lagrange-Reginald-O-P.

[99] Garrigou-Lagrange, "Where Is the New Theology Leading Us?"

man, really? — and particularly to enter into the new, contemporary philosophy." Not resting in a "stagnant" system but continually questioning with a theology that has evolved with the ever-changing needs of "modernity."

Garrigou-Lagrange also mentions a note from a French professor of theology who warned that the New Theology was "modernism in thought as in action."[100] Another colleague of Garrigou-Lagrange told him: "Those who have attempted to attend the classes of the masters of modernist thought in order to convert them have allowed themselves to be converted by them. Little by little, they come to accept their ideas, their methods, their disdain of scholasticism, their historicism, their idealism and all of their errors."[101]

The great French Thomist warned that if the principles of the New Theology, which he viewed as distinctly Modernist, were accepted and promoted, disaster would follow, especially with regard to the doctrines of Original Sin and the Eucharist. I do not think it necessary to prove these predictions true with citations, as I am sure the reader knows full well that most baptized Catholics hardly concern themselves with baptizing their children for reasons of salvation but, rather, because it is a way of entering into the "community of faith"; and one need not do any research to know that the average Catholic — if he does attend Mass — has little or no belief in the Real Presence of Christ in the Eucharist.

Before we transition to a discussion on the philosophical and theological undergirding of the New Theology, I admit that many who have an affinity for the work of theologians associated with the approach will likely be scratching their heads. This historical sketch of how the New Theology began will probably not match their experience, and this is true. But herein lies the crux of the matter; the New Theology has *evolved*, and today, when we think of scholars associated with it, we

---

[100] Garrigou-Lagrange, "Where Is the New Theology Leading Us?"
[101] Garrigou-Lagrange, "Where Is the New Theology Leading Us?"

think of men such as Bishop Barron, who are clearly on the conservative side of things and who often speak of Thomas Aquinas with great eloquence. But it is this evolution in the New Theology that is at the heart of the matter — namely, that its proponents can change their approach with the winds of change itself. In the early period, it was fashionable in academia to be an outright liberal, but since anyone with half a brain can see that this has been an utter disaster in the Church, we now find adherents of the New Theology edging to the "right" of the spectrum. Also — and this is only anecdotal, so take it for what it is worth — I have found that it is difficult to have a concrete and defined conversation with its proponents. For example, I can present the information heretofore presented, which undoubtedly shows that the New Theology started as a reintroduction of Modernism, but the New Theologian can say, "Yes, but that is because it is misunderstood by its critics." The same can be said by adherents to all forms of theology imbued with modern philosophy because they all rely heavily on the subjective.

Granted, we can at times parody a set of beliefs that we do not agree with, and I hope I have not done that here, but, objectively speaking, the New Theology started as a version of Modernism. Ironically, given the subjective nature of Modernism, this gives New Theology disciples the leeway to suggest that critics don't "understand what it really means," and this is another way of saying, "We New Theologians get it, and you don't." This, again, is indicative of its subjectivity, which permits redefinition and a "moving of the goalposts."

With Thomism, or any Scholastic approach, while we may abuse the method or use it poorly, it is hard to skirt the issue; Thomas means what he means, and his words are surgical and unambiguous. This is not so with the modern methods, and this is at the heart of the issue.

Furthermore, the perennial philosophy of the Church is as ancient as the Church herself, whereas the New Theology is *new*. In historical terms, Scholasticism is an organic outgrowth of something that began centuries ago and was distilled carefully as theologians surgically defined dogmas in continuity with the past; the New Theology began yesterday, and its proponents seem to desire to be "understood." Respectfully, they do not have that right, as like the modern revolutionary does not have the same rights as the king.

A False Synthesis of Greek and Modern Philosophy

The New Theology is, in essence, a synthesis of the Church Fathers — largely the Greek Fathers — and modern philosophy.[102] It is not hard to see that modern philosophy would be at the heart of the New Theology, as the New Theology is a new thing supposedly for "modern man." But the question must be asked: Why synthesize it with Greek theology? Simply put, the New Theologians needed a theology that was foreign to the West but still Christian to mix with their philosophy, which was Western in nationality but neither Western nor Eastern by blood.

---

[102] If you do a little digging, you will find that the disciples of the New Theology readily admit that Ratzinger and other New Theology theologians are enamored of modern philosophy. For example, in an article that was published by Bishop Barron's *Word on Fire*, we read the following: "[Hegel] produced one of the greatest synthesis of human thought.... In contrast to Hegel's great harmony in which all of humankind is moving in one, grand, collective movement, Kierkegaard emphasizes the individual, the particular, the unique, the tragic and the salutary moment." It should be noted that not only was this article complimentary of both Kierkegaard and Hegel, the author, Fr. Emery de Gaál, suggests that Ratzinger's views on the topic considered in the article are consistent with Kierkegaard's. Both of these non-Catholic philosophers presented many conclusions that are completely inconsistent with the Catholic Faith, even if some good can be found in their work, as good things can be found in virtually all works by all men. That it is seen as a positive that Ratzinger's thought was consistent with Kierkegaard's, or that Hegel was a great synthesizer of human thought, is troubling, no matter which angle we assess it from. The article discussed here: Fr. Emery de Gaál, "Ratzinger versus Kierkegaard on Desecularization," *Word on Fire*, June 26, 2023, https://www.wordonfire.org/articles/contributors/ratzinger-versus-kierkegaard-on-desecularization/.

Fr. Greenstock explained that New Theologians were fond of the Greek Fathers, and many of them did a great service to the Church by translating various works. Nevertheless, the intention was not merely an innocent academic one. This is because Greek, or Eastern, Christian theological terms were foreign to Latin Catholic theology in many ways and not part of the tradition. This allowed the introduction of terms that were Catholic but could be used in confusing ways. Also, the accusation on behalf of New Theologians was that these terms had been lost because the Western Church was "tied excessively to Thomism in all its forms."[103]

Now, it was not Greenstock's opinion that understanding Greek theology on its own terms was bad; of course it would not be bad to understand Eastern Christian thought in its own sphere. Rather, Greenstock showed that the intention was not merely to understand Greek thought but to introduce terminology that was not *Latin*, the language of Scholasticism. Also, for all the excellence of Eastern Catholic thought, "in some cases, the method of approach adopted by the Greek Fathers led them into difficulties which were not solved satisfactorily until the time of Aquinas."[104] Again, this is not to say anything negative or condemnatory about Greek Christian thought, as Western theologians had their own issues to deal with until the arrival of Aquinas. The point is that Aquinas took the *best* of Greek thought (Aristotle) and Western thought (Augustine) and performed a legitimate, dare I say, *synthesis* — not in the way of contradiction, as with modern philosophy, but in the way of *purification*, through an intellectual baptism of the greatest thought of antiquity and the pre-Scholastic era.

Again, the two traditions are not enemies but instead are like different instruments in an orchestra. If the West is like a cello, large and powerful yet capable of the most beautiful melodies, the East is like the violin, which, although smaller, has a certain agility and the ability

---

[103] Greenstock, "Thomism and the New Theology."
[104] Greenstock, "Thomism and the New Theology."

to play a greater diversity of tunes and styles — even some styles that may sound foreign to foreign ears but heavenly to native ears.

The East and West have grown separate but with roots in the same soil, like two towering trees with equal grandeur and magnanimity but distinct in appearance. The West is an oak, and the East is a cedar of Lebanon. But modern philosophy is riddled with the dialectic evolutionism of Hegel, and therefore, the modern theologian has used the Hegelian method to attempt to graft the branches of the cedar to modern philosophy in chimeric fashion. This could be done only with Eastern Christian thought, not because Byzantine theology is modernist but because it is, in a way, ethereal insofar as it is mystical and delightfully strange. Latin thought, especially Thomistic, is as practical and clear as cool, still water, and therefore all that is contained by the water is seen in great detail. Eastern thought is like a swift river descending Balkan hills, with light from the Eastern sun shining and sparkling in different nooks and crannies. It would be wrong to say it is not clear, but due to its nature, it is harder to see what lies beneath the water unless one really *knows* the river and the landscape.

The New Theology is a chimera, and because of this, it has proven itself to be infertile and stunted. Yes, there are disciples of the New Theology, almost always in academia, but the experiment has failed. A young child can understand Thomism put in simple terms as he studies his First Communion catechism, but only an academic can even attempt to understand the New Theology.

16

Modernist Reform Activated: The Conciliar Revolution in Action

In the section of *Pascendi* where Pius X warned of what Modernist reform would look like in practice, he cautioned the Church that a variety of overhauls were desired by Modernists. The various warnings will constitute different subsections and will be teased out and considered against the backdrop of the Second Vatican Council and the reforms that have taken place since the 1960s. Not every warning can be discussed in this chapter, however, because some of the topics, such as the penchant of Modernists to subject dogma to modern science, have been discussed at length in other chapters. In this chapter, we will consider Pius X's warnings about the "mania" of Modernist reform; the threat of modern catechetical methods; how Modernism promotes a governing style of the Church that has led to the dreaded synodality; and how Modernism flips the moral order and stressed activity over spirituality. Pius X did warn that an overhaul to liturgical and sacramental rites would take place, but this topic will have its own chapter.

It is worth noting again that Modernism is as much an *attitude* or a *mood* as a heresy of *suggestion*. So, for example, if we were to assess the New Mass — the *Novus Ordo Missae* or the Missal of Paul VI — it is not necessary to prove that the missal or rubrics themselves express objective heresy to see a Modernist spirit present therein. No, we may look at the new liturgy and assess what is *suggested* by the very act of the massive reform that took place.

We might ask: Why was the Mass changed so drastically? Why were the liturgical reformers so concerned with appealing to Protestants? Why was the Mass changed by a type of committee in a way never before seen? If the New Mass is truly the Roman Rite, then why does it look *nothing* like the Roman Rite of so many centuries? And so on. Whether one agrees that the New Mass is the true Mass of Vatican II — more on that later — we must all agree that it was the Fathers of Vatican II who made the New Mass, and the Fathers of Vatican II who thrust the Mass on the Church, and the Fathers of Vatican II who *acted* as if the New Mass was the Mass of Vatican II. For all intents and purposes, the New Mass is at least the Mass of the *spirit of Vatican II*, if not the Mass of the conciliar documents themselves.

At any rate, we will discuss the New Mass in light of *Pascendi*'s warnings in more detail as we proceed, but this short example serves as a reminder of the tricky and ethereal nature of Modernism that has seemingly infiltrated every nook and cranny of the Church, even if doctrinal and liturgical orthodoxy may be saved, in some cases, with technicalities.

The Mania of Modernist Reform

About the mania of Modernist reform, Pius X states: "From all that has preceded, some idea may be gained of the reforming *mania* which possesses them [Modernists]: in all Catholicism there is absolutely nothing on which it does not fasten" (38, emphasis added).

Modernism foments in its adherents a type of *mania*. The word "mania" is derived from the Greek word *mainesthai*, which means "to be mad." Mania is a form of madness, a type of insanity. If Pius X is correct when he asserts that Modernist Reform is a type of insanity — and I believe he is correct — then we ought to consider *madness* in order to understand the works of the Modernists.

Madness is a rejection of reality or some vital portion thereof. Therefore, heresy is always madness (a.k.a. insanity), and Modernism lives up to that classification with flying colors.

All heresy is insanity, as all heresy is a rejection of what is *real* and binding. The heretic says to himself, whether he knows it or not, "God has revealed this doctrine through the Church that He established, but I reject this dogma, or I reject this Church." Thus, Arius rejected the Trinity and relegated Christ to the level of a god, even if a very high god. Thus, the Donatists rejected the true nature of grace and the effect of grace on the repentant soul, even of the worst cowards and sinners. Thus, Luther rejected a whole swath of dogmas, along with the plenitude of the biblical canon. Thus, Calvin did the same as Luther and also rejected the liberty of the will with his damnable double predestination.

The ancient and Protestant heretics, as vile as they were, were not as mad as the Modernists. For all we can say about the heretics of former eras, they were absolutists and unwavering. They were principled in their heresies, and they had enough self-respect — even if misguided — to start their own religions. Arius did not pretend that one could see Christ as God and not God at the same time. The Donatists had enough gumption and zeal to call Catholic priests heretics who disagreed with their heresy; this is what a logical person would believe, even if that logical person is wrong. Luther rejected Tradition and therefore followed his maniacal instincts to their logical end and rejected all authority but himself; he may have been a devil, but he was a devil with devilish integrity. Calvin's ruthless, fatalistic determinism was anything but squishy and ethereal; he was a maniacal puritan and legalist, but he really was a puritan and legalist.

For all these reasons, a Catholic can debate a heretic of the old school because the heretic of the old school believes in doctrines that can be debated. The Modernist, however, cannot be reasoned with because his mania has festered to the point of imbecility and unreason, like an intellect that has deteriorated after years of undetected syphilis. He not only destroys Catholicism, but he "ruins and destroys all religion" (*Pascendi* 13).

Thus, a Modernist reformer after the Council can ransack a parish of its statues and high altars like an iconoclast but without professing the iconoclast heresy. Thus, the postconciliar Modernist can treat the Roman Rite like an experimental specimen, vivisecting the glorious patrimony of saints and martyrs under the guise of creating a Catholic liturgy that no Catholic would recognize as Catholic.

The Modernist maniacs became so drunk with their heresy that they spoke of the conciliar era with notable positivity, while upwards of a hundred thousand men left the priesthood. Religious orders were liquidated and sexual abuse cases reached all-time highs, yet we were told we were in a "new springtime" and a "new Pentecost."

The *mania* is everywhere, and it has gripped even the highest of churchmen. How else do we explain an era in which heretics and pedophiles were promoted and praised and traditionalists were looked at with suspicion and called schismatic?

Imagine a history book written two hundred years from now, in an age when the Church has recaptured her former glory. How would this recent era be described? An honest historian, taking into account the *facts* of what has befallen the Church, and not the revisionist explanations about any good intentions the reformers may have had, would have to describe the Conciliar era in a way similar to the following:

> The Second Vatican Council — unique in that it was designated as distinctly pastoral — was supposed to have ushered in an era of great renewal for the Church. Despite the continual messages of hope and optimism that came from the clerics and popes who oversaw the Conciliar Age, however, the Church continued to decline at a rate perhaps never before seen. Hundreds of millions of Catholics from all nations stopped attending Mass. Hundreds of thousands of priests and religious left their professed states,

and nations that were once Catholic descended into virtually godless states of complete societal decay to the point where so-called Catholic politicians advocated for the mutilation of children to treat gender dysphoria and for the "right" of mothers to destroy their unborn children. To make matters worse, these apostate politicians were not excommunicated by popes and bishops, as in former times, but were welcomed by pope after pope for private audiences in the Vatican; in fact, it was the traditionalists — those faithful to the Deposit of Faith — who were most likely to be penalized by the Vatican and who were mercilessly persecuted for decades because they represented the strongest subgroup of Catholics who resisted the reign of terror that had befallen the Church. Catholic Churches were essentially ransacked of their art and statues the world over, and a liturgy — which was seen by the most sensible liturgy scholars as uncatholic and even offensive — was forced upon Catholics; priests who did not want to implement the new liturgy were removed from their posts and replaced by liberal priests who would minister to dying congregations. Catholic education became unrecognizable, and good Catholic schools became rarer and rarer, but the Vatican seemed more concerned with ecology and religious syncretism than with the sound catechesis of young people. Sure, there were bright spots here and there, as there always are, but the situation was so dire that many sensible Catholics wondered — not without reason — if the end of the world was nigh.

Truly, as Pius X said, there "is absolutely nothing on which [Modernism] does not fasten."

Modern Catechesis

If Modernists intended to change the way Catholics thought and believed, then Catholics would have to be catechized in a way that allowed the infiltration of Modernism into their intellects. So Pius X asserts that in Modernist catechisms "no dogmas are to be inserted except those that have been duly reformed and are within the capacity of the people" (38).

By "duly reformed" and "within the capacity of the people," he means the Modernist notion that seemingly "out of touch" doctrinal expressions must be rejected and replaced with expressions that conform to the predominant thought of the era. Of course, as we saw with the New Theology, though the reformers believed they were presenting a stream of thought that was for the "everyman," nothing could be further from the truth. Modernism began in academia and not in the pious conversations of normal Catholics chatting in a pub or a barbershop.

The change of direction in how Church catechisms were produced took root after Vatican II, and a notable thing happened during the pontificate of Pope John Paul II. In 1979, he wrote the following in *Catechesi Tradendae* (*On Catechesis in Our Time*) in a section called "Continual Balanced Renewal":

> Finally, catechesis needs to be continually *renewed by a certain broadening of its concept,* by the *revision* of its methods, by the search for *suitable language,* and by the utilization of *new means* of transmitting the message. *Renewal* is sometimes unequal in value; the synod fathers realistically recognized, not only an undeniable advance in the vitality of catechetical activity and promising initiatives, but also the *limitations or even "deficiencies" in what has been achieved to date.* These limitations are particularly serious when they endanger integrity of content. The message to the People of God rightly stressed that *"routine, with its refusal to accept any change, and improvisation, with its readiness for any venture, are equally dangerous"* for catechesis. Routine leads to stagnation, lethargy and eventual *paralysis.* Improvisation begets confusion on the part of those being given catechesis and, when these are children, on the part of

their parents; it also begets all kinds of deviations, and the fracturing and eventually the complete destruction of unity. It is important for the Church to give proof today, as she has done at other periods of her history, of evangelical wisdom, courage and fidelity in seeking out and putting into operation *new methods* and *new prospects* for catechetical instruction. (emphasis added)[105]

As is to be expected with everything after the Council, the focus is on "renewal" and making everything "new" with "new methods." And John Paul II makes it very clear in the same document that the need for continual renewal in catechesis stems from the Second Vatican Council, which, citing Paul VI, he referred to as "the great catechism of modern times."[106] Again we see this insistence that "modern" Catholics are somehow different from other Catholics, and because of this, we need "new methods." Of course, the results of these "new methods" seeking "renewal" have resulted in utter catastrophe. What is so different about "modern" Catholics that they cannot be catechized like their ancestors? Were Catholics at the time of Augustine clamoring for new doctrinal expressions because they were different from Catholics at the time of St. Paul? What about Catholics at the time of St. Joan of Arc — did they view themselves as so different as to require different catechesis from what St. Francis received?

According to John Paul II:

The aim of catechesis is to be the teaching and maturation stage, that is to say, the period in which the Christian, having accepted by faith the person of Jesus Christ as the one Lord and having given Him complete adherence by sincere conversion of heart, endeavors to know better this Jesus to whom he has

---

[105] John Paul II, apostolic exhortation *Catechesi Tradendae* (October 16, 1979), no. 17.
[106] *Catechesi Tradendae* 2.

entrusted himself: to know His "mystery," the kingdom of God proclaimed by Him, the requirements and promises contained in His Gospel message, and the paths that He has laid down for anyone who wishes to follow Him.[107]

Now, perhaps I am a bit simplistic in my understanding of the purpose of catechesis, but it is my understanding that the aim of catechesis is to *catechize*, which means to teach the doctrines of the Church. A typical dictionary search on the topic renders results such as "to instruct systematically, especially by questions, answers, and explanations and corrections." This definition of what it means to catechize is consistent with how virtually all Church-approved catechisms have been formatted since time immemorial.

The Catechism of Pope Pius X, the Baltimore Catechism, Butler's Irish Catechism, and others, all accepted for generations as adequate teaching resources, were formatted in a question-and-answer format. While no one can fault John Paul II for associating catechesis with a conversion of heart, his explanation of the aim of catechesis is utterly confusing. It seems to me that this notion of converting hearts through catechesis, while noble in a sense, is an example of "putting the cart before the horse." This is in line with the notion of *living tradition*, which views Catholic Tradition as valid only when Catholics have the same *experiences* as the early Christians. It is emotionalist, psychological, and not rational, ultimately.

Conversions of heart are largely a subjective and personal affair, meaning that they happen to individuals for reasons that are unique to them. A person can attend Mass his whole life, but only in his forties does he finally come to understand the Real Presence in a way that pierces his heart. But *before* any interior conversion can take place, a man needs to wrestle with the truths of the Faith in his intellect. St. Paul tells us, "Faith then cometh by hearing; and hearing by the word

[107] *Catechesi Tradendae* 20.

of Christ" (Rom. 10:17), and we understand that we hear the Faith, and the Faith that we hear comes from Christ: "He that heareth you, heareth me" (Luke 10:16).

Faith is a virtue — a theological virtue, in fact — and virtues are formed by the conditioning of conduct and habit. Following the Aristotelian model of the acquisition of virtue, the Church has always understood that believers and catechumens must be instructed in a formulaic manner with the truths of the Faith. Again, this is why catechisms have always followed a question-and-answer format, starting with the most rudimentary and fundamental aspects of religion, moving to the higher and more complex realities in turn. This is also how the Scholastic presentation of doctrine works; thus, the format of St. Thomas's *Summa Theologiae*, which is formatted in many ways like a catechism.

John Paul II's understanding of catechesis seems to be the opposite, as he states that catechesis is to be the "maturation stage" after a "conversion of heart." Again, this is putting the cart before the horse, and it is a catechesis following a *religious experience*, which is a distinctly Modernist and subjectivist perspective. Sure, a man may have a dream about Christ or the Blessed Mother and his heart may be on fire with a burning love for God, and that man may then seek out a parish priest to learn the Faith. This is the exception and not the rule, however, and it is not the experience of the vast majority of Catholics throughout history.

It is ineffective and shortsighted because it is ultimately based on something like an emotional high, which will peter out as time passes. Furthermore, one is just as likely — nay, more likely — to experience an interior conversion when he hears a strong sermon on the typological fulfillment of Christ as the New Adam, or when he attends a catechesis session with a soundly trained priest, than he is in an emotionalist and vapid environment. Also, a person cannot manufacture a true conversion experience because he is not the Holy Ghost, and a person cannot force someone to respond to particular graces bestowed upon a soul at

God's discretion. It is as if the architects of modern catechesis believe that someone's interior conversion can be forced by way of emotionalist experiences and that this would be more effective than an organized and understandable presentation of saving truth.

Two of Christ's disciples walked with Him to Emmaus after the Resurrection, and the Gospel tells us that they didn't recognize Him, even though they walked with Him (Luke 24:16). But then a remarkable thing happened: Christ "opened" the Scriptures to them, and their hearts began to burn within them, and they subsequently recognized Him when Christ "took bread, and blessed, and brake, and gave to them" (Luke 24:30). From this, we can see that Christ saw fit to explain the Faith to the disciples as a prerequisite for a true recognition of Christ in the Mass (the breaking of bread). So many Catholics (and perhaps you are one of them) have gone through life in the "new springtime" with a forgettable commitment to the Faith, only to be awakened to the burning of their hearts because they stumbled upon an audiotape of a scholar opening up the Old Testament to show that Christ is written of throughout it. If I may provide an anecdote, I remember listening to a lecture series about Thomism, and when principles of essence and existence were explained, I was taken aback. In fact, I was in a gym, and I took a knee after putting my dumbbells on the ground and began to laugh. I laughed because the change was so profound that it was almost absurd. Reality had changed, and my heart had felt it, but it was the result of the presentation of the doctrine of St. Thomas Aquinas, and nothing more.

Historically, parents baptized their infants, and when their children obtained the use of their reason, they would be instructed in the Faith by their parents, educators, or priests. It has never been the custom to expect a child to have a profound conversion of heart before he is instructed from the St. Joseph's Catechism before his First Holy Communion. This shows us that it has always been understood that the intellectual basis was considered the *foundation* for the conversion of heart and would precede it. Furthermore, much of modern catechesis is so wordy and ethereal in terminology that it cannot even be understood by a small child.

Even in missionary territory, the modus operandi was always to send missionaries to a foreign land where they would learn the native language so they could create a catechism and open a school where the children could be formed.

Constantly Updated

While I will not argue here at length about the modern catechism of John Paul II, we would do well to remember that the text has been revised numerous times, most recently to reflect Pope Francis's belief on the death penalty. The revision reads:

> Recourse to the death penalty on the part of legitimate authority, following a fair trial, *was long considered* an appropriate response to the gravity of certain crimes and an acceptable, albeit extreme, means of safeguarding the common good. Today, however, *there is an increasing awareness that the dignity of the person* is not lost even after the commission of very serious crimes. In addition, a *new understanding* has emerged of the significance of penal sanctions imposed by the state. Lastly, more effective systems of detention have been developed, which ensure the due protection of citizens but, at the same time, do not definitively deprive the guilty of the possibility of redemption. Consequently, the Church teaches, in the light of the Gospel, that "the death penalty is inadmissible because it is an attack on the inviolability and dignity of the person", and she works with determination for its abolition worldwide. (2267, emphasis added)

Again, there is an emphasis on newness, updating what was believed for centuries, and an insinuation that the Church has "learned" something in a way that contradicts what she taught for twenty centuries. Apparently, when God said to Noah, "Whosoever shall shed man's blood, his blood shall be shed" (Gen. 9:6), He was speaking without the knowledge of what the Church would learn under Pope Francis.

But this is consistent with Modernism, as we see yet again the concept of the evolution of dogma and vital immanence on full display: the truth was understood in revelation in one way during a certain time period, and then that understanding changed when the experience of believers in a different age changed. The same errors that underpin the conciliar revolution are on full display in the modern *Catechism of the Catholic Church*.

Now, none of this is to say that some new catechisms, such as *Credo* from Bishop Schneider, are not warranted or welcome, as there are certainly cultural and historical events that perplex Catholics and require guidance in light of contemporary problems. But the catechism of John Paul II was not only a new version of the catechism but a catechism based heavily on the statements of the Council, which supposedly defined nothing new but to which total assent has been demanded.

When Pope Pius X produced his catechism in 1905, it was merely a way of transmitting the perennial doctrines of the Church in a simplified question-and-answer format for laymen. This was done because the Roman Catechism was produced to aid priests in their catechetical efforts and is admittedly beyond the literary comprehension level of some readers, especially during a time when literacy was less common.

Interestingly, Benedict XVI said the Catechism of Pope Pius X was "the fruit of the *personal catechetical experience* of Giuseppe Sarto [Pius X]."[108] Amazing! Pope Pius X wrote his catechism because of "personal experience." It seems that Cardinal Ratzinger was so permeated with the Modernist zeitgeist that he read Modernism into the motives of the man who condemned the whole system!

---

[108] "Cardinal Ratzinger on the Abridged Version of the Catechism," Zenit, May 2, 2003, https://web.archive.org/web/20080218102213/http://www.zenit.org/article-7161?l=english.

EWTN's website has an edition of the Roman Catechism available to the public, and the edition includes a foreword by Fr. Francois Laisney, who wrote:

> After the Second Vatican Council, a number of new catechisms appeared which did not present Catholic Doctrine as it should be presented, and these new publications even included some very grave errors. Coupled with the new methods, whereby children are not required to memorize, two generations of children have grown up not knowing the Catholic Faith.... May this edition of Saint Pius X's *Catechism* help priests, teachers and parents to impart the knowledge and love of the Doctrine of the Catholic Church to their pupils and their children in all its entirety and beauty. It is our hope that it will also help adult Catholics to revise and deepen their own knowledge of the Faith.[109]

Fr. Laisney could not have been more accurate in his assessment.

Government by Synodality and the Church of Mercy

The mania of Modernist reform brought with it a penchant for radical reform of Church governance and disciplinary and penitential requirements. Relaying what Modernism requires, Pius X writes:

> Ecclesiastical government requires to be reformed in all its branches, but especially in its disciplinary and dogmatic parts. Its spirit with the public conscience, which is not wholly for democracy; a share in ecclesiastical government should therefore be given to the lower ranks of the clergy, and even to the laity, and authority should be decentralised. The Roman Congregations, and especially the index and the Holy Office,

---

[109] Foreword to *Catechism of St. Pius X*, EWTN, https://www.ewtn.com/catholicism/library/catechism-of-st-pius-x-1286.

are to be reformed. The ecclesiastical authority must change its line of conduct in the social and political world; while keeping outside political and social organization, it must adapt itself to those which exist in order to penetrate them with its spirit. (*Pascendi* 38)

Have we not seen all these things take place? Of course we have. The governmental structures of the Church have been radically reformed since the Council, especially by way of national conferences of bishops, which now de facto act as national churches with their own disciplines and norms that can be completely different from those of other countries. As an example, after the Council, any emphasis on obligatory fasting disappeared faster than the Index of Forbidden Books.

Likewise, the Holy Office has become unrecognizable in recent years. In 1542, Pope Paul III established the Supreme Sacred Congregation of the Roman and Universal Inquisition to deal with the rise in heresy after the Protestant revolt and to concern itself with the affairs of the Inquisition. This is not the book to dispel the myths about the Holy Inquisition that have been disseminated, but let it be known that the Inquisition was *doctrinal* in nature, and if you appreciate your modern legal system with its concepts of innocence until proven guilty and that all the accused are defended in court, you should thank your local Inquisitor for that.

At any rate, in 1908, Pius X renamed this the Supreme Sacred Congregation of the Holy Office, as its affairs were no longer of the same ilk as during the times of the Inquisition. Nonetheless, it was not "downgraded" in any doctrinal sense; the change in name reflected a change in operation.

Immediately after the Council closed, the Supreme Sacred Congregation of the Holy Office was renamed the Sacred Congregation for the Doctrine of the Faith. And with the 1983 *Code of Canon Law*, promulgated by John Paul II, it was renamed the Congregation for the Doctrine of the Faith, as any reference to the "sacred" was dropped from

Curial offices. Under Pope Francis, it has been renamed the Dicastery for the Doctrine of the Faith.

It is no longer sacred and no longer a congregation. This is Modernism in action.

You may recall how nominalism is essential for Modernism, and we should remind ourselves just how much *words matter* and how important the *definitions* of words are. Under Pope Paul III, there was no question of what the purpose of the Supreme Sacred Congregation of the Roman and Universal Inquisition was; it was supreme, it was sacred, it was Roman, and it was universal, and it was for the purpose of the Inquisition, and because it was a congregation, it acted with an authority vested by the office of the papacy itself. When Pius X renamed it the Supreme Sacred Congregation of the Holy Office, there was no change in its power or the weight of its judgments. The Holy Office was the final court of appeal during cases of heresy when it was acting under the auspices of the Inquisition, and when the Inquisition was no longer taking place, the change in name reflected this change. But, under Pius X, it was still "supreme," and no one expected that its authority would go away. In fact, until the changes that took place after the Council, one could still expect rulings on doctrine from the Holy Office, and they were not infrequent. They were clear and authoritative and served a great purpose.

Typical of good Church governance, when the Holy Office would release a letter, it would clearly demonstrate which heresies were *condemned*. This changed when the office was changed after the Council. The Congregation for the Doctrine of the Faith (CDF) ceased condemning heresy and instead presented theological explanations in the positive sense. Now, while many of these explanations may have been correct, and I am sure many have been, it is also true that nothing was condemned. The psychological effect of this on the theologians of the Church has been notable. By not condemning heresy but only presenting orthodoxy, even if relative orthodoxy, the CDF ceased being a judge and was instead a teacher. Yes, teaching is good, but criminals are not judged by teachers but by judges. Heretics are spiritual criminals, and they harm the faithful with their errors and therefore should be judged and condemned. Instead, we live in an age in which the good students get a gold star when they do well, and the bad students can still pass the class, even if they don't get a gold star for themselves. Heretics are now free to galavant around the Church like shoplifters in California.

As John XXIII said at the outset of the Council: "The Church has always opposed these errors, and often condemned them with the utmost severity. Today, however, Christ's Bride prefers the balm of mercy to the arm of severity. She believes that present needs are best served by explaining more fully the purport of her doctrines, rather than by publishing condemnations."

Of course. The Church has changed her mind, and because modern man is different, she no longer condemns his heresies but is merciful toward him. Now, mercy is not possible without justice, so what we see is not mercy but *apathy*. It is *merciful* to condemn a heretic or a heresy because it helps the heretic and the faithful who are fooled by him to become aware of their error, which they cannot take with them to the grave if they wish to save their souls. By not condemning heresy and error, the prelates of the Church have performed an even greater crime than the heretics: the heretics are like drug dealers, which is bad enough, but the authorities who pander to them are like politicians who legalize or permit the sale of narcotics, and they should be judged all the more severely. In the Church of Mercy, it is only the traditionalists who are condemned with any severity, and it is because they are judged as being too severe about heresy. The irony.

Synodality

Pius X's allusion to a change in Church government desired by the Modernists with lower-ranking clergy and laity being put in positions of authority is nothing other than the craze of synodality. Pope Francis's recent Synod on Synodality, a title that reads like a parody but is all too real, is nothing more than the Modernist spirit of a democratic and parliamentary Church incarnate. The scenes from the first session of the Synod on Synodality in the fall of 2023 were like images of a bad dream inspired by Lewis Carroll's *Alice in Wonderland*. However, this synod has been all too real, and perhaps we can call it *Theologians in Synodland*.

In attendance was everyone from conservative cardinals sitting with stern faces as they tried to stomach the indignity of sitting at the same table as feminist nuns with shoulder pads and pantsuits, to liberal priests wearing masks — because their vaccines are apparently ineffective — mixing it up with representatives from the "periphery." It could have been a synod in Bunyan's Vanity Fair.

Of course, keeping with the Greek obsession of the Modernists, who justify every attack on Rome with a nod to Athens, we have been told that a Synod on Synodality is nothing but a manifestation of something that has been going on in the East for centuries. This is not true, however, and Greek Byzantine Catholic bishop Manuel Nin has condemned this notion of a Byzantine-inspired synod as balderdash. He explained that if the West understands synodality as where "everyone, lay and clerical, act together in order to arrive at some ecclesiastical, doctrinal, canonical, disciplinary decision, whatever it may be, it becomes clear that such synodality does not exist in the East."[110]

But this notion of a continual synod did not originate with Pope Francis, or in the East, for that matter. In 1983, in a discourse titled "Theological Basis of the Synod of Bishops," Pope John Paul II wrote:

> The Synod of Bishops sprang up in the fertile terrain of the Second Vatican Council, was able to see the sun thanks to the sensitive mind of my predecessor, Paul VI, and began to bear its fruits right from the first Ordinary Assembly in 1967, held

---

[110] Edward Pentin, "Greek Catholic Bishop: Synod on Synodality Is Not Like Eastern Synods," *National Catholic Register*, August 24, 2023, https://www.ncregister.com/blog/bishop-manuel-nin-synod-on-synodality-unlike-eastern-synods.

in the same hall where we are now. Since that time, meeting at the regular intervals, but also sometimes trying another type of meeting, the Synod of Bishops has contributed in a most noteworthy manner to the implementation of the teachings and the doctrinal and pastoral directives of the Second Vatican Council in the life of the universal church. *The synodal key to reading the Council has become as it were a place for interpretation, application and development of the Second Vatican Council.* The rich list of subjects treated in the various Synods alone reveals the importance of its meetings for the Church and for the implementation of the reforms intended by the Council. (emphasis added)[111]

Granted, the notion of a continual synod has become a parody under Pope Francis, but the notion is not his, and it was instituted by Pope Paul VI and continued and *praised* by John Paul II. Furthermore, the express purpose of the synodal process is for the "interpretation, application and development of the Second Vatican Council." So, after Vatican II, Pope Paul VI instituted a continual synodal process that was tasked with interpreting Vatican II over time, and the idea was that these interpretations would be applied as the process continued. How is this anything other than Modernism? If Vatican II was so clear, which its proponents tell us it was, why must bishops meet in perpetuity to discuss and implement the thing?

The General Secretariat of the Synod of Bishops stated the following about the method of synods: "Briefly stated, the method of work alternates between analysis and *synthesis*, in *consulting interested parties* and decisions being made by competent authorities, according to a *dynamic* of feed-back which permits the continual verification of results and the making of *new proposals*. Each part of

---

[111] Holy See Press Office, "General Information on the Synod," updated June 10, 2012, vatican.va/news_services/press/documentazione/documents/sinodo/sinodo_documentazione-generale_en.html.

this process takes place within the climate of *collegial communion*" (emphasis added).[112]

If there was a game wherein one tried to fit as much Modernist phraseology in a single paragraph, this paragraph may be the all-time champion. So the process of synodality is a matter of synthesis and consultation that is dynamic (vital), which leads to *new* proposals, and it all takes place in a setting of "collegial communion." Again, it is as if the Modernists read *Pascendi* and misunderstood Pius X's warnings as an instruction manual rather than a condemnation.

Again, synodal madness *did not* start in the East, and the popes who either oversaw the Council or sought to implement the Council all agree that Vatican II is the source of the continual synod of bishops; Pope Francis is only following their lead. Pope Francis has done some egregious things, but he is merely the fulfillment of the spirit of Vatican II in all its glory, and his method is that of the synodal process, which was initiated by Paul VI and heralded by John Paul II as being the correct application of the Council.

Perhaps zealous defenders of the Council will object that Pope Francis does not truly understand Vatican II and is not "doing" Vatican II correctly. Well, to these people I say: perhaps they should ask the pope to call a synod as per the recommendations of Pope Paul VI — who oversaw Vatican II — and ask the attendees to consider their interpretation of the Council and vote as to whether they have the right, dynamic interpretation.

Activity over Spirituality

"With regard to morals, they adopt the principle of the Americanists, that the active virtues are more important than the passive, both in the estimation in which they must be held and in the exercise of them" (*Pascendi* 38). What Pius X warns of here is a trend stemming from Modernism that active virtues should be emphasized over passive

---

[112] Holy See Press Office, "General Information on the Synod."

virtues, something that can be easily seen throughout the Church since the Council. Who can deny that the corporal works of mercy have usurped the spiritual works of mercy?

A local bishop or priest may disregard the need for orthodoxy in his diocese or parish, but he will doubtless promote various political activities or charitable ones. It is not wrong for clerics to be involved in politics or to emphasize charity. But we are now at the point when a soup kitchen is more important than the confessional or a catechism class. Furthermore, this insistence on activity over spirituality has led to a ghastly confusion about Catholic social principles. Insistence on the active virtues over the spiritual ones has provided cover for liberal Catholics to support anti-life political parties so long as they help migrants and are concerned with the climate. A proper understanding of solidarity as a sound Catholic principle has been hijacked by Marxist unions that present their activity as consistent with Catholic teaching.

With Pope Francis, we have perhaps seen the most egregious example of this trend; his pontificate has essentially made secular environmentalism into a superdogma as he wags his finger at Catholics who have a different stance on the debatable science of so-called climate change — formerly called global warming and even global cooling. In addition, American bishops have bent their knee to the Marxist plot to usurp sovereign borders under the guise of caring for migrants. Of course, caring for disenfranchised persons is perfectly Christian, but it is not a justification for heresy with regard to the natural law and the sovereignty of nations.

Christ was extremely clear that physical things must be subjected to spiritual things: "And fear ye not them that kill the body, and are not able to kill the soul: but rather fear him that can destroy both soul and body in hell" (Matt. 10:28).

In the Church in the age of Modernism, it is the *body* that is most important, and God does not require spiritual or moral perfection in the religious sense. Thus, the bishops writ large submitted to the Covidian insanity of lockdowns and vaccine mandates, and Pope Francis has expressed more than once that those who object to novel politically motivated injections are unintelligent simpletons. Who can forget when Pope Francis called taking the Covid jab an "act of love," or when he called the same action a "moral obligation" that people refused because of "baseless information"?[113]

When we consider the warnings of Pius X about Modernist Reform in light of what has been discussed in this chapter, is there any doubt that those warnings became realities under the guidance of the popes of the "new springtime"? I have often heard it said that all this madness is taking place either because people have not heeded the true words of the postconciliar popes or because Vatican II has simply not been "done right." Well, that is a very hard sell given what we have seen in this chapter, as it seems to me, at least when I assess what the popes themselves have said, that they were convinced that they were simply following Vatican II — even if synodality requires that we meet to discuss what Vatican II means with each passing year.

In the next chapter, we will discuss how Modernist reform led to a liturgical revolution, and I think you will see that what has happened with the rise of the New Mass was, like everything else discussed in this chapter, the furthest thing from a coincidence and not alien to Vatican II.

---

[113] Devin Watkins, "Pope Francis Urges People to Get Vaccinated against Covid-19," Vatican News, August 18, 2021, https://www.vaticannews.va/en/pope/news/2021-08/pope-francis-appeal-covid-19-vaccines-act-of-love.html; Associated Press, "On COVID Vaccinations, Pope Says Health Care Is a 'Moral Obligation,'" NPR, January 10, 2022, https://www.npr.org/2022/01/10/1071785531/on-covid-vaccinations-pope-says-health-care-is-a-moral-obligation.

17

Modernist Worship: The Liturgy of the Revolution

This is the last chapter in a series of four chapters considering Pius X's warnings about what would result from Modernist reform and how this was made possible by the Modernist spirit and statements of Vatican II. As mentioned above, I will devote this chapter to the warning about Modernist reform of the liturgies and ceremonies of the Church.

Not satisfied with all it has destroyed, Modernists have been hell-bent — pun intended? — on a complete overhaul of the liturgical life of the Church. On this facet of Modernist Reform, Pius X explains how Modernists view worship: "Regarding *worship*, the number of external devotions is to be reduced, or at least steps must be taken to prevent their further increase, though, indeed, some of the admirers of symbolism are disposed to be more indulgent on this head" (38, emphasis added).

We will discuss the liturgical revolution in some detail below, but it is worth considering what Pius X warns of here in plain terms about things we all know. The number of external devotions has been drastically reduced, and this cannot be denied. For example, there used to be various versions of the Rosary that different communities would say;

the Dominican Rosary and the Franciscan were common, and each emphasized different facets of the spiritual life. In addition, there were many other chaplets that were common in different regions, but today, they are mostly lost. These did not fall out of fashion without encouragement from the mentality nurtured in the conciliar era, including a major change in the nature of indulgences, which gave the impression that these devotions were no longer seen as important. The change in indulgences was an effective method to "prevent their further increase."

Also, Catholics historically attended Vespers on Sunday evenings, as they were a beautiful and prayerful sung affair, but striking reforms to the Divine Office helped this to go away. When the Office was translated into every vernacular language, the traditional Latin hymns that carried with them a sacred musicality were lost; it can hardly be argued that awkward English translations of ancient hymns and passages — which do not naturally rhyme if not in Latin — can inspire an environment of sacred musicality.

Finally, it is fascinating that Pius X foresaw that some "admirers of symbolism," although steeped in Modernism, would be more indulgent. We have seen this with how the Traditional Mass has been permitted. For example, when Pope John Paul II permitted the establishment of traditional communities in 1988, he said, "respect must everywhere be shown for the feelings of all those who are attached to the Latin liturgical tradition."[114] This statement may seem harmless enough, but the emphasis is on feelings and attachment. In other words, while it may be true that traditionalists do have strong feelings of attachment to the Old Rite, the emphasis on these sentiments as a reason for permitting the Traditional Mass — in limited communities — is based on the subjective and not the objective; he did not establish regulations for such communities because the Old Mass was objectively more sacred and so forth but because he was indulgent toward those for whom the Old Rite symbolized deep meaning.

---

[114] *Ecclesia Dei* 6.

Now, the reader could disagree with the rest of my forthcoming assessment of the New Mass, but it is clear that at least the *mentality* of Modernism has been actualized with the sweeping liturgical reforms that followed Vatican II.

In any event, I fear that in this chapter I will not do justice to all that could be said about the liturgical revolution that has plagued the Church since Vatican II, given that it is but one chapter in a larger work. Nevertheless, it is impossible to discuss Modernism without at least discussing the New Mass, even if relatively briefly. Furthermore, this chapter will focus solely on the introduction of the New Mass and not on the wholesale change to the rubrics and ceremonies of all seven sacraments. A complete look at every sacrament would require a much longer work, and given the fact that Catholics have most contact with the Mass, it seems appropriate to discuss the Modernist revolution in liturgy from that vantage point.

But it is worth keeping in mind the words of Dr. Peter Kwasniewski, who has written strikingly on the unprecedented change to every aspect of the liturgies of the Roman Rite:

> Every bit of the Mass, every aspect of the Divine Office, every sacramental rite, every blessing, every piece of clerical and liturgical clothing, every page of Canon Law and the Catechism — all had to be revamped, reworked, revised, usually in the direction of diminution and softening: "the Word was made bland, and dwelt in the suburbs". The beauty and power of our tradition was muted at best, silenced at worst. No form was safe, stable, or deemed worthy of preservation as it stood, as it had been received.[115]

The topic of Vatican II and the Novus Ordo — the Mass of Paul VI — is a contentious topic, to say the least, and a certain sensitivity

---

[115] Peter Kwasniewski, *The Once and Future Roman Rite* (TAN Books, 2022), 321..

must be noted. This is because the majority of Catholics and clerics either attend the New Mass or say the New Mass. Therefore, millions upon millions of Catholics have had or continue to have frequent contact with the New Mass, and not infrequently, I find that criticism of the new liturgy is taken as criticism of persons, given their contact with and participation therein. Let it be said here that I speak only of the New Mass itself, and I make no judgments on persons who say it or attend it. Many Catholics do not have ready access to the Traditional Latin Mass, and there are priests who will read this who are stuck between a proverbial rock and a hard place, given their positions as pastors in typical diocesan parishes. Simply put, we live in a *valley of tears*, and that many laymen and priests experience a grave crisis of conscience by their contact with a liturgy that has resulted from so much upheaval is an indictment on the authorities in the Church who have established the crisis and not those who have inherited it.

Anathema to Traditionalists or Pope Paul VI?

Now, before we even assess the New Mass in light of the Modernism spoken of in *Pascendi*, it must be addressed that sharp criticism of the liturgy itself—not merely excesses or how it has been implemented in some settings—can make some Catholics uneasy. This is completely understandable and speaks to a sound Catholic conscience animated by filial devotion and piety toward Holy Mother Church. Stating that there are problems with a published liturgy of the Church raises questions for some, most notably in the realm of the indefectibility of the Church: How could a Church undefiled give the faithful a "bad" Mass?

This intuition is also buttressed by a powerful statement from the Council of Trent that seems to be an infallible truth that Catholics can never say that a ceremony—which would include a liturgy—of the Church is a hindrance or defective. The Council of Trent proclaimed in session XXII, canon VII: "If any one saith, that the ceremonies, vestments, and outward signs, which the Catholic Church makes use of in the celebration of masses, are incentives to impiety, rather than offices of piety, *let him be anathema*." This cannot be taken lightly. At face value, this would seem to anathematize traditionalists, who go so far as to say there is something inherently *wrong* with the New Mass. But it is not that simple.

This is because Trent had already proclaimed in session 7, canon 13: "If anyone says that the *received and approved* rites of the Catholic Church customarily used in the solemn administration of the sacraments may be despised or may be freely omitted by the ministers without sin, or may be *changed into other new rites by any church pastor whosoever*, let him be anathema" (emphasis added).

The pope is a pastor. He is the Vicar of Christ, the bishop of Rome, the patriarch of the West, the primate of Italy, and the archbishop and metropolitan of the Roman Province. Therefore, we must consider these two anathemas from Trent in context. First, the Council of Trent was called primarily to condemn the errors of Protestantism, which included the promulgations of various reforms that took place within the Church. Luther and the others said horrible things about the Mass, and many Protestants believe the Mass is an act of idolatry, among other things. Clearly, this anathema was aimed at them.

Also, Councils, when they speak infallibly, speak of particular issues and must not be taken to mean more than they mean. The Novus Ordo did not exist in the sixteenth century, therefore, it could not have been in mind when this canon was uttered.

Now, if we consider the second statement from Trent that condemns *any church pastor who* would change a rite *into other new rites*, we must also proceed with caution, while still understanding the severity.

Defenders of the New Rite of Mass may suggest that it is merely a revision of the Old Mass, and a revision is not the same as changing something into a new rite. A revision is not the same thing as a wholesale change, and there have been revised liturgies in the past or liturgies tailored to particular communities that were in some ways different from the rite used generally. This is the case with the Dominicans, for example, who were permitted to use their own rite. However, the

Dominican Rite, while different in some ways from the Traditional Latin Mass, has obvious continuity with it.

Also, at the time of the Council of Trent, the issue of various liturgical rights within the Latin Rite of the Church as a whole was considered. The Council decided to safeguard liturgies that were at least two centuries old and to suppress what was not. The Dominican Rite, as well as others, was older than that. Also, the Dominican Rite was not published as a *replacement* of the Roman Rite in use at the time but as a *different* rite that was permitted for Dominicans for reasons that pertained to the charism of their order. So, while it could not be said that a new rite per se is bad, the anathema from Trent must be taken seriously in that it speaks of the impermissibility of *changing* an existing rite into a new rite.

I think, if we consider the New Mass as opposed to the Traditional Latin Mass, we should find the change troubling. This is because the Novus Ordo was clearly published to replace the usage of the Traditional Latin Mass, and it was presented as a *change* to the Traditional Rite and considered to be the new Roman Rite.

On November 26, 1969, the pope spoke to a General Audience about the New Mass and said: "We ask you to turn your minds once more to the *liturgical innovation of the new rite of the Mass*. This *new rite* will be introduced into our celebration of the holy Sacrifice...... A *new rite of the Mass*: a change in a venerable tradition that has gone on for centuries."

Paul VI went on to ask the question: "How can we celebrate this *new rite* when we have not yet got a complete missal, and there are still so many uncertainties about what to do?" (emphasis added).

This is a striking statement that cuts to the heart of the failed attempts to explain away the New Mass as merely a revision. Paul VI called the New Mass a "new rite" a total of seven times during his speech and admitted it was a new rite that would replace the Traditional Mass.

Also, if we consider the statement from Trent that anathematizes the Protestant notion that the Mass itself is bad, we can look to how this must have been understood by orthodox churchmen of high reputability. When the rubrics of the New Mass were written, Cardinal Alfredo Ottaviani, who was the head of the Holy Office during and after the Council, produced in conjunction with other prelates, including Archbishop Lefebvre, what is colloquially called the "Ottaviani Intervention." The intervention blasted the text of the Novus Ordo as it was presented for review before publication. Among other things, the intervention stated: "The *Novus Ordo* represents, both as a whole and in its details, a striking departure from the Catholic theology of the Mass as it was formulated in Session XXII of the Council of Trent."

Notice that Ottaviani and the others were well aware of session 22 of the Council of Trent — which anathematized the notion that the rites of the Church could be incentives to impiety — yet they were convinced that the proposed New Mass would be harmful to souls via a departure from defined theological principles. In addition, Paul VI did not respond to the intervention by anathematizing the authors or by appealing to the Council of Trent for justification. Furthermore, if Trent can be used to anathematize traditionalists, then what can we say about Paul VI when we consider the anathema leveled against "any church pastor *whosoever*" who seeks to make fundamental changes to liturgical rites? Again, the pope is a pastor of the Church, even if the supreme pastor.

I do not contend here that I have the authority to say a pope is anathema, but I *do* contend that given what has been discussed, we cannot brush aside sharp criticism of the New Mass itself as anathema, if we consider the context of the Council of Trent and the understanding of Cardinal Ottaviani and others. Furthermore, Trent anathematized the accusation that the *received and approved* rites could be spiritually harmful. The New Mass was approved, but it was certainly not received, considering it was, as Paul VI said, a "liturgical innovation," and it could certainly not fall under the auspices of the condemnation of Trent, considering all that could have been in the minds of the Fathers of that Council would have been what was received and approved at that time.

The Mass of Vatican II?

Now, many Catholics will admit that the New Mass has not been received well by the majority of the Church, which is evident by the fact that, among other things, Catholics writ large have stopped attending Mass and belief in the Real Presence has plummeted. In response to this obvious fact, there are some who contend that the New Mass is not the *true* Mass of Vatican II; by that, they mean that the Novus Ordo does not correspond adequately to the text of Vatican II's document on the liturgy, *Sacrosanctum Concilium* (*SC*). The insinuation is that if the New Mass were *truly* in line with *SC*, then all would be fine. I believe this is incorrect, however, and that there are problems and ambiguities in *SC* itself that make it hard, if not impossible, to say that the New Mass does not meet *SC*'s criteria.

Granted, discussion about *SC* is complicated, as it is clear, on the one hand, that *SC* can be interpreted in a way that leaves room for the Traditional Latin Mass while, on the other hand, one can justify striking liturgical innovations by appealing to it. As liturgy expert Gregory DiPippo wrote:

> And the fact remains that, however it got to be so, *Sacrosanctum Concilium* is indisputably full of ambiguities. It says that "a broader place (amplior locus) can be given" to the use of the vernacular in the liturgy (36.2), without stating how much broader. Does this exclude or include the possibility that such a place will in fact be so broad as to eliminate Latin from the liturgy altogether? The text does not say. It says that "The Church acknowledges Gregorian chant as specially suited to the Roman liturgy: therefore, other things being equal, it should be given pride of place in liturgical services." (116) Which "other things", and how shall we know them to be equal? The text does not say. Does this exclude or include the possibility that the Church will "lose a great part of that stupendous and incomparable artistic and spiritual thing, the Gregorian chant?" as the

Pope himself, less than six years after *Sacrosanctum Concilium* was issued, stated what would happen? (General audience, Nov. 26, 1969). The text does not say. Further examples could be adduced almost endlessly. Is there a single document of the Council about which similar questions cannot be asked? The text does not say.[116]

The fact that the text of *SC* allows itself to be interpreted in a number of ways speaks to a disastrous lack of precision, which allows for contradictory conclusions and for a doubt about its meaning. Furthermore, the open-ended permissions to add as much or as little vernacular as is desired, or to use as much or as little Gregorian chant as desired, for example, leaves the door open for a liturgy that is unrecognizable to Catholic history; we might even say an *evolved* liturgy in the true sense of what it means for something to evolve from one thing to another. The ambiguity, doubt, and spirit of evolution can only remind us of Modernism.

Furthermore, there are other passages from *SC* that should strike us as in accord with the Modernist spirit. For example, there is talk of loosening liturgical rules for the "good of the whole community" (37); a wide range of the vernacular language can be used in "readings ... directives ... to some of the prayers and chants," and the usage of the vernacular in all these areas is to be decided by national bodies of bishops (39); there is talk of needed "radical adaptation of the liturgy" in "some places and circumstances" (40), and so on. From these few examples, we could easily imagine a liturgy that would be a complete rupture from what came before. The emphasis on the community's needing fewer rules speaks to a liturgy with numerous options that can be switched here and there; the use of the vernacular in so many places could mean that the majority of the liturgy would no longer be in Latin;

---

[116] Gregory DiPippo, "The Hopeless Ambiguity of Sacrosanctum Concilium," New Liturgical Movement, October 22, 2020, https://www.new liturgicalmovement.org/2020/10/the-hopeless-ambiguity-of-sacro sanctum.html.

radical adaptation of the liturgy means just what it says — revolutionary alterations. So walking into a parish playing modern music that is part of the culture, with the whole thing being in English with perhaps the exception of when the congregation sings "*Miserere nobis*," and where the liturgy looks radically different from anything you have ever seen is completely justified by *SC*.

What we see here is the making of a liturgy that is in a state of flux and adaptation to culture, experience, changing aesthetic tastes, and the communal experience; what we see here is *Modernism*.

Now, some may object that there are many good passages in *SC*, and they would be correct. Plenty of beautiful statements are included in the document, especially when it speaks of the nature of the Eucharist, for example. Even Cardinal Ottaviani and the other authors of the intervention argued that the New Mass was in many places opposed to directives from *SC*, and they were right. It could be argued that the New Mass does not satisfy the directives of *SC*, and it could be argued that it does, as many conservative-minded priests and theologians have attempted to do. The thing is, they are both correct; the New Mass can be seen, on the one hand, as produced in opposition to the Vatican while, on the other, as in line with the Council.

SC contains what have been called "time bombs" — that is, ambiguous statements later to be exploited — and statements that are pleasing to pious Catholic sentiment. This is what Modernism does. Call to mind what was spoken of in an earlier chapter about how Modernists can produce works in which you find statements of sound theology on one page and on the next you find the opposite (*Pascendi* 18).

Furthermore, the official name of the missal published by Paul VI that contains the rubrics for the New Mass is called *Missale Romanum ex decreto Sacrosancti Oecumenici Concilii Vaticani II instauratum*, which in English is "The Roman Missal renewed by decree of the Most Holy Second Ecumenical Council of the Vatican."

Quite frankly, the New Mass was produced as a response to the desire for liturgical revision spoken of at Vatican II, and the pope who oversaw the majority of the Council published a missal with a title stating that it was from the Council. While the New Mass may not be the "ideal" liturgy that could have emanated from Vatican II in the minds of some, it is the liturgy that did emanate from Vatican II. We must conclude that it is the Mass of Vatican II, because it could come from nowhere else.

Is the New Rite the Roman Rite?

This book has been critical at times of Pope Benedict XVI, but we must all admit that he did a very good thing for the Church by liberating the Traditional Latin Mass in 2007 with his letter *Summorum Pontificum*. His accompanying letter to bishops, *Con grande fiducia*, expressed his opinion that the New Mass and the Old Mass were "two forms" of the Roman Rite. I believe it is appropriate here to give Benedict the benefit of the doubt and assess his actions through a political lens, even if I think it is wrong to call the two liturgies the "Roman Rite." If the Old Mass is the Roman Rite, then it stands to reason that the New Mass is not, and vice versa. Thus, to avoid an administrative problem, it has been suggested that Benedict sought a ceasefire between the adherents of the Old and the New for purely political reasons. Fair enough.

We are hard-pressed to call the New Mass a *Catholic Rite*, however, let alone the *Roman Rite*. Again, we must hearken back to our nemesis William of Ockham and his heresy of nominalism. As has been discussed, nominalism denies the natures and essences of things and views words and definitions in a subjective sense as purely categorical and practical. A nominalist can call virtually *any rite* the Roman Rite if he so chooses. So long as a rite is said by Roman Catholic priests, the nominalist can say the rite is Roman. But this is not so.

If an Italian makes Chinese food and calls it lasagna, we cannot say it is lasagna just because an Italian called the Chinese thing an Italian thing. Lasagna, along with all things, exists in a world of forms and natures and essences. In the same way, we cannot call the New

Rite the Roman Rite unless it really is *Roman*. It is not enough that it was written in Rome by Roman Catholics; it must *be* Roman to be called Roman.

The implacable German liturgy scholar Martin Mosebach wrote: "No one who has eyes and ears will be persuaded to ignore what his own senses tell him: these two forms are so different that their theoretical unity appears entirely unreal."[117] Mosebach can say this because he is not a Modernist; thus, he is a Realist philosophically. He trusts his senses, as we all should, and when we *see* the New Mass, we *know* that it is not like the Old Mass. Not only is it unlike the Old Mass, but any talk of their sameness appears "entirely unreal."

For a liturgy to be truly considered the Roman Rite, it must first meet the criteria required for something to be a Catholic rite. What is required of a liturgy that it be considered wholly Catholic? And by saying "wholly Catholic," I mean that it corresponds to what is seen throughout history in the approved liturgies of the Catholic Church, and not just in the Latin West. We can refer to these liturgies as "authentic," in the sense that they authentically belong to the Church and her tradition.

There are eight criteria that are met in every authentic Catholic liturgy.

1. Every authentic liturgy celebrates the Mass with the priest and the congregation facing the East, which is called *ad orientem*. In fact, this custom is so old that it was defended, by saints such as Basil the Great and John Damascene, as being directly from the *Apostles*.
2. All the authentic liturgies of the Church use an ancient and fixed Eucharistic Prayer, which is also called an *anaphora*. In cases in which a rite may have more than one anaphora, there are fixed days of the liturgical year when different ones are to be used.

---

[117] Cited in Kwasniewski, *Once and Future Roman Rite*, 164

3. In all authentic liturgies, we find the use of an elaborate Offertory, in which it is made clear that what is being offered is *sacrificial* and for the forgiveness of sin.
4. All authentic liturgies require that the Blessed Sacrament is treated with utmost veneration and reverence. Laymen do not handle the consecrated offerings, and the Eucharist is placed directly into the mouths of the faithful. And the priest ensures that each and every particle of the Host is cared for with precision.
5. In every authentic liturgy, we find a clear hierarchical structure, as the roles of bishops, priests, deacons, subdeacons, and so on are clearly outlined, and those outlines are never transgressed. These roles are reserved for men, and the laity do not participate in roles designated for ordained ministers.
6. All authentic liturgies make use of buildings designed to foster, by way of architecture, what is presented in the theology of the Mass.
7. All authentic liturgies chant the liturgical texts according to received and ancient musical customs that developed organically. And, for almost each day of the liturgical year, there are fixed orations, that may be recited or chanted, that present the breadth of Catholic doctrine and belief. Lectionaries follow the same rules — a one-year cycle — so that the prayers read at the altar or chanted are harmonious with the cycle of readings from Holy Scripture. Of course, the Roman Rite can be celebrated as a Low Mass, during which there is no chanting; the same liturgical rubrics are followed, however, except for the opening *Asperges me* antiphon that is sung at the beginning of the ceremony. Whether celebrated Low or High, the antiphons and many prayers of the Mass are still set to chant melodies.

8. All authentic liturgies employ elevated or sacred language, such as Church Latin in the West and Koine Greek in Greek liturgies. In cases where some eastern liturgies have adopted the use of vernacular for some moments in the Mass, the language is used in a heightened way and does not come off as how the faithful commonly speak.[118]

Can we say that the New Mass meets these stipulations?

Regarding the saying of Mass *ad orientem*, this is not required by *The General Instruction of the Roman Missal* (*GIRM*), published for the Mass of Paul VI, even if it is permitted. As far as fixed Eucharistic Prayers are concerned, it is simply not the case that the New Mass requires the use of a fixed prayer, and there are several to choose from. And, it is not as if the variety of prayers are assigned to different days of the liturgical year, as a priest can simply choose to use whichever one he wants, whenever he wants.

Concerning the use of an elaborate Offertory that makes it clear that a sacrifice is taking place, well, in the New Mass they are referred to as the "Prayer over the Offerings," rather than "Offertory prayers." The Prayer over the Offerings of the New Mass is as follows: "Pray, brothers and sisters, that my sacrifice and yours may be acceptable to God, the almighty Father"; "May the Lord accept the sacrifice at your hands for the praise and glory of his name, for our good and the good of all his holy Church"; "Receive, O Lord, we pray, these offerings of your servants and of your whole family, that, cleansed by the purifying work of your grace, we may be conformed to the mysteries of the redemption. Through Christ our Lord. Amen."

Now, it is true that there is mention of sacrifice, but is it clear *what* is being sacrificed and *why*?

---

[118] These points have been summarized from Dr. Peter Kwasniewski's presentation thereof in *The Once and Future Roman Rite: Returning to the Traditional Latin Liturgy after Seventy Years of Exile* (Gastonia, NC: TAN Books, 2022), 41–44.

Well, in the preparatory prayers of the New Mass, what is being offered is called "the work of human hands," and it is offered so that it can become "the bread of life" and "spiritual drink."

There is no mention of the offerings being offered as a sacrifice for the forgiveness of sins, even though the priest does pray silently that God forgive his sins while he washes his hands during the preparatory prayers. And there is no clear delineation between what is being offered by the priest and what the people present offer of themselves — hence, "my sacrifice and yours."

Let us compare these to the prayers of the Old Rite, but I will not include the totality of the texts because there are *five*, and each of them is longer than those of the New Rite.

The first is the *Suscipe, Sancte Pater*, which begs God the Father to accept the "spotless host," and the priest prays that God may accept it as an offering for his sins. The second is the *Offerimus tibi, Domine*, when the "chalice of salvation" is offered, and the priest beseeches God for clemency (mercy). The third is the *In spiritu humilitatis*, in which the priest prays, "In a humble spirit and with a contrite heart may we be accepted by Thee, O Lord, and may our sacrifice so be offered in Thy sight this day, that it may please Thee, O Lord God."

Now, before we continue, it will already be clear to the reader that the prayers of the New Rite are not clear that a sacrifice for sin is offered, whereas the opposite is true in the Old Rite. Also, while in both the priest prays that we may be accepted by God, there is a clear delineation in the Old Rite between the sacrifice being offered and the prayer to be accepted.

The fourth prayer in the Old Rite is the *Lavabo*, which is said when the priest washes his hands:

> I will wash my hands among the innocent: and will compass Thy altar, O Lord: that I may hear the voice of Thy praise, and tell of all Thy wondrous works. I have loved, O Lord, the beauty of Thy house, and the place where Thy glory dwelleth. Take not

away my soul with the wicked, nor my life with men of blood: in whose hands are iniquities, their right hand is filled with gifts. But as for me, I have walked in my innocence: redeem me, and have mercy on me. My foot hath stood in the right way: in the churches I will bless Thee, O Lord. Glory be to the Father, and to the Son, and to the Holy Ghost. As it was in the beginning, is now, and ever shall be, world without end. Amen.

This prayer is clearly elaborate when compared with the New Rite prayer for the washing of his hands which states, "Wash me, O Lord, from my iniquity and cleanse me from my sin."

Can there be any argument that the prayer from the Old Rite is clearer and more majestic than the New Rite prayer? Furthermore, the Old Rite prayer is taken from Psalm 25 (26 in some translations), in which King David prays to be cleansed so that he may approach the Tabernacle and "compass" (go around) the altar. So even in the *Lavabo* of the Old Rite, it is clear that what is being offered is a sacrificial offering for sin.

The fifth prayer is the *Suscipe, Sancta Trinitas*, wherein the priest states:

> Receive, O Holy Trinity, this oblation which we make to Thee in memory of the Passion, Resurrection, and Ascension of our Lord Jesus Christ, and in honor of Blessed Mary, ever Virgin, of Blessed John the Baptist, of the holy Apostles Peter and Paul, and of all the Saints; that it may avail to their honor and our salvation; and may they vouchsafe to intercede for us in heaven, whose memory we celebrate on earth. Through the same Christ our Lord. Amen.

"Oblation" means "sacrifice," and it is clear in this prayer that the sacrifice is offered to the Holy Trinity for the salvation of mankind. The Holy Ghost is not even mentioned in the preparatory prayers and prayers over the offerings of the New Rite, let alone the Holy Trinity.

As far as reverence and unmistakable veneration for the Blessed Sacrament, this was radically reduced with the publication of the Novus Ordo. Priests are not required to keep their index fingers and thumbs — what are called "canonical digits" — pressed together after they touch the consecrated Host when celebrating the Novus Ordo, but they are in the Traditional Latin Mass. This shows that less reverence is expected, and the risk of particles being carelessly lost increases. Also, Communion on the hand has been a common practice in the New Mass since it was published.

The hierarchical structure is obliterated in the New Mass, as laymen can do almost everything except preach, read the Gospel, and say the words of the Mass. Also, the minor orders were suppressed after Vatican II, so there is no role for a subdeacon, and women are often on the altar doing things that only men have done for eons.

While the New Mass does not require hideous architecture that is foreign to classical Church buildings, when the New Mass was published, a type of iconoclasm took place that "wreckovated" churches and altered them in heinous ways. Altar rails and high altars were removed, and often churches were made "in the round" so the congregation could sit around the altar as at a stadium. It may not be so that this was officially required for the New Mass, but we cannot help but wonder if the New Mass itself inspired — at least in part — these ghastly developments.

It is possible to find chant in the New Mass, but at the time of Paul VI, it was not so, as the Mass was published before Gregorian chant could be adapted to the new prayers, which were also changed drastically. In fact, only 13 percent of the orations of the Old Mass were kept unaltered, with many of them radically changed or removed entirely.[119]

---

[119] Matthew Hazell, "All the Elements of the Roman Rite? Mythbusting: Part II," *New Liturgical Movement*, October 1, 2021, https://www.newliturgicalmovement.org/2021/10/all-elements-of-roman-rite-mythbusting.html.

Furthermore, the received lectionary cycle, which harmonized with so many aspects of the liturgical year, was removed and replaced with the new three-year cycle, in which there is often no connection between the readings and the feast day.

Finally, the sacred language of ecclesial Latin was suppressed, even if the original texts were written in Latin. And it was manifestly *not* Paul VI's intention that the New Mass be said in Latin or that Gregorian chant be normative. He said:

> It is here that the greatest newness is going to be noticed, the newness of language. No longer Latin, but the spoken language will be the principal language of the Mass. The introduction of the vernacular will certainly be a great sacrifice for those who know the beauty, the power and the expressive sacrality of Latin. We are parting with the speech of the Christian centuries; we are becoming like profane intruders in the literary preserve of sacred utterance. We will lose a great part of that stupendous and incomparable artistic and spiritual thing, the Gregorian chant.[120]

Well, at least Paul VI was honest about the New Mass — because it clearly represents a complete break with the received tradition of the Church, and we can say with confidence that all the criteria required for a liturgy to be considered Catholic are either missing or contorted to the point where we can hardly notice the continuity or similarity with what came before.

With all this said, we have the right to question whether the New Mass is *Catholic*, let alone the Roman Rite. We can agree with Dr. Peter Kwasniewski who wrote: "The *Novus Ordo* encapsulates the errors of modern philosophy: in its prejudice against the universal anthropological language of symbols ... its rubrical sparseness and vagueness, it shows itself to be characterized by nominalism ... rationalism, and

---

[120] Pope Paul VI, General Audience, November 26, 1969.

relativism."[121] In short, it has all the hallmarks of what is encapsulated in Modernism.

The New Mass suffers from a lack of continuity with all of Christian worship since time immemorial. Now, some may object and point to the fact that the architects appealed, albeit *selectively*, to some liturgies that were celebrated in the earliest times of Church history. While this is true in some cases, it is also a feeble defense of the New Mass because it is not necessary for the Traditional Latin Mass, or any received liturgy, to be *exactly* the same as an earlier liturgy for it to be more authentic. Over centuries, with the aid of the Holy Ghost guiding the Church, the ancient apostolic liturgies were cemented in their forms substantially and passed on for generations. By the time of St. Gregory the Great, who canonized the Roman Rite, we find a liturgy that is strikingly similar to the Traditional Latin Mass we see today and utterly different from the New Mass. St. Gregory died in 604, and the liturgy was then already many centuries old. Furthermore, even if we could find a liturgy in the earliest times that resembled something like the New Mass, there is a reason why it was not kept and transmitted and why we received the Roman Rite in all its glory as it had been fostered since time immemorial.

Appealing to the distant past, to a time of primitive religion, to justify change for the sake of change is nothing more than a Modernist mentality that misrepresents tradition completely. The Modernism that inspired the creation of a New Rite with veritably no linkage to Catholic tradition and custom can be seen in virtually every aspect of the liturgical innovation inspired by Vatican II. We can say with Pius X: "What is there left in the Church which is not to be reformed according to their principles?" (*Pascendi* 38).

The Modernist Spirit of the New Mass

Aside from the obvious rupture with Catholic tradition, the lack of Catholicity in the New Mass, and the errors of modern philosophy that

---

[121] Kwasniewski, *Once and Future Roman Rite*, 45.

encapsulate the creation of the New Mass, there is a spirit of Modernism that is transmitted by the New Mass.

Catholic author Michael Baker wrote that the debasement of the New Mass

> flows from the Council's misconception of the priesthood as a "function of the People of God", as if that ineffable office depended for its legitimization on the faithful; the view that Our Lord, at the beginning, "established ministers among his faithful."[122] But Christ did no such thing. He chose and prepared the Apostles as priests long before there were any faithful — *in order that there might be* faithful.[123]

We see here the same error that John Paul made when speaking of catechesis: an appeal to the *experience* of religion in the community, whence flows the teachings and then the teachers. This is a reversal of the process of divine revelation; it is "bottom-up," not "top-down." It is also biblically incorrect, as we know full well that Christ *chose* His Apostles and called them by name — even giving new names — and they were sent forth to teach "all nations; baptizing them in the name of the Father, and of the Son, and of the Holy Ghost. Teaching them to observe all things whatsoever I have commanded you" (Matt. 28:19–20), Christ did *not say*, "Go ye therefore and become part of the faithful, whence I will find my prelates."

Baker adds that the "*Novus Ordo* indulges novelty and experimentation for its own sake."[124] This is manifestly true, even in the case of the "reverent" New Mass. Some proponents of the New Mass object to criticism of it and suggest that since the New Mass can be celebrated in a "traditional way," with chant, incense, nice vestments, and so forth,

---

[122] Second Vatican Council, Decree on Ministry and Life of Priests *Presbyterorum Ordinis* (December 7, 1965), no. 2.
[123] Baker, "What's Wrong."
[124] Baker, "What's Wrong."

this should satisfy traditionalists who are overly concerned with aesthetics. This mentality, however, only betrays the Modernist spirit that emanates from the New Rite: the very idea that, if you were to make the New Mass *look* like the Old Rite, this would somehow make the two rites similar is a type of "liturgical nominalism." Recall that nominalism — the error of Ockham — asserts, essentially, that we call things by names because of what they look like or what we perceive them to be but not because of their natures or essences, which nominalism denies. In this sense, if we simply dress up the Novus Ordo to *look* like the Traditional Mass, we are basically saying, "Well, it looks like what you want, so it should satisfy what you are looking for." This mentality completely disregards the fact that the New Mass, whether dressed up or not, is still the New Mass and the problems remain. This mentality is superficial and seems to suggest that everything is fine as long as traditionalists have a superficial experience that reminds them of the Old Rite, which is subjective and an appeal to experience as the primary mode of religion; subjectivity, nominalism, and an appeal to religious experience as primary modes of spirituality are all hallmarks of Modernism.

In fact, Paul VI seems to have suffered from a Modernist mentality when trying to justify why, from the beginning of the liturgical revolution, Latin and Gregorian chant would disappear with the advent of the New Mass. He said:

> The answer will seem banal, prosaic. Yet it is a good answer, because it is human, because it is *apostolic*. Understanding of prayer is worth more than the silken garments in which it is royally dressed. Participation by the people is worth more — particularly participation by *modern* people, so fond of plain language which is easily understood and converted into everyday speech. (emphasis added)[125]

---

[125] Pope Paul VI, General Audience, November 26, 1969.

Of course! It is apostolic to do things that are modern! Who knew?

This statement by Paul VI not only reeks of Modernist tendencies — given the insistence on the experiential reality of understanding the liturgy in one's own language and the hat tip to modern man — but it is philosophically absurd. How can it be apostolic to do things the way Modern man supposedly desires? Modernity is a historical time period that is different from the Apostolic Age; thus, a man from modernity is necessarily formed by a different set of cultural and linguistic circumstances. Also, isn't the idea that the primary liturgy of the Church should substantially change with the altering fads of culture reminiscent of the Modernist obsession with the evolution of religion? Furthermore, this mentality would suggest that the New Mass should be revised over and over again to change with the changing cultures. Should we create a Revised New Mass or a Newer New Mass to appeal to the TikTok generation?

Another Modernist tendency of the New Mass, according to Baker:

> [Is the] error contained in the Council's directive that among the "functions" of the priesthood, the first place is to be given to preaching, *sub textum* "proclaiming the Gospel of God to all." This contrasts dramatically with the Church's millennial understanding of what characterizes the priesthood, confirmed by the Council of Trent: "If any one says that there is not in the New Testament a visible and external priesthood; or that there is not any power of consecrating and offering the true body and blood of the Lord, and of forgiving and retaining sins; but only an office and bare ministry of preaching the Gospel ... let him be anathema (Session XXIII, Canon I)."[126]

The abundant liturgical tradition of the Church has been seemingly reduced to a service typified by a conversation between the priest and

---

[126] Baker, "What's Wrong." The citation from Vatican II is from *Presbyterorum Ordinis* 4.

the congregation. How apropos that the first half of Mass in the New Rite is called the "Liturgy of the Word" as opposed to the "Mass of the Catechumens," as it was always called.

What is ironic is that a true Modernist could accept the Old Mass, or any old thing that represents a custom of shared transcendence, because Modernists believe that the collective experience of the people constitutes a proof of religious truth. Although a Modernist would reject the immovable nature of traditional doctrines, he could look to history — even if he is agnostic about history — and see the witness of so many pious Catholics whose "religious subconscious" was watered by traditional liturgical customs. Hence the words of Pius X on Modernist liturgical reform: "Some of the admirers of symbolism are disposed to be more indulgent on this head" (*Pascendi* 38). This is why the permissions given to say or attend the Old Mass by the postconciliar popes were never a sure sign of the orthodoxy of the popes who permitted them. Benedict surely did the most to reestablish the Old Rite, but this is in keeping with Benedict's aesthetic character and preferences, as he demonstrated a very refined artistic taste, even with some Modernist theological tendencies.

But the Novus Ordo was thrust upon Catholics nonetheless because Modernism requires continual evolution and change to keep up with the times. But the Modernists who did so were so blinded by their commitment to Modernist doctrines that they couldn't see that the "collective religious sentiment" of the people — as they would understand it — did not want the Novus Ordo. For this reason, it was dead on arrival and offensive to the religious sense — properly understood — of the faithful; the millions upon millions of Catholics who simply stopped going to Mass after the arrival of the New Rite speaks volumes.[127]

---

[127] In 1970, weekly Mass attendance was much higher than now, with roughly thirty million Catholics in America attending Mass each week. In 2019, that number had fallen to just over fifteen million Catholics

By Their Fruits You Will Know Them

Let us end this consideration of the Modernist reform of the liturgy with a brief meditation on the word of Our Lord:

> Beware of false prophets, who come to you in the clothing of sheep, but inwardly they are ravening wolves. By their fruits you shall know them. Do men gather grapes of thorns, or figs of thistles? Even so every good tree bringeth forth good fruit, and the evil tree bringeth forth evil fruit. A good tree cannot bring forth evil fruit, neither can an evil tree bring forth good fruit. Every tree that bringeth not forth good fruit, shall be cut down, and shall be cast into the fire. Wherefore by their fruits you shall know them. (Matt. 7:15–20)

I had the great privilege of being raised with the influence not only of my parents but of my Nonno and Nonna (grandfather and grandmother) as well; my mother hails from Italy, and I had the pleasure of living in Tuscany for a time as a child. I have fond memories of spending time with Nonno in the cellar, helping him make wine, and I recall harvest time in the foothills of the Apennine Mountains, where I helped my great-uncle Silvano collect the fruits of his labor. In addition, I spent loads of time shadowing my great-uncle Lorenzino, who harvested and produced olive oil — liquid gold! — from his grove,

---

in America attending each week. In raw numbers, that is about a 50 percent decrease, but when you take into account the fact that the U.S. Catholic population had increased to more than eighty million by 2005, the relative decline is even more bleak. In addition, since 2005, the number of self-identified Catholics in the United States has dropped by almost 11 percent. And from 2000 to 2019, the number of weekly Mass-attending Catholics dropped by 31 percent in that period alone. Similar trends are seen all over the world and are even more severe in many Western European nations. Eric Sammons, "The Church's Dunkirk Moment," Eric Sammons, August 17, 2020, https://ericsammons.com/the-churchs-dunkirk-moment/.

which had been handed down in his family. I learned of the fruits of the Mediterranean and how they were cultivated; thus, I have always understood this passage from Our Lord with what I think is a correct contextual understanding.

One summer day a few years ago, my wife and I accompanied some friends to a local winery in Ontario, and the sommelier was giving us a lesson in wine tasting. I whispered to a friend that since the winery was only three years old, the grapes must have come from somewhere else, as at least fifty years were required before any consistent vintage could be harvested. My friend thought I was mistaken and asked the sommelier when the vines were planted. She said, "Three years ago," and my friend looked at me triumphantly. She then added that the plants had come from France and were about forty-eight years old, and therefore the winery would have to continue to produce blended wines until the grapes were fully mature. I smirked at my friend, and he laughed sheepishly. The sommelier regaled us with a story about how regions of France had lost the mass of their vineyards due to disease, and to avoid this problem, it is necessary to destroy any diseased plant the moment the disease is discovered, lest it spread and destroy the whole crop.

We cannot know the fruits of something until it has had time to mature, and since Christ was speaking in the context of the Mediterranean fruits of the Levant — grapes, figs, and olives — we can assume that anyone who heard Him would understand the meaning in that sense. In 2019, the New Mass turned fifty, and the fruits are sour. Since the very beginning, the vintage of the New Rite has been rejected en masse, evidenced by the hordes of Catholics who never came to Mass again after 1970.

The disease of Modernism has spread to every branch of the tree through the preaching, liturgical abuse, and sacrilege incarnated in the practice of the New Rite. Sanctuaries were destroyed, statues were beheaded, and the piety of twenty centuries was cast into the fire to make way for the *nouvelle régime*. As Christ said, "A good tree cannot bring forth evil fruit, neither can an evil tree bring forth good fruit." The new tree has been kept alive only by artificial means, like the body of Lenin, which is preserved by formaldehyde as an ode to communism; the old tree has been kept alive on its own merits and sanctity, rediscovered by new generations like an incorruptible saint discovered under an altar.

The two trees cannot exist side by side, and the one has proven to yield bad fruit throughout its maturation process. Only one can remain, and it must be the tree that yields the fruit of Tradition; the other must be cast into the fire.

18

The Pride of Modernism Rages More Than Ever

Pope Pius X published *Pascendi* in 1907, at a time when Modernism still existed in the realm of ivory towers and dissident communities of priests. Granted, the turn of the last century was not a golden age in the Church, given that what was left of Christendom was reeling from a century of revolutions. Nevertheless, what Pius X did was expose the greatest heresy the Church had ever seen, and he did it with exactitude. With the advent of the First World War, however, what was left of the old order of civilization — basically, Europe and the Catholic way of life — was struck with a seemingly fatal blow. The Holy Roman Empire, at the time under the guardianship of the Habsburg dynasty, was trampled and reformulated by the new international powers, and various political ideologies with strikingly religious character stepped in and captured the hearts and minds of many millions of people. In fact, it is said that Pope Pius X died of a broken heart in 1914, just weeks after the Great War was declared. He tried with all his might to stop it, but it was not enough.

In any event, due to this calamity, the Church suffered immensely, as did her academic institutions. So many heroes died in the subsequent years as yet another war ravaged the human race, and the situation became more grave. As a result, so many good men died, and we can only assume that with the death of so many patriots came the death of so many vocations. Furthermore, the prevailing narrative was, and still is, that the old sensibilities of "medieval Europe" had been the cause of the conflicts in Europe. Instead, the new zeitgeist was one of democracy and freedom, where the age of kings and emperors was dead, and the dawn of the individual and his conscience was born.

Because of these realities, and many others, the hydra of Modernism was fostered in the intellectual institutions of Europe, where the animating spirit was "progress" and everything "modern" was pursued with religious zeal.

For these reasons, by the time Vatican II was convened, a new class of theologians, educated in modern philosophy and psychologically gripped by the seeming progress of the postwar age, took center stage and officialized the Modernist revolution.

What we face now is a super heresy, even more monstrous than the Modernism defined by Pius X. In his day, though the situation was grave, the average Catholic still had contact with the unchanging Faith of time immemorial in the Holy Sacrifice of the Mass and the devotions that have made many saints. Now, after the sweeping changes to the Mass, the catechisms, the governance of the Church, and much else, we see Modernism in its fullest and ugliest form.

Daily, Catholics are reminded of this if they pay attention. Who would have ever thought that a pagan idol — the pachamama — could have been paraded into St. Peter's Basilica? Who could have imagined the absurd and laughable, yet all too real, Synod on Synodality. The elevation of Pope Francis to the See of Peter has been received by so many as a chastisement, yet we know that what happens now did not start with him. While he may in some ways be the most egregious offender, he is the logical conclusion of the revolution that has reached its climax.

Recently, Rome approved the so-called Mayan Rite, which is a *new spin* on the New Mass, tailored for the vestige of Central American paganism. At the same time, it is those dedicated to the Traditional Mass who are dealt blow after blow from Rome as the Mass of All Time is relegated to a side issue that can be celebrated — in some cases — in the later afternoon at a shrine far from their parish.

How can we explain a hierarchy largely motivated to crush what is left of Tradition while vocations plummet and parishes are sold to the highest bidder and are often made into mosques or restaurants?

We can pose the question with Pius X: "If experiences have so much value in their eyes, why do they not attach equal weight to the experience that thousands upon thousands of Catholics have that the Modernists are on the wrong road?" (*Pascendi* 39).

Nevertheless, the revolution continues, and Catholics are often left wondering where they can attend Mass or educate their children so they may avoid the poison that seems to infect everything in its path. Truly, as Pius X said, Modernism is the *synthesis of all heresies*. "Were one to attempt the task of collecting together all the errors that have been broached against the faith and to concentrate the sap and substance of them all into one, he could not better succeed than the Modernists have done. Nay, they have done more than this, for, as we have already intimated, their system means the destruction not of the Catholic religion alone but of all religion" (39).

That said, as complicated as the Modernist system is, and it is truly complex, the motivating factor is the same thing that precipitated the fall of the human race at the beginning. The root of the whole enterprise is *pride*.

The Devilish Pride at the Foundation

It is said that all sin is rooted in pride, and the logical conclusion of pride is the sin of Lucifer, who will not serve God and will be worshipped as a god even if it means being worshipped in Hell by the damned. The Modernists have uttered their *non serviam* — "I will not serve" — like Lucifer before them, and they will take as many souls to Hell with them as they can.

They will not yield to the Tradition of the wisdom of Catholic history but will prostrate themselves at the altar of novelty. They will not hear the cries of so many Catholic parents begging them to provide their families with the old-fashioned Catholicism that gave us saints as numerous as the stars in the night sky. They seem incapable of any true self-reflection — despite all the conciliar talk of self-discovery — as they continue to do *new thing* after *new thing* and act as if it is the "rigid" refuseniks who hold on to their Latin prayers who are the problem.

They are truly out of touch, stuck in a Modernity that is stuck in the revolutionary spirit of the 1960s.

The spiritual cause is simple:

> Pride sits in Modernism as in its own house, finding sustenance everywhere in its doctrines and an occasion to flaunt itself in all its aspects. It is pride which fills Modernists with that confidence in themselves and leads them to hold themselves up as the rule for all, pride which puffs them up with that vainglory which allows them to regard themselves as the sole possessors of knowledge, and makes them say, inflated with presumption, "We are not as the rest of men," and which, to make them really not as other men, leads them to embrace all kinds of the most absurd novelties. (*Pascendi* 40)

The pride of Modernism blinds men to reality, which leads Modernists, ultimately, to disobey God.

> It is pride which rouses in them the spirit of disobedience and causes them to demand a compromise between authority and liberty; it is pride that makes of them the reformers of others, while they forget to reform themselves, and which begets their absolute want of respect for authority, not excepting the supreme authority. No, truly, there is no road which leads so directly and so quickly to Modernism as pride. (40)

"For it is a master-stroke of Satan," wrote Archbishop Lefebvre, "to get Catholics to disobey the whole of Tradition in the name of obedience."[128]

Therefore, we must obey the Faith of All Time and not fall prey to Modernist errors. This is, of course, a great cross for us to bear, as we face a Leviathan that has enraptured the intellects of the vast majority of theologians and prelates for decades. Furthermore, the laity have been increasingly made into Modernists through the propagation of their system as Catholic education has only degraded universally. "They seize upon chairs in the seminaries and universities, and gradually make of them chairs of pestilence" (*Pascendi* 43).

Yield Not to Despair and Trust in Providence

For some reason, God has ordained that we live in times such as these, and we must remember what Pius recalls for us:

> For Catholics the second Council of Nicea will always have the force of law, where it condemns those "who dare, after the impious fashion of heretics, to deride the ecclesiastical traditions, to invent novelties of some kind ... or endeavour by malice or craft to overthrow any one of the legitimate traditions of the Catholic Church"; and Catholics will hold for law, also, the profession of the fourth Council of Constantinople: "We therefore profess to conserve and guard the rules bequeathed to the Holy Catholic and Apostolic Church by the Holy and most illustrious Apostles, by the orthodox Councils, both general and local, and by every one of those divine interpreters the Fathers and Doctors of the Church." (42)

We must avoid the temptation to fall into despair or negativity about the Church, which is the Mystical Body of Christ and is inviolate

---

[128] Marcel Lefebvre, *Open Letter to Confused Catholics*, chap. 18, https://www.sspxasia.com/Documents/Archbishop-Lefebvre/OpenLetterToConfusedCatholics/Chapter-18.htm.

in her supernatural character, despite what evil men have done. If we give in to this temptation, we give in to the plan of the Modernists, who wage their war of attrition. The Modernists *want* us to "bring contempt and odium on the mystic Spouse of Christ, who is the true light, the children of darkness have been wont to cast in her face before the world a stupid calumny, and perverting the meaning and force of things and words, to depict her as the friend of darkness and ignorance, and the enemy of light, science, and progress" (42).

For this reason, Catholics must fight the temptation to gain the respect of men, especially the men of the Church who are plagued with this spiritual disease, a respect that "would only provoke nausea in a real Catholic" (*Pascendi* 35). Instead, we must expect attacks and calumnies as a way of life, for "the Modernists vent all their gall and hatred on Catholics who sturdily fight the battles of the Church" (42). And it is to be expected that whenever a traditionalist stares down the Modernist monster, he will be labeled a "Fundamentalist" or a "Pharisee," which only demonstrates the stupidity of the Modernists, who do not realize that they are the true Pharisees; a Pharisee is not a man who holds fast to Tradition but a man who uses the letter of the law with no spirit. These are the Modernists, who deny the activity of the Holy Spirit in the dogmas of twenty centuries while they contort words to condemn souls to a state of perpetual confusion.

Nay, they are *worse* than Pharisees, for at least Christ could say of the Pharisees, "All things therefore whatsoever they shall say to you, observe and do" (Matt. 23:3). We cannot do what the Modernists say *or* do. The Pharisees did not, for example, make the liturgy of the Temple unrecognizable.

Imagine what Christ would say to the Modernists; in fact, we do not have to imagine: "And then will I profess unto them, I never knew you: depart from me, you that work iniquity" (Matt. 7:23).

While it may be impossible to see it with human eyes, there *will* come a time when Modernism will be vanquished, even if it seems to happen at a snail's pace. If we recall, for example, the time of the Arian heresy, we may be tempted to consider it a short time because we read about it in a single paragraph or discuss it in a single conversation. In reality, the entire fourth century was essentially riddled with Arianism before the heresy was eventually condemned.

Modernism is the synthesis of all heresies, and a much graver heresy than Arianism, so it should not surprise us that we have been dealing with it for a century or more. It is much harder to root out bad ideas and doctrines than it is to promulgate sound theology and philosophy, in the same way that the road to health after contracting a disease can take years, whereas getting in shape can take weeks or months.

If we are to root out the Modernist tumor from the Church, the authorities must have the humility to *go back* and discover where the diseased cells first began to multiply.

If we consider another analogy, those leading us must realize that we are *lost* in a dark forest, and, therefore, turning around and retracing our steps is the right thing to do.

And if the authorities admit that we are lost and diseased, they will demonstrate the initial humility that will allow them to see the cause of the crisis and adopt the solution.

Thankfully, Pope Pius X, like a good physician, did not merely diagnose the disease, but he gave us a sure remedy.

19

The Solution

Pius X ends his encyclical by providing practical guidance to the bishops of the world, to whom his letter was addressed. Though there may be some bishops who will read this, surely the majority of readers will be laymen. That being said, we can take Pius X's proposed remedies and apply them to our own lives and to those of our children. It must also be noted that it is never too late to reverse course, even if we have imbibed the heresies of the Modernist doctrine in one way or another. Coming into contact with these errors is unavoidable, and it is likely that most of us have believed this or that error of the Modernists at some point.

Virtually no institution can claim to be totally immune from Modernist influence, especially not the mainstream institutions of the Church, as we all swim in a Modernist swamp as our natural habitat. Therefore, we must make Pius X's solutions our own and strive to rid ourselves of the disease, even if it seems impossible.

As was mentioned in chapter 16, all heresy is a type of madness, and Chesterton told us what to do with madness when he wrote in *Orthodoxy*, "Every remedy is a desperate remedy. Every cure is a miraculous cure. Curing a madman is not arguing with a philosopher; it is casting out a devil."

We must *amputate* Modernism from our lives: "And if thy right hand scandalize thee, cut it off, and cast it from thee: for it is expedient for thee that one of thy members should perish, rather than that thy whole body be cast into hell" (Matt. 5:30).

Now let us consider Pius X's remedies.

Study Scholastic Philosophy

"In the first place, with regard to studies, We will and ordain that scholastic philosophy be made the basis of the sacred sciences" (45).

You will recall from the chapter on the philosophy and theology of the Modernists their disdain for Scholasticism. "There is no surer sign that a man is on the way to Modernism than when he begins to show his dislike for this system" (42). It stands to reason, as Pius X does reason, that the way to fix the problem is to do the opposite of what the Modernists do. If Modernists become Modernists — at least in part — by rejecting St. Thomas, then we should study St. Thomas; if Modernists become subjectivists by imbibing the errors of Modern philosophy, then we should study Scholasticism.

Now, far be it from Pius X to suggest that by merely studying the Scholastics uncritically and without recourse to true development in the field, we will have perfect intellectual security. Citing Leo XIII, Pius X states: "It goes without saying that 'if anything is met with among the scholastic doctors which may be regarded as an excess of subtlety, or which is altogether destitute of probability, We have no desire whatever to propose it for the imitation of present generations'" (45).

We need not view the Scholastics as infallible oracles of divine revelation, but we *must* accept that the *method* of Scholasticism is unimpeachable; hence its exaltation at numerous councils. If a man studies Aquinas and learns the Scholastic method, he cannot easily be swayed by the errors of our time. Thomism may not be a *panacea*, a cure-all, but it is the closest thing to a cure-all that exists.

Some may object that Thomas is not the main theologian for Eastern Catholics, and therefore it cannot be said that Catholics universally must study Aquinas. While I admit that Eastern theology has a different tone in many ways, it must also be admitted that the East has been plagued by Modernism just like the West. Byzantine Catholicism is not immune to the errors of Modernity, even if they have kept stronger liturgical traditions. In fact, we can see how the Scholastic precision of Rome has helped the Byzantines avoid the continual schisms and heresies that plague the Eastern Orthodox churches, many of whom are still debating theological truths sorted out centuries ago. Thomas is the Universal Doctor of the Roman Catholic Church, and Pius X, along with numerous other popes, prescribed Thomas for the universal Church.

It can be difficult for laymen to read Aquinas without commentary or in older prose, which is understandable. Luckily for us, not all that is modern is bad, and modernity has given us the ability to access publications and productions that do us great service.

The works of arguably the greatest Thomist and theologian of the twentieth century, Réginald Garrigou-Lagrange, are more available in English than ever. Traditional priests and theologians produce a variety of podcasts and videos imbued with the spirit of Scholasticism. And anyone can access a traditional catechism electronically, as well as the increasing library of good catechisms published by Sophia Institute Press. Simply put, as bad as things are in the world of academia, we have innumerable traditional resources at our fingertips that can be studied with zeal.

Although this is merely anecdotal, in my own experience, aside from priests trained in what few good seminaries remain, the strongest theological minds I have encountered belong to regular men who read shelves and shelves of old books and who make the study of the perennial thought of the Church their hobby. And this must not come off as an onerous or burdensome task; it is far from it! Finding the perennial wisdom of the Church is like discovering a secret garden amid a forest of thorns. It is a joy and a refreshment to the soul. It is a great adventure, with never a dull moment.

Reject the Materialist Spirit of the World

We must also guard against the temptation to spend all our time in the profane — nonreligious — sciences. While there is much good to be found in the world of the natural sciences, there are also great dangers, given the materialist underpinnings of modern natural science. Who can deny that the errors of subjectivism and evolutionism are the foundation for much of modern natural science? Is there anyone who lived through the Covid era who can say that we should "trust the science"? Pius X quotes his predecessor's warning on this very topic:

> If you carefully search for the cause of those errors you will find that it lies in the fact that in these days when the natural sciences absorb so much study, the more severe and lofty studies have been proportionately neglected — some of them have almost passed into oblivion, some of them are pursued in a half-hearted or superficial way, and, sad to say, now that they are fallen from their old estate, they have been disfigured by perverse doctrines and monstrous errors. (47)

The natural sciences exist in a realm of constant doubt and flux, which is appropriate in some instances in order to test hypotheses, but theological truths, especially those of defined dogmas, are not up for debate. It does not matter if a dogma was defined in the year 50 or the year 1950, it is a dogma in perpetuity and cannot be denied. We will not be damned because we misunderstand the theory of relativity or how viruses mutate, but we will be damned if we die as obstinate heretics.

Be Vigilant and Employ Censorship

Pius X implored bishops to be vigilant over publications produced in their jurisdictions and actively to censor heretical works. He warned that the danger of reading heretical material "would be equal to that caused by immoral reading — nay, it would be greater for such writings poison Christian life at its very fount" (50). He also implored bishops to censor the writings of some laymen in a way that would put numerous supposedly reputable apologists out of work in our day:

> The same decision is to be taken concerning the writings of some Catholics, who, though not badly disposed themselves but ill-instructed in theological studies and imbued with modern philosophy, strive to make this harmonize with the faith, and, as they say, to turn it to the account of the faith. The name and reputation of these authors cause them to be read without suspicion, and they are, therefore, all the more dangerous in preparing the way for Modernism. (50)

Of course, if you are not a bishop, then you have no authority over what is published in your diocese and little, if any, over what is taught in local schools. But you *do* have authority over your domain, whether that be your personal domain as an individual or the domain of your children's education.

We must avoid heretical works and even works suggestive of heresy. "We bid you do everything in your power to drive out of your dioceses, even by solemn interdict, any pernicious books that may be in circulation there" (51). Exceptions may be made in certain circumstances wherein research may be required due to necessity, such as it was necessary for Pius X to read the works of heretics in order to understand what should be condemned. But there is always a danger in reading bad books, as there is a danger in listening to bad music or watching bad movies.

At traditional seminaries, there is a section in libraries called "Hell" where seminarians will find the works of heretics such as Martin Luther and the works of false religions. Only with permission from their superiors can seminarians access these works, and only when it is absolutely necessary. I recall a story told to me by a priest about how a superior dealt with a seminarian who had spent considerable time reading "Hell" books for research. The seminarian relayed that he worried the bad literature was having an effect on his thinking and causing doubt about his

Faith. Rather than telling the seminarian to study more Aquinas in that instance — which was not necessary because of his classroom formation — he told the seminarian to go outside and play sports every day.

This is a testament to the perverse nature of "Hell" books; they are like viruses that infect the mind and must be quarantined. Furthermore, the wisdom of this superior was seen in his prescription of outdoor activity. This is because all thought that attacks the Scholastic method turns one *inward* and away from the *real*. The solution to bad thinking and intellectual viruses can certainly be the study of good thinking, but it can also be an activity that stops bad thinking from happening. We can all gain wisdom from this anecdote and should all consider spending less time in virtual reality and more time in *real* reality.

Read Good Books

It should also be noted that there are plenty of works written by "conservative" authors in the political sphere that many orthodox Catholics will read. These books will doubtless contain references to things such as "freedom of speech" and "freedom of the press" as positive attributes of a society that should be fought for. However, they are positions condemned by many popes, even if the condemnations have gone out of fashion.[129]

World-famous authors produce self-help books and guides to economic and personal success; while there are many good things in these books, they are often steeped in the philosophical errors of the authors.

---

[129] One condemnation is found in Proposition 79 of the *Syllabus* of Pius IX, which presents the following statement as condemned: "Moreover, it is false that the civil liberty of every form of worship, and the full power, given to all, of overtly and publicly manifesting any opinions whatsoever and thoughts, conduce more easily to corrupt the morals and minds of the people, and to propagate the pest of indifferentism." This means that to hold this view is condemnable, and it is clearly understood from this statement that those who hold it believe there is no danger in publishing erroneous and false works.

Even in the realm of Catholic books, Pius X warns us that an imprimatur is not enough to ensure orthodoxy in a book:

> Nor are you to be deterred by the fact that a book has obtained the Imprimatur elsewhere, both because this may be merely simulated, and because it may have been granted through carelessness or easiness or excessive confidence in the author as may sometimes happen in religious Orders. (51)

There are plenty of works circulating today written by priests and approved by bishops that are certainly unorthodox and Modernist; this cannot be denied. It stands to reason that going back to perennial works is sufficient for a sound Catholic formation. When considering which books to read, take into account the reputation of the publisher and the formation of the priest or theologian who wrote the book. There are many modern authors who produce amazing works that are really distillations of Traditional doctrine for new readers. Once you find an author whom you can trust, it is advisable to read his corpus.

Furthermore, no one is required to be a theologian to save his soul — being a theologian in our day may present *obstacles* to saving your soul! There is no reason to spend considerable time reading new books when the Roman Catechism and St. Louis-Marie Grignion de Montfort's *True Devotion to Mary* are collecting dust on your bookshelf. Have you read the Bible, or at least the whole New Testament?

Find Beauty

Also, we needn't overburden our intellects with philosophy and theology; good reading has made many saints, but how many more have been made by praying the Rosary and the Divine Office? And how many more by listening to Palestrina?

Our world is filled with an overabundance of factoids and news stories that will drive us mad if we let them. We need to unplug from rationalism and fill our souls with heavenly and beautiful things. Have you ever noticed that styles of art that are called Modernist — in the aesthetic and not theological sense — are just as ugly as their theological counterpart? The great unnamed saints of history who built cathedrals and palaces did not accomplish what they did because they were experts in computer sciences or algorithms; they created the greatest architecture the world has ever seen — or will ever see — because they built for the sake of *beauty*.

The Gothic cathedral is a building only after it was first a dream. Modernists cannot build Gothic cathedrals because they cannot dream of cathedrals — nay, Modernists cannot even really dream; they can only analyze dreams. They cannot truly create because they can only produce; they cannot truly live because they can only *experience vitality*.

Lest anyone suggest that the pursuit of beauty is impractical, we should compare the longevity of the aqueducts and Notre Dame to the shelf life of modern buildings that are ugly and always being repaired. Our ancestors built *for God*, and consequently, what they built will last until the consummation of the world.

Modern man has lost all sense of beauty, especially natural beauty, which can be seen plainly in the grotesque vestments modern priests wear, such as the drab green cloaks they wear during what is now called Ordinary Time that look as if they are made of polyester curtains. Traditional priests, on the other hand, during the Time after Pentecost, wear silken chasubles that appear as summer fields turning from shimmering green to shining gold. Do everything in your power to find priests who have a sense of true beauty. The loss of the sacred has meant the loss of beauty; therefore, if we desire to recapture the sacred, we must chase after that which is beautiful.

Ditch modern music and its syncopated rhythm, and allow the heaven-sent flittering of Baroque crescendos to recalibrate your spirit. An afternoon spent in a sunroom with an espresso and Vivaldi will do more to rid your soul of Modernism than almost anything. A walk through a crimson forest in October will teach you more about creation than any theologasting blowhard lecturing you about theistic evolution. The smell and feel of an old Chesterton novel will satisfy your soul more than any viral video. The touch of a transcendental vintage to your lips will teach you why Puritans are heretics more than any apologist could hope to.

You may think that studying the inner workings of the universe is the best way to see the Divine Hand, but we do not call God the Mathematician or Architect like the Freemasons; He is the Author of creation, and His great work is a poem and a song. Chaucer and Dante will guide you through the Heavens better than any physicist could. Of course, this is *not* to say that studying the created world is necessarily rationalistic; but our age of rationalism has exalted the calculator and the computer above the sacred vessels used in Mass and the biologist above the priest. We must recalibrate our souls to eternity, which is their destination. In eternity, we will contemplate God in a way that is impossible to use on this side of the divide; thus, we ought to spend more time in the world of imagination, where impossible things come true.

Chesterton said it best in *Orthodoxy*: "Imagination does not breed insanity. Exactly what does breed insanity is reason. Poets do not go mad; but chess players do.... Poetry is sane because it floats easily in an infinite sea; reason seeks to cross the infinite sea, and so make it finite. The result is mental exhaustion.... The poet only asks to get his head into the heavens. It is the logician who seeks to get the heavens into his head. And it is his head that splits." Now, Chesterton was often a provocateur, and we could retort to him that in our era of Modernity we see all sorts of artists go mad. But I think the spirit of what he says is true, given that he was concerned with the milieu of his time, which was the same as Pius X's. When we read the poetical and imaginative works of ancient writers and sages — even pagans — we so often find brilliance and beauty that leave us with peace in our souls. However, so much modern literature and art has been infected by the modern philosophy that has made modern man so mad, and their works invoke lust and despair.

Free yourself, dear reader, from Modernism by purifying yourself of the unholy intellectual and artistic milieu that birthed this monster. Modernism is from Satan, and Satan is a dragon and must be stabbed in the heart and beheaded. Take up the sword of St. George, and amputate this gangrenous growth from your soul once and for all.

Conclusion: The Immaculate Virgin, the Destroyer of All Heresies

In the last paragraph of his magnum opus, Pius X writes:

> Meanwhile, Venerable Brethren, fully confident in your zeal and work, we beseech for you with our whole heart and soul the abundance of heavenly light, so that in the midst of this great perturbation of men's minds from the insidious invasions of error from every side, you may see clearly what you ought to do and may perform the task with all your strength and courage. May Jesus Christ, the author and finisher of our faith, be with you by His power; and may the *Immaculate Virgin, the destroyer of all heresies*, be with you by her prayers and aid. (58, emphasis added)

Like every good sermon, Pius X's work ends with an invocation of the Virgin Mary and employs her heavenly aid as the *destroyer of all heresies*.

Pope Pius X began his pontificate with the encyclical *E Supremi*, wherein he laid out his plan for the Church to "restore all things in Christ" — *instaurare omnia in Christo*. This was soon followed by his second encyclical, *Ad Diem Illum Laetissimum*, a letter explaining his

Mariology and commenting on the Immaculate Conception for the fiftieth anniversary of Pius IX's proclamation of the dogma.

There is a heavenly symmetry in the order of these two documents, as it shows the faithful that to restore all things in Christ, we must immediately turn to the Blessed Virgin Mary in all her glory. We are reminded of the dependency of Christ Himself as a Divine Infant on the tender care of the Blessed Mother as she nursed Our Savior. We may call to mind the journey of Mary and Joseph to Bethlehem in the dark cold of the desert, illuminated by her sacred womb, whence the Light of the World shone forth like the first monstrance.

> Wherefore in the same holy bosom of his most chaste Mother Christ took to Himself flesh, and united to Himself the spiritual body formed by those who were to believe in Him. Hence Mary, carrying the Savior within her, may be said to have also carried all those whose life was contained in the life of the Savior.[130]

Our life is in Christ, and therefore our life is in some mystical way sustained in the virginal womb of Mary. The Devil knows this; thus we have the perennial combat between the Serpent and her heel (see Gen. 3:15).

The history of heresy has been the history of attacks on Mary as much as it has been attacks on Christ; this is because, just as Christ would not have for us a religion without his Mother, He will not have for us orthodoxy that is not Marian.

When the Gnostics arose in the early centuries, they attacked the Incarnation along with the incarnate nature of human life as a whole. Arius arose with his diabolical denial of the divinity of Our Lord, which was also an attack on the divine maternity. After Arius had been vanquished, Nestorius arose to claim that Mary was not the Mother of God

---

[130] Pope Pius X, encyclical *Ad Diem Illum Laetissimum* (February 2, 1904), no. 10.

but the Mother of Christ; he was not willing to call her the *Theotokos*, the "God-Bearer."

Out of the desert rose the heresy of Islam, the continual scourge of Christianity in her native lands. Worse than the tip of the sword with which Mohammed's legions converted or martyred millions was again the denial of Christ's divinity, relegating Him to the realm of a prophet.

Then, as if the ancient Gnostic Manes had been reincarnated, arose the Albigensian heresy just over a thousand years after Christ walked the earth, pitting body and soul against one another in a dualistic suicide. The Incarnation was attacked, and by extension so was the Virgin Birth. Once again, Our Lady was not the Mother of God because Christ was not a real man, because matter was evil and spirit was good.

Every heresy that attacked Our Lord attacked his Mother, and in every battle with every heresy, we must march into war with the banner of Our Lady: "Who is she that cometh forth as the morning rising, fair as the moon, bright as the sun, terrible as an army set in array?" (Cant. [Song of Sol.] 6:9).

By defining the Holy Trinity and establishing the divinity of Christ, the Church established the divine maternity of the Blessed Mother and the mystical espousal of Our Lady to the Third Person of the Holy Trinity. In the rejection of Nestorius's error, the Church defined for every generation that Our Lady is the Mother of God, and therefore any heretic who will not have Mary as his Mother will not have Christ.

Islam, scourge as it was, was no match for Don Juan at Lepanto and his fleet brandishing Our Lady of Guadalupe standing on the crescent moon.

The Albigensians sought to lead Europe to suicide with their dualistic death cult but were defeated by Our Lady through St. Dominic, who gave us the mysteries of the Rosary to use like a knotted cord for driving demons out of the Temple of God.

The history of heresies can also be seen as the history of Our Lady *defeating* heresies and heretics, and we must hold with sincere faith that the Blessed Mother will defeat Modernism.

> For can anyone fail to see that there is no surer or more direct road than by Mary for uniting all mankind in Christ and obtaining through Him the perfect adoption of sons, that we may be holy and immaculate in the sight of God?[131]

In this present age, mankind edges further and further toward the precipice from which there is no return. Our world has not only gone mad; it has gone beyond madness; we cannot even define that a man is mad because the very definition of a definition cannot be defined. Our drunkenness of rationalism has made us imbeciles who are both the inmates and nurses of the Cartesian asylums of our own intellects. The situation is not only dire; it is *impossible*.

How can one reason with a Modernist? Consequently, how can the faithful reason with a class of prelates who do not believe they are Modernists because they have likely never even read *Pascendi*? We are like sober men having conversations with vagabonds who have been drunk for so long that they appear sober yet unresponsive.

But is not this state of impossible escape from heresy and apostasy the very theme of the Old Testament? How long did the Hebrews labor under the yoke of slavery, burning under the Egyptian sun like an egg under a broiler? How long did the Hebrews wander in the desert, with their insatiable thirst for water, prefiguring the living water of Christ that would satiate the very depths of our souls?

How bitterly did King David cry when God took his firstborn as an atonement for David's murderous sin? How much more bitterly must Adam have cried — the real Adam, not some evolutionary monstrosity — when that first drip of sweat slipped down the awning of his brow while he worked among the thorns for his daily bread?

That we have been given the cross of Modernity and her heresy to bear in this valley of tears is not proof of God's abandonment but is instead a tribulation ordained for our benefit; for if we are to be sons

---

[131] Pope Pius X, *Ad Diem* 5.

of God, we must be *strong sons* who will not bend to the whims of the passing of time like the fanatics who sold orthodoxy for worldly acclaim.

And that we languish under this heavy cross is only proof that God has not left us orphans but has instead said to us, "Behold, your Mother."

We must *cleave* to the Virgin Mary during these times, never letting go of the Holy Rosary, which is both our comfort and the tether that fastens us to the Ark of Salvation. Pius X tells us that "through the Virgin, and through her more than through any other means, we have offered us a way of reaching the knowledge of Jesus Christ.... Nobody ever knew Christ so profoundly as she did, and nobody can ever be more competent as a guide and teacher of the knowledge of Christ."[132]

If the Old Testament patriarchs were saved by the blood of Christ, which came in chronological history long after their deaths, then they were saved by the blood that nourished Christ in the Virgin's womb; the blood that flowed from the Immaculate Heart into the Sacred Heart, bruised for our offenses.

Thus, the Crusaders of old marched into battle singing the Salve, rejoicing at the prospect of dying for Christ, as Mary rejoiced "that her Only Son was offered for the salvation of mankind."[133]

To end this era of confusion and decay, we must exalt the Virgin Mary as high as has ever been done. We must not give in to the madness of ecumenism that degrades the worship of the Mother of God to mere veneration. "For to be right and good, worship of the Mother of God ought to spring from the heart."[134]

By exalting her to her proper place, we become veritably immune to heresy:

> Now this plague, which is equally fatal to society at large and to Christianity, finds its ruin in the dogma of the Immaculate Conception by the obligation which it imposes of recognizing

---

[132] Pope Pius X, *Ad Diem* 7.
[133] Pope Pius X, *Ad Diem* 12.
[134] Pope Pius X, *Ad Diem* 17.

in the Church a power before which not only has the will to bow, but the intelligence to subject itself. It is from a subjection of the reason of this sort that Christian people sing thus the praise of the Mother of God: "Thou art all fair, O Mary, and the stain of original sin is not in thee." (Mass of Immac. Concep.) And thus once again is justified what the Church attributes to this august Virgin that she has *exterminated all heresies in the world*. (emphasis added)[135]

Thus, we may approach the end of the book with the words of Pius X, to whom we owe so much:

> Is it forbidden us to hope for still greater things for the future? True, we are passing through disastrous times, when we may well make our own the lamentation of the Prophet: "There is no truth and no mercy and no knowledge of God on the earth. Blasphemy and lying and homicide and theft and adultery have inundated it" (Os. iv., 1-2). Yet in the midst of this deluge of evil, the Virgin Most Clement rises before our eyes like a rainbow, as the arbiter of peace between God and man: "I will set my bow in the clouds and it shall be the sign of a covenant between me and between the earth" (Gen. ix.,13). Let the storm rage and sky darken — not for that shall we be dismayed. "And the bow shall be in the clouds, and I shall see it and shall remember the everlasting covenant" (ibid. 16). "And there shall no more be waters of a flood to destroy all flesh" (ibid. 15). Oh yes, if we trust as we should in Mary, now especially when we are about to celebrate, with more than usual fervor, her Immaculate Conception, we shall recognize in her that Virgin most powerful "who with virginal foot did crush the head of the serpent (Off. Immac. Conc.)."[136]

---

[135] Pope Pius X, *Ad Diem* 22.
[136] Pope Pius X, *Ad Diem* 33.

As daunting as it may have seemed at the outset of the book, we have reached the end of our journey through Modernism. Truly, it is a damnable heresy, which is why no effort can be spared if we are to understand what it is and how it has plagued our beloved Church during this decades-long dark night of the soul. Nevertheless, as Pius X commends us to do, we must hold on to the Virgin Mary, for she is never far from her son.

We might imagine a statue of Our Lady and the Infant Christ; if we were to take away Our Lord from that statue, she would still stand; if we were to take away Our Lady, the Divine Infant would fall. Of course, this does not demonstrate that Our Lady possesses power beyond Christ's; it demonstrates that, in His infinite wisdom, He deemed it necessary to demonstrate that not only is He all-powerful, but His humility knows no bounds. We must be humble servants of Jesus Christ, and to do so, we must be humble sons of the Blessed Mother.

The storm of Modernism will continue to rage all around us until Our Lord commands the tempest to cease. We must fasten ourselves to the Catholic Church — the only Ark of Salvation — with every fiber of our being. And there is no surer way to tie ourselves down to the ship than by the Holy Rosary. If we hold on to Mary, we will never let go of Christ.

Pope St. Pius X, *ora pro nobis.*

About the Author

Kennedy Hall is a Catholic author and podcaster. He has published numerous bestselling books, which can be found at his website: www.kennedyhall.ca/books. He lives in Ontario, Canada, with his wife and six children.

CRISIS Publications

Sophia Institute Press awards the privileged title "CRISIS Publications" to a select few of our books that address contemporary issues at the intersection of politics, culture, and the Church with clarity, cogency, and force and that are also destined to become all-time classics.

CRISIS Publications are direct, explaining their principles briefly, simply, and clearly to Catholics in the pews, on whom the future of the Church depends. The time for ambiguity or confusion is long past.

CRISIS Publications are contemporary, born of our own time and circumstances and intended to become significant statements in current debates, statements that serious Catholics cannot ignore, regardless of their prior views.

CRISIS Publications are classical, addressing themes and enunciating principles that are valid for all ages and cultures. Readers will turn to them time and again for guidance in other days and different circumstances.

CRISIS Publications are spirited, entering contemporary debates with gusto to clarify issues and demonstrate how those issues can be resolved in a way that enlivens souls and the Church.

We welcome engagement with our readers on current and future CRISIS Publications. Please pray that this imprint may help to resolve the crises embroiling our Church and society today.

Sophia Institute Press® is a registered trademark of Sophia Institute.
Sophia Institute is a tax-exempt institution as defined by the
Internal Revenue Code, Section 501(c)(3). Tax ID 22-2548708.